BLACK, WHITE OR BRINDLE
Race in rural Australia

GILLIAN COWLISHAW

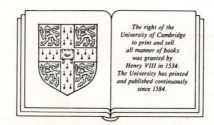

The right of the
University of Cambridge
to print and sell
all manner of books
was granted by
Henry VIII in 1534.
The University has printed
and published continuously
since 1584.

Cambridge University Press
Cambridge
New York   New Rochelle   Melbourne   Sydney

FOR SALLY AND NICK

Published by the Press Syndicate of the University of Cambridge
The Pitt Building, Trumpington Street, Cambridge CB2 1RP
32 East 57th Street, New York, NY 10022, USA
10 Stamford Road, Oakleigh, Melbourne 3166, Australia

Typeset by Love Computer Typesetting, Sydney.
Printed in Hong Kong

Australian National Library cataloguing in publication data
Cowlishaw, Gillian K. (Gillian Keir), 1934–
    Black, white or brindle: race in rural Australia.
    Bibliography.
    Includes index.
    1. Aborigines, Australian — Social conditions.
    2. Aborigines, Australian — New South Wales — Social
    conditions. 3. Australia — Race relations.
    I. Title.
994'.0049915

British Library cataloguing in publication data
Cowlishaw, Gillian K.
    Black, white or brindle: race in rural Australia
    1. Australia. Rural regions. Race relations
    I. Title
305.8'00994

Library of Congress cataloguing in publication data
Cowlishaw, Gillian K.
    Black, white or brindle: race in rural Australia/Gillian
    K. Cowlishaw.
            p.   cm.
    Bibliography: p.
    ISBN 0 521 34660 6
    1. Australia — Rural conditions. 2. Australia — Race relations.
I. Title.
HN843.5.C68 1988
307.7'2'0994--dc19

ISBN 0 521 34660 6

Contents

Tables

'I don't care if a person is black, white or brindle;
if they behave properly I'd invite them into my
house.' A comment from a town I call Brindleton.

Introduction

This is the story of the town of Brindleton where the population is divided into two kinds by a process, the origin of which is so obscure to its supporters and its victims alike, that it is considered natural by both.

Any population is divided in many ways. There are men and women. There are professional people who live comfortable lives they consider normal, and there are the indigent who, these days, rely on welfare payments. There are the owners of property, who employ those who sell their labour. There are children and adults. But it is the racial division that is the most contentious, the black, the white and the brindle. Colour, though often denied importance when such matters are discussed in Brindleton, none the less is constantly referred to with the intensity or venom of deep-seated anxiety.

The racial categories of black and white, Aboriginal and European, are widely used, and are usually considered to be an accurate reflection of natural categories[1] in Australian society. However racial categorisation of human beings based on biological inheritance is not valid. The genetic characteristics which are popularly supposed to define racial categories are a tiny proportion of the common human genetic material. The variation in genetic characteristics within any population is greater than the genetic differences between any two populations. Further it has been accepted for many years that any genetically given physical differences have no necessary relationship with psychological or social characteristics. If it is agreed that biology does not determine racial groupings, but that these 'racial' categories are related to cultural characteristics, then we must ask exactly what these characteristics are and how they developed. Furthermore, given the major changes in cultural practices over the last hundred years, has the relationship between the races changed also? Besides any biological or cultural contrasts, the third element in the situation is the hostility between the races. Are we to accept that this antagonism is a natural consequence of any biological or cultural differences that exist? I want to show that race, culture and hostility are all socially created and that there is nothing natural and inevitable about

---

[1]The term natural is used with the common-sense connotation of inevitability, and being outside the power of human agency.

1

the racial tension which is endemic in western New South Wales and elsewhere in Australia.

Science, even social science, is supposed to explain the world. But the world, or some bit of it, has first to be seen in need of explanation. Those aspects of the world that we take for granted have to be seen as problematic before they become the object of research. The intense feeling surrounding racial divisions are seen by those who experience them as a natural consequence of the actions and attitudes of those involved. However outsiders commonly express a certain shock and disapproval at the expressions of hostility. That is, to outsiders the racial tension is problematic and in need of explanation. It is therefore easier to consider the reasons for the hostility than for the racial division itself which is seldom seen as problematic by insiders, outsiders or academics. However it is necessary to trace the origin of the racial categories, for it is in the particular creation and perpetuation of the races that the explanation for the hostility must be grounded. The emotion surrounding the process of racial categorisation can be understood, in part, as a consequence of the struggle to maintain the categories in a situation where they serve to reinforce the power structure but are constantly disputed.

Being black in Australia has always meant being a member of a group with limited access to education, health, welfare services and the protection of the law, an insecure place in the labour market and a precarious control over one's own existence. These characteristics have come to be a part of being Aboriginal. Thus, when asked who was an Aboriginal, Shirley Smith's definition was of shared suffering. She said an Aboriginal person was anyone who had been 'Down there with me on the thirty two acre mission' (Read, 1984).

The events which are to be described in the following pages are taken for granted by those who experience them or, in the case of the past, know about them. These actors in the drama would, in most cases, not accept my attempt to 'problematise' them. This, however, has not deterred me because, for some other participants, these events themselves constitute a problem of immense proportions.

In exploring how the situation comes to be as it now is, I will begin with a number of themes which can be grouped under the following headings. I will discuss how the land was 'taken up' in the middle of the 19th century by the settlers, as they called themselves. What was the nature of the endeavour they were undertaking, and how did they themselves see their actions? In other words, who were these new owners and what did they do? Also, given that the pastoral industry dominated the west, what niches were there for others? That is, what work was generated for those who did not have some of the land? Who did the work which was a necessary part of the pastoral endeavour? In other words, who were the workers and what did they do? Finally, who were the Aborigines and what did they do? Were the previous owners of the land incorporated into the new regime as owners, workers, or in some other capacity? In each case we must rely largely on evidence from the first category of people, but in doing so we need to unravel the assumptions and biases inherent in their writing.

Another set of themes which lie deeper in the text are those encapsulated in the title; the black, the white and the brindle. How has the racial division been understood and re-created over the years? The blacks possessed the land and then the whites came in the form of surveyors, squatters, shepherds and shopkeepers. All the new-comers were men at first, which gave rise to the theory among the Aborigines that the cattle, which these men so jealously guarded, took the place of their wives (Hardy, 1977:30). In fact the Aboriginal women did, and hence the brindle came into being.

Interest in the differences between human groups flourished when, with the invention of large sailing ships, world travel became possible. Those who were in the process of developing systems of heirarchical classification of human beings naturally placed others who seemed to show markedly different characteristics lower in the hierarchy than themselves. However at the same time these same sailing ships were breaking down the very barriers that had created the particular 'races' whose characteristics were being delineated. In a few cases social barriers almost entirely replaced the geographical ones, but in most colonial situations there was extensive and continu-ing 'miscegenation'. This is not the place to discuss the variation in that process. A new grouping of Eurasians is the dominant popu-lation in, for instance, Malacca. In India social barriers between British and Indian were strict but did not preclude the appearance of a substantial number of 'Anglo-Indians'. South African Boers have lately been shown to have had considerable genetic mixing with black compatriots in their earlier humbler days (Nurse *et al.*, 1985). In colonies such as Australia, where the natives soon became a min-ority, miscegenation had somewhat different consequences from those countries where the European colonisers remained a minority such as in most of Africa and Asia. While a dedicated band of anthropologists were collecting bones, measuring heads, and trying to find the definitive characteristics of the Australians, the brave pioneers and Aboriginal women were messing up the categories.

This subject, the so-called process of miscegenation[2] or mixing of the races, is an extremely emotive one and, perhaps for that reason, an ill-understood one. In this study miscegenation will be taken from the hidden recesses of shameful matters which are deplored but not examined. The mystery serves to disadvantage those who are some-times thought to be protected by not mentioning their 'mixed' ancestry. It seems to me that by refusing to enquire into the nature and consequences of miscegenation the whole notion of racial groups has been perpetuated in the face of a serious empirical problem. Great biological and cultural changes have taken place since the middle of the 19th century in the population of Australia, yet the importance of racial structuring has not been undermined. That is, races have been created and re-created by a process of exclusion and differentiation rationalised by the emphasis on the importance of certain supposedly defining and inherent characteristics.

Of course the differences between the indigenes and the invaders were not only physical ones. The other differences are often referred to as cultural. The languages were different. In a comparatively short time some language learning took place, though it seems to have been biased in one direction and limited in degree. Other habits were markedly different also, from clothing and food to general notions about what constitutes a family, a home and a proper way of life. In each case some habits and practices were exchanged by some indi-viduals immediately. But it is not the exchange or replacement of genetic or cultural material which was the basis of the conflict which marked this era. Rather it was the replacement of one system of production by another which made a battle for the land inevitable. Race was at the forefront of consciousness, so that the conflict was called racial. But the cause of the war was not the existence of racial differences, however defined, but rather the desire of one race to make radical changes in the use of the land.

A popular assumption in recent accounts of the frontier conflict is that the Europeans were particularly violent and inhumane due to their racist attitudes. Reading of the savage massacres which occurred in many areas it is tempting to think of such men as of a different kind

---

[2]The term miscegenation came into common use in 1864 when a bogus pamphlet was published in New York which raised the issue of race in an aggravated form during an election (Bloch, 1958). Literally it refers to the genetic mixing of two races, thus implying that races are genetically discrete groupings.

from ourselves. But it is also true that the success of their enterprise depended on the removal, by one means or another, of the contenders for ownership of the land. If a war is defined as an all out violent struggle to possess the land, then this was a war. Aborigines disputed the invaders' rights; they resisted their occupation; they opposed their hegemony, though not in a manner that the invaders would call war. Their resistance was sufficiently effective to make their total defeat necessary if the pastoral enterprise was to succeed. As in other wars, the physical violence was supported by a web of ideas and explanations of which we know only the victor's side. These ideas are largely to do with the rectitude of the desire to use the land in the way they were doing and the injustice of the black's attempts to stop them. In fact it was even possible not to recognise that the land was being defended. Contemporary comments from the early days often present Aborigines as simply savages whose nature was such that they killed white people if they could. As there was never a surrender, the violence had to continue, and continues today in different forms. But a further contention is that the actions of individuals, while played out within this framework, were not wholly determined by it. Interpersonal relations were not determined by race. There were many individuals who had close and complex relationships with others of a different race. There were those whites who deplored the savagery towards blacks on grounds of both morality and personal feelings. The relationship between employer and black worker was different from that between black and white worker. And those relationships between men and women, one black and one white, often considered to be entirely violent and exploitative, were and are sometimes tender and long-lasting attachments. Today, as yesterday, the struggle continues. The tactics and positions taken by the protagonists show some variation, but elements of similarity in the conflict across 100 years give some indication of its real nature.

The violent separation of Aborigines from the land, the popular notion of their primitive and inferior nature and the development of scientific racism, have all been discussed as aspects of the destruction of Aboriginal society (e.g., Rowley, 1972a,b). But there is a fundamental and continuing feature of the relationship between Aborigines and whites that is perhaps more pervasive. That is, the very system of categorisation of people by race. Relationships and individuals had to be defined by race, not just psychologically, but socially, economically, politically and in virtually every aspect of their lives.

Not all whites have been hostile to blacks, but virtually all consider them as inherently different and problematical. Such categorisation allows racism to be perpetuated.

Much popular understanding of Aborigines' disadvantages in Australia today and in the past relies on a notion of racism as an irrational or ignorant hostility to Aborigines. Such negative prejudice is seen as due to erroneous generalisations about the inherent characteristics of a group of people. That is, individuals show racial prejudice if they display hostility towards members of a group defined in terms of ·inherited characteristics. The classic racist believed that people with dark skins were inferior in moral or intellectual standards. Much work in 20th-century anthropology has emphasised the error of this belief, first denying that there was any general inferiority associated with racial differences and, more recently, rejecting the notion of race as a useful way of categorising human beings. The fact that racial hostility persisted was seen as due to ignorance or irrationality, and thus characteristic of the uneducated blue-collar workers rather than the educated 'middle class'. Such a view leads to the kind of research done by Lippmann (1973).

This attitudinal definition is narrow and severely misleading. Those who pass the tests for racial prejudice with a clean bill of enlightenment — by asserting that they think blacks should have equal educational opportunities and equal access to jobs — are adhering to popular middle-class notions of race relations and perhaps merely providing a measure of their distance from racial problems. Rather than opposing the disadvantages blacks experience, the liberal middle class opposes the supposed racists who are ignorant and hostile to the innocent Aborigines. They defend the social processes that create disadvantage though they claim not to be hostile to black people (cf. Wellman, 1977). The existence of racism does not depend on expressed hostility but on the consequences of actions and beliefs. Further the actions and beliefs of individuals need to be seen as part of a series of processes whereby racial inequality is structured into the whole social matrix.

Racist beliefs can be seen as culturally sanctioned responses that, perhaps unintentionally, defend the advantages that whites enjoy which are denied blacks. My account of the process of reproduction of racial categories shows that those who espouse a hard line concerning Aborigines — some of whom are classic racists — are not the creators of the problems of racial tension, although they are an important element in defending the status quo against challenge. It is extremely difficult to resist the process of categorisation which in effect says that there are fundamental differences between Aboriginal people and white people. Whether they advocate kindness or further cruelty to Aborigines, whites are cooperating with the process. In a racially divided town all become racists if they adopt the definitions and divisions which surround them.

What, then, is at the basis of the racial division in Brindleton? If we cannot understand this inequality as stemming from racial prejudice, where do we seek its source? My answer is that racism must be seen as a series of differentiations and exclusions that are built into a much wider system of inequality. The more fundamental process is that of class differentiation. I am not arguing that Aboriginal disadvantage is simply a consequence of being labourers or erstwhile members of the working class. Rather Aborigines, already stigmatised by race, were inserted into a class system where to subsist they must sell their labour. They did so, often reluctantly, and only in specific areas and at specific periods was their labour in demand. In even fewer areas was it well rewarded. They became grouped into particular niches in the labour market. Such a process of differentiation creates its own logic: the outcome seems to explain its origin.

The process whereby some groups are stigmatised fits very well with a competitive social system. The stigma of being Aboriginal seems to explain why Aborigines are disadvantaged, and also allows the disadvantage to continue. The more parsimonious explanation is that Aborigines are only one group that is disadvantaged by exactly the same processes as others, that is, through unequal access to resources of all kinds — an inequality that is endemic in this society. The result is poverty, powerlessness and the attendant social inferiority which is experienced widely throughout our society.

This is not of course to say that Aborigines are the same as others who are at the bottom of the class structure or that there is nothing specific and important about racial inequality. Stuart Hall said, 'The class relations which inscribe the black fractions of the working class, function as race relations. The two are inseparable. Race is the modality in which class is lived. It is also the medium in which class relations are experienced.' (Hall *et al.*, 1978: 394) That is, race is not some independent or separate factor in a class-based society. But nor can racial categories be treated as misleading interpretations of class-based inequality. There are very powerful and particular social processes and ideological forms built around the interactions between Aborigines and whites in Australia, and this will be explored here.

The story begins before Europeans came to western NSW. In outlining both the nature of Aboriginal society and the takeover by the pastoral industry in only one chapter it is clear that a mere sketch of these events can be provided, a sketch, moreover, which emphasises only certain aspects of the process. It is the creation of a new way of life for all involved which I have taken as the theme. I have attempted to show how various endeavours came to fruition while others failed; how the price of success for the pastoralists was the defeat of the Aborigines and the despoiling of the land. While these things have been argued before separately, I have tried to show the relationship between them and how the process operated. When the new system was established changes continued to take place. The pastoral industry faced disasters stemming from the climate and the economy. The Aborigines also faced continuing disasters, but as well began to develop systematic responses. That is, the Aboriginal culture changed. Chapter 2 indicates the main themes in this period of history, themes which dominated until the era which I call the enlightenment, beginning in the 1960s. In writing the first two chapters, placing the specific study of Brindleton in its historical context, I have discovered the pitfalls involved in playing the historian. There is a tremendous problem with evidence in any research which wants to reinterpret history with attention to those things which were considered of no importance, or which were actively hidden, when they occurred. There is a bias in the evidence, with information about the richest and largest properties easy enough to come by. Smaller enterprises and poorer people have fewer experiences recorded. Virtually none are in their own words. However when such small people 'make nuisances of themselves' the cacaphony of complaints, the outraged diatribes, provide some information about their activities. Also one can gain some meagre insights from the omissions themselves, especially for instance in the field of miscegenation. This particularly sticky field is the subject of attention throughout.

The second part of the work requires less explanation or apology. I have begun the study of the town I call Brindleton in the late 1960s when there were major government initiatives intended to reverse the disadvantages experienced by Aborigines in Australia. The effects of such policies and other changes on a country town are described and analysed. They are not what might be expected. The

relationship between Aboriginal groups and the townspeople is replete with conflict which none of the residents can avoid. The way
individuals and groups become enmeshed in various struggles, and
their attempts to solve or rationalise them, is a major part of the study.
Further it attempts to illuminate the real nature of that conflict. I hope
to have shed some light, however faint and feeble, on a situation
which fills many with sorrow, anger or despair. In Chapter 6 I give a
more specific account of the process of racial differentiation, or
racism, and a critique of theories of racism. The book is prefaced on
the notion that academic and literary work is not separate from the
social world in which it is produced. While such a statement is a
truism in some circles, other social scientists seem often to begin with
the opposite assumption. The concluding section will look at academic contributions to the understanding of matters raised in this
work.

Acknowledgements

I cannot acknowledge by name here many of those people in western
NSW towns who talked to me, explained their views and provided me
with information of various kinds. Some also extended hospitality to
me and showed interest in the research. These people are from many
different sections of the community, and hold contrasting and often
conflicting views of the issues this book is concerned with. I have tried
to represent this range of views faithfully. However there is no doubt
that some individuals will strongly reject my interpretation of events.
For this reason it seems wise to omit any names of those who assisted
me lest they be in some way held responsible for the result. I would
like to add that any criticism that is implied in my analysis of various
people's reactions to the situations described here is made with the
knowledge of my own comfortable distance from the conflicts in
Brindleton. Perhaps in future deeper insights will be recorded by those
who are more permanently and personally involved.

I can acknowledge those who read and made invaluable suggestions and comments, especially Barry Morris and Margaret Barbalet
who read the whole manuscript. Chris Eipper, Jeremy Beckett,
Andrew Metcalfe and Jan Cooper helped with constructive criticism
of sections of the work. My colleagues at Mitchell College have also
been cooperative and understanding of my propensity to be absent
from my usual place of employment for extended periods. I thank the

Institute of Aboriginal Studies for the grant which supported me during part of the research and writing.

PART ONE

THE HISTORICAL
PERSPECTIVE

Chapter 1

The pastoral invasion

OLD AND NEW LANDHOLDERS

The earlier landholders

Many local histories of Australian towns have brief sections describing the original inhabitants of the local area in terms of their particular languages or 'tribal' names, the kind of tools or weapons found in the local area, and sometimes the particular form of ceremony or marriage rule. This focussing of attention on particular features or practices which appear to define the nature of the people is misleading. It serves to obscure the nature of the Aboriginal society as it existed previously and as it has altered. The pattern of social relations which makes up the way of life of a people needs to be seen as a whole. The description of a particular artefact or practice implies idiosyncracy and peculiarity and does not allow a consideration of the ways in which the invaders affected the social arrangements that previously had prevailed. One could as well describe Australian society today only in terms of its motor cars or football matches.

In considering the change from one method of making a living from the land to another, from a society built on a subsistence economy to one based on a capitalist system of production, it is necessary to begin with a discussion of the economic characteristics of Aboriginal hunter-gatherer society. One reason for such a beginning is that the removal of the economic basis of life alone was sufficient to fundamentally dislocate Aboriginal society. Another, is that the system of production is a significant determinant of other features of the society.

It is difficult to describe a society in neutral terms, but I would ask the reader to recall that romanticising a society different from one's own is as misleading as denigrating it. If we hear of a society where sharing is endemic, where private ownership is rare, and where there is no wealth and therefore no poverty, we are likely to sigh with envy. But these characteristics do not mean an absence of injustice and conflict or perfect equality. Perhaps particular frustrations and joys characterise particular societies, but the happiness or otherwise of the population is not the issue here, even were information on such states of mind available. The characteristics of the social structure are all we can hope to grasp. The following brief description is of some general features of Australian society before Europeans arrived.

Aborigines were foragers, sometimes called hunter-gatherers. That is, production mainly consisted of seeking out and harvesting those products of the land which were valued as food, returning to the camp, and preparing and distributing them. Tools, clothing, shelters, decorative objects, ceremonial objects and a number of other material goods were also produced and exchanged, sometimes along extensive trading networks. Songs, dances, and of course a complex social organisation were produced and reproduced regularly. Land was not privately owned. Like most human societies, Aborigines had relationships with land through kin groups. That is, certain lineages had the responsibility to interact in certain ways with certain areas of the land. All of the land was related to all of the people in some way. Thus, everyone had the land and its products.

Two kinds of relationship with the land, spiritual and economic, are usually distinguished, though it would be more accurate to talk of two aspects of the relationship with the land. The spiritual relationship is stressed by Aborigines who still live in the areas of their forebears, and have retained their knowledge. It is expressed in myths and rituals, but also entails practical obligations to perform certain ceremonies which are believed essential to the continued well-being both of the land and the lineage. The intricacies of these ceremonies, their meaning and the networks of kin groups which are involved in various intertwined obligations concerning their performance are the subject of a great deal of anthropological writing (e.g., Maddock, 1982). The economic relationship with the land has been analysed too, but it seems more straightforward and has not attracted the curiosity of theorists to the same degree. Little attention has been paid to the matter of the actual control of production and distribution, even in recent structural Marxist analysis (e.g., Keenan, 1981).

Perhaps the aspect of the economy of the Australian Aborigines which people today find most striking is the virtual absence of private ownership. There was no exclusive exploitation of resources to the advantage of some and the detriment of others. Accumulation of material resources was not possible, and so power over others could not be accrued by such means. Economically then, the society was comparatively egalitarian. While poverty is the experience of some in a society where inequality is built in, hunter-gatherers experienced substantial material equality. That is, a most important consequence of the economy of the Aborigines was the lack of significant economic differences between people. While it cannot be said that there were no status or power differences between groups, categories or individuals, it can be said that these differences did not depend on the control of material resources. The land, the major means of production, was communally owned, and it was not possible for an individual, much less a group, to be excluded from it.

A brief description of the way food was collected and the arrangements for its distribution should clarify these points. The only division of labour was by sex and age. Commonly throughout Australia women collected the plant foods, foraging in groups for a part of the day and returning to camp to prepare and cook their harvest. Women also hunted smaller game and fished. The division of labour was related more to the use of tools and weapons than to a prohibition of particular quarry. Women did not use spears. Men did not use digging sticks or grinding stones. From a very young age, girls were inducted into the labour force, joining their mothers and other kin and learning the tasks gradually over a number of years. As women became old their production decreased, but their knowledge remained valuable and there was, of course, no retiring age.

No comprehensive empirical study of the process of distributing food in Aboriginal society was ever carried out, partly because this process was disrupted along the frontier of land dispossession, and anthropologists followed far behind the frontier — by about 100 years in southeast Australia. But also the informality of the distribution of women's products has allowed the myth of primitive communism, through sharing, to remain. The ideology of generosity and generalised reciprocity obscured the exchange relationship. Generalised reciprocity of course does not mean in practice 'to each according to his need'. Women tried to control the distribution of the things they collected and prepared, for to be owed is always preferable than to owe. Also, the food women collected was the staple and reliable source of sustenance for all, and with women engaged more regularly and for a greater part of their lives in foraging it is probable that they supplied more food than did men. However men hunted the larger game. This form of production was less reliable but more prestigious, and the distribution of meat was more formally determined by a set of kinship-based rules which ensured a wide distribution. It also gained more attention from anthropologists.

Western NSW provided a rich and varied diet before the sheep and cattle arrived. Unlike coastal regions, where yams were abundant, the staple food of the interior was grass seed, especially native millet which was picked green and sun dried before being threshed and ground on large flat grinding stones. These stones were one of the major variety of tools and were not easily transported. In the area where this work is centred, the explorer Mitchell saw miles of grass, full with seed, being harvested on the Darling River. Seeds of pigweed were also gathered, and nardoo spores were used during drought periods when more desirable grain was not available. The thick bulrush root was also a major source of carbohydrate, harvested by men and women together, and many other fruits and roots were eaten. Men also netted, trapped and speared emus, wallabies, fish and ducks in their season (Allen, n.d.).

Accounts of Aborigines

The Aborigines' society was of only passing interest to most of the explorers and settlers in the late 19th century, and so there is a paucity of reliable information or even detailed observations of any kind. Those who did exhibit curiosity often thought that Aborigines did not know any better way to behave or were victims of irrational superstitions, a view that has changed only superficially in some areas. Even accurate observations can be misleading clues to social structure if considered in isolation. Of course Aboriginal judgements of the behaviour of whites may have been similar.[1]

Scientific interest at that time was marked by a search for similarities and differences by which to trace the origins and dispersal, or evolution, of the particular groups observed. Such preoccupations were part of very general notions of evolutionary change, and Aborigines were seen as our contemporary ancestors. Language, ritual and myths, or rather random elements of them, were the major sources of information about the human past in Australia (Curr, 1886,1887; Woods, 1879). The inaccuracy of the conclusions drawn from these collections of disparate observations is especially apparent in the simplicity of the process pictured and in the short timespan believed to be involved.

There was also a popular concept of the 'savage mind'. This savage mind had a pre-socialised wildness, and showed limited rationality. Logic and rationality were the mark of the civilised European, the

---

[1]One can imagine the information about whites related about the Aboriginal camps. White people hate their children because they smack them; white people are characterised by extreme selfishness and will allow each other to starve rather than give enough food to others without payment; white women don't know how to wash the clothes or cook and have to get someone to do their work; white people smell peculiar.

definitive characterisitic of the more highly evolved. In terms of human history such rationality was thought to be relatively recent, and the savages had not yet achieved it though there were indications, some said, that they had rudimentary reasoning ability. Ridley, a missionary, assumed that faith in the initiation ritual would fade with association with whites (*SMH*, 14/12/1855:3), reflecting the prevailing view, perhaps surprising in a religious man, that European society is based on self-evident and rational principles. When Sturt announced of the Aborigines that 'on the whole I should say they are a people at present at the very bottom of the scale of humanity' (*HB*, 2:19), he was simply stating a widespread and popular view and one which remained extant for many years.

Comments from western NSW smack of such popular conceptions, or misconceptions, about the nature of humans and human society which prevailed at the time. For instance, the settler Teulon's comment that Aborigines do not foster bitterness and wrath for long, perhaps because of indolence (Curr, 1886:204), appeals to a notion of an essential nature, in this case of indolence, peculiar to a race of people. Further, Aborigines confuse our beliefs with their own traditions (ibid., 200), presumably because of a lack of rationality in their own beliefs. Teulon also asserted that they usually died of '. . . that mysterious inability . . . to live, to which those succumb who are (and have discovered that they are) not "the fittest" '(ibid., 197). This reference to a supposed inexorable law of nature whereby the fittest survive depends on a misunderstanding of the biological use of the term fitness. Such a misuse was common, but it may be Teulon's own addition that the unfit recognise their inferiority and curl up and die. Despair, or the lack of the will to live, were called upon, even by scholarly writers, to explain the decline of the Aboriginal population (e.g., Berndt, 1945:51-2).

There were others who tried to give an account of the practices of the tribes 'before detribalisation had proceeded very far' and commonly the information is a rather inadequate description of kinship or polygyny, initiation ceremonies or religious beliefs. Most local whites, then as now, seemed content with a little information about some curious Aboriginal practice or belief which served to distinguish and distance them from the more 'civilised' or, these days, 'normal', whites. To a degree, this kind of interest was 'anthropological' in that it was informed by an idea, which must have stemmed from anthropological writings, that initiation ceremonies, moities and totems were exotic beliefs of scientific interest. But such interest was often accompanied by a casual, and really quite astonishing, lack of interest in the actual lives of the people being displaced. For instance, in a description of the flood of 1864, the observation is made in passing that 'the blacks disappeared with their piccaninnies, dogs, opposum rugs and warlike weapons to the mountain twenty miles off' without any apparent interest by the newcomers in recording how people who must have experienced floods before, coped with such dramatic occurrences (Foott, 1958:56).

There was occasional recognition that the Aborigines' food sources were being denied them, and comments on half-castes showed an awareness that miscegenation was occurring, but no systematic public interest was taken in these processes. Indeed, much of the pattern of interaction between the indigines and the invaders was deliberately hidden from public scrutiny, as we shall see below. The fisheries at Brewarrina did provoke many tributes to the ingenuity of the Aborigines and the effectiveness of this fishing technique. However, a newspaper account of the fish traps in 1874 says 'It has been said that years ago some whiteman must have planned the traps but this is not admitted by the blacks . . . the labour has been as clever as is the idea that the natives formed the work' (*T & C Journal*, 2/5/1874:715).

Demographic evidence is too scattered and unspecific to allow any firm conclusions about the Aboriginal population in the mid-19th century (cf. Smith, 1980). There were many observations of large numbers of Aborigines in the area we will be concentrating on. Teulon estimated that the Barkinji, who, he says, occupied 100 miles of the river, numbered 3,000 before the whites came to the Darling River in 1845, that 1,000 were left when he arrived in 1863 and that, in 1884, there were only 80 left (quoted in Curr, 1886:189). Extensive observations of smallpox by the earliest explorers may indicate that such diseases were the major direct cause of population reduction (cf. Butlin, 1983). Another cause was deliberate and continuing violence. The one large massacre that is known of in the area was claimed to have killed 400 people (Kerrigan, 1882, quoted in Kamien, 1978:15). It certainly appears that there was a massive reduction of the Aboriginal population in this region before the 1880s. Any more precision about its cause and extent is probably impossible to achieve, though it is clear that it is unnecessary to call upon Teulon's mystical notion that it was the 'new garment' of European ways that caused the population decline (Curr, 1886:190). Disease and war are apparent enough as causes. There is also no doubt that there remained an

Aboriginal population in the district, and it is with them that I am concerned.

While systematic interest in the nature of Aboriginal society was rare, Aboriginal geographical knowledge was certainly valuable to the surveyors. A recognition of this is to be found in the place names which remain interspersed with those deriving from explorers and important personages in the colonial administration. In the 1830s and 40s, maps recorded many Aboriginal names and surveyors were told that 'The natives can furnish you with names for every flat and almost every hill' (*HB*, 3:44). However these names were later recognised as only ephemeral titles often changing from year to year. The Surveyor-General's instructions in 1851 said, 'Map names altho' derived originally from Aborigines are for the use of Englishmen, and once adopted it matters little what they mean, our use of them when they fit our mouths is, to distinguish geographical features' (quoted in Heathcote, 1965:34).

The new owners

Explorers, government surveyors and squatters did not come in that order to western NSW. Sometimes squatters came first and surveyed the land they would lease. Surveyors were often explorers, commissioned by governments to seek the exploitable resources in the interior of the continent and to provide information as to the suitability of the land they traversed for pastoralism. One of the tasks of the government was to regulate the access of its citizens to the land. This was attempted with acts of parliament, which seldom fulfilled their intention due to little government control or knowledge of the remoter regions of the colony. The basis of land alienation is, of course, that those with the money can have it. But in the western district in the mid-19th century, the money consisted of relatively small amounts for the leases, and the capital to stock the property. What was in short supply was the expertise required to manage stock in the outback. Rewards were great for initiative, but the initiative and skill of the stock and station manager were as necessary as the initiative of the investors.

Huge areas of land came to be controlled by large landowners, by companies and by banks, before 1860. The Robertson Land Act of 1861 attempted to create a more equitable access to land and to limit land speculation. This attempt to support the selector of limited means against the more wealthy pastoralists failed (Heathcote, 1965:44). In fact, the Act resulted in the provision of better services such as transport to the pastoral industry (J. Cooper, pers. comm.). There occurred extensive private monopolies of the water supplies and pockets of superior country (Heathcote, 1965:40). It was claimed that the squatters were forced to protect their leases from unscrupulous speculators because the Act allowed for selection of the most essential part of a holding by anyone willing to pay. This seldom occurred in the western region because few small selectors could venture so far. The pastoralists successfully claimed that the land had no value apart from improvements (ibid., 66). As a result rents were geared to stock-carrying capacity, a telling example of the squatter's influence over legislation.

Runs of 32,000 acres, or 25 square miles, were laid out when surveys were done, but groups of these runs began to be considered one property. Identifying the recorded 'owners' of these huge areas gives no indication of who was living in the district and managing the properties, because owners were often the banks who held the mortgage or already established squatters from other districts. Such large investors have always pulled major strings in the western fiddle. Legislation, rather than determining the pattern of land holding, was a method whereby the government tried to rectify the worst excesses of the squatting process. As the squatters themselves dominated the legislative assembly, the process was modified, rather than radically altered, in the early years.

In 1857, settlement on the upper Darling began in earnest with the arrival in quick succession of a number of managers of the large runs that were being taken up on the river frontages. Many managers doubled as surveyors, obviously in their own interests.[2] One of these early settlers, and one of the few owner occupiers, was Vincent J. Dowling, of a landowning family. In May 1859, at the age of 27, he established the 300,000 acre Fort Bourke station with 2,000 head of cattle which he and some hired men drove from Maitland. He explored a great area, particularly of the Paroo River, and applied for most of it (Jervis, 1948:87). The diary he kept for a number of years records the hardship and loneliness he experienced and provides some insight into the activities and the values of such men. Dowling recorded the condition of the land and the presence of water as he travelled along the rivers and across the drier country, frequently

---

[2]Because surveying was slow many lessors were unsure of their boundaries for years (Heathcote, 1965:101-3). The Surveyor General gave instructions for determining distances as follows; 'a horses forefeet move about 950 times to the mile, walking or trotting, and a stone should be transferred from one pocket to the other at every 100' (Surveyor-General, 1847, *HB*, 3:56.)

blazing his initials in trees. But he had little appreciation of the fact that the 'well grassed plains' he observed with obvious relish in many places would not sustain his cattle during the frequent droughts. It is even less likely that he was aware of the more ominous fact that the grass he eyed as cattle fodder was the bearer of the grain which formed the Aborigines' staple diet.

The establishment of pastoralism continued in the 1860s, with more managers arriving and often taking up land themselves or continuing as managers for banks, pastoral companies or individuals. It was these early managers who became landowners and town businessmen, and who founded the families in the district which became the local 'squattocracy'. A few, like Dowling, were from landowning families elsewhere, but such men, again like Dowling, did not remain in the district. Most began with little or no capital, little education, and a few were illiterate. Managers, stockmen, skilled tradesmen and even one police constable became owners of tracts of land, though many of these did not succeed in retaining their position as owners.

The first arrivals drove the cattle in and herded them near the river. Until the stock became accustomed to an area, long hours were spent searching for them and chasing them back from their wanderings. Sheep became the more profitable stock, and gradually ousted the cattle. The early years were often very harsh ones for the stockmen, whether they were the rare owners, the managers or other employees. At first 'masters and men alike sheltered in bark huts or "gunyas" adapted from those of the aborigines' (Ward, 1966:87). The relatively cheap land could provide excellent profits, and some of the stations soon began to reflect this prosperity in thriving communities. The home camps, where at first the manager and stockmen lived on meat, pigweed, flour and tea (when the latter two were available), were transformed into homesteads with communities consisting of a manager and stockmen, sometimes with wives, shepherds and jackaroos, as well as some Aborigines. Slowly local towns developed.

The prosperity of the early 1860s did not last. The harshness of the environment became apparent in the 1864 flood and in the drought conditions which followed. The flood ruined some. As the water rose one household abandoned its dwelling for a small hillock which also became the refuge for a range of animals including snakes. Two young employees rowed off for provisions but, instead of returning, emptied the homestead of all the family's goods and rowed off elsewhere never to be seen again. The family lived on the sandbank for seven weeks (Foott, 1958:56-7). Such dramatic and bizarre tales became characteristic of the outback, and they are one basis for the general view that there was some special quality about the life and the people which could not be understood by those who lived 'down inside' the settled and protected areas.

The hunger for land, or perhaps greed for profit, was combined with ignorance of the climatic extremes. During the drought of 1865, the Bogan River Company turned 40,000 sheep into the bush. Squatters left the Bogan deserting their stations, especially those with 'back-blocks', that is, land back from the river with no permanent water available. The preciousness of water was made starkly apparent. According to King, the severe drought caused a slackening of speculative enthusiasm and a healthy culling of inferior stock (King, 1957:89). It may not have appeared thus to those whose land reverted to the mortgagee. A letter from the branch manager of the Commercial Bank to his superior, in 1869, indicates the alarming financial conditions of the pastoralists but says, reassuringly, that the debts to the bank are amply secured (*HB*, 2:128). Thus it was that many of the stations passed into the hands of the banks, who remained the holders of large mortgages throughout the history of the western region and who were thus, in a sense, the real owners of the land. An awareness grew that large holdings were necessary if the bad seasons were to be weathered.

Horror and despair at the effect of drought was widely felt. Sheep by the thousands died by the roadsides. Managers walked off properties and the workers were paid with valueless cheques. Some starved (*HB*, 9:154). Bean gives a gruesome account of unidentified skeletons — all that was left of many a traveller who deviated slightly from the track or whose water bag was pierced by a twig (Bean, 1916:26). But the financial suffering of the owners, and the physical suffering of the workers, are both seen as due to the drought rather than to a particular system of production. It was not recalled that the previous owners had had quite different experiences and had probably never suffered hunger. Nor was drought recognised as endemic. The despair of February 1869 had changed to satisfaction by June when 'a stockholder sent flocks of 5,000 wethers to the southern market' (*MM*, 17/6/1869). The drought was considered an abnormal phase, though some of the large holders began to sell their leases to their managers. Lessons about conservation of resources were not learned, despite the fearful dust storms which blew the topsoil away causing much discomfort. Overstocking was usual. One person observed that if a squatter did not overstock his run 'his neighbour's cattle will soon do it for him' (MM, 18/5/1869). The subsequent droughts, the long-term effects of cattle, sheep and rabbits on the land, and the dramatic depreciation in value of the properties, were still to come.

In 1947 James Jervis read a paper before the Royal Australian Historical Society on 'The West Darling: Its Exploration and Development'. He said 'It is high time that history paid its tribute to those bold spirits who opened up the Far West' (Jervis, 1948:66). Without doubt, timidity would have been a rare quality among those who went west in those years. But the bold spirits were also motivated by land hunger, and the illegality of many occupations, the greed for ever larger properties, the rapaciousness of the speculators and the complacency of the banks, makes the story a less admirable one. Jervis himself gives evidence of the way properties changed hands with indecent rapidity (ibid., 171ff.). A bold spirit can also be seen as a land shark, and the opening up of the country could be said to have led to its bleeding to death.[3]

There is one other aspect of this period of history that must qualify any tribute paid to those who were involved, and that is the effect on the original owners. How is it that humane men, claiming to be civilised, became savage wreakers of destruction on the people they called savages? Some early settlers who kept diaries provide some insight into this process, which really consisted of responding to the logic of their enterprise. If they were to establish the pastoral industry the blacks, in their present form at least, had to go. An increasing hardening in the settler's attitude to those blacks who showed resistance occurred along with the development of, at best, a humane and paternalistic attitude to those whose labour they managed to make use of. Thus a distinction between good and bad blacks began to emerge. There was little speculation about the reaction of the Aborigines to the 'settlers', and a decreasing willingness to consider that they might be defending themselves. In 1872 a newspaper article on unoccupied areas asked 'Why this country should have been left to the dominion of the savage so long' (quoted in Jervis, 1948:154). Another report said that some stations were abandoned 'on account

---

[3]There is a virtual industry celebrating the 'pioneering spirit' which attempts to fabricate a heroic past from a small part of the story of settlement. The whole story is much more interesting and less morally pure.

of native outrages and the enormous cost of carriage' (ibid., 150). We shall see below the nature of 'outrages' in the district at that time.

STRUGGLES AND VIOLENCE

The necessary lesson

Frontier conflict, black resistance and massacre are now common terms used in the historical accounts of settlement in Australia. In this section I want to discuss the nature of the struggle, the extent to which it was violent, and the way that violence has been understood both in the early period of settlement and since. There are a number of aspects of the situation which need to be considered separately.

There was conflict between government and settlers, with the former trying to control what the latter deemed a necessary part of their pastoral mission: removing of the black threat. Not only did violent killings occur, but also threats of violence and other forms of restraint that did not allow for resistance. Violence was understood to be necessary. The extent of resistance or collaboration needs to be considered. Resistance, it is often argued, has remained a feature of Aborigines' existence until today, but here I will illustrate these issues with some of the events of the frontier years.

Before settlement in western NSW occurred, debate had been going on for decades between the government and the squatters on the matter of treatment of the natives. Rowley says that when policy passed from the home government into local hands, 'no indigenous people have been more completely at the mercy of typical settler democracies, where the standards of parliament are those of the settlers' (Rowley, 1972a:23). Among the settlers the prevailing belief developed that the price of the land was the removal of the Aboriginal resistance, and there developed 'the philosophy . . . of the one good bloody lesson as the basis for peace in the frontier regions' (ibid., 42). This was considered more humane than continuing skirmishes. An 1865 newspaper report says: 'So completely has the native mind become embittered against the white population, that if the country is to be populated by Europeans, the safety of their own lives lies in the extermination of the Aborigines' (*Empire*, 27/10/1865:5).

There was not even the discussion of the possibility of peaceful means of domination at this stage of colonisation. It was usual to talk of guilty 'tribes' or 'mobs', and Rowley has documented how the assumption of guilt by association led to massacres of whole groups in the isolation of the scrub (Rowley, 1972a:42). Official attempts to control the frontier were sometimes postponed in case settlers became more incensed and therefore more violent.[4]

It is not the aim of this section to count the bodies in the western region. Any quantification would be extremely difficult because of the care taken to disguise the extent of violence meted out to the blacks, and to exaggerate the violence done by them. An affair called 'the murder of Lee's party' illustrates the divergent ways events may be interpreted and the way a myth is made. In 1841 a Mr Lee was occupying land on the Bogan River — illegally, because it was outside the limit of settlement. It was a drought period, and so he was 'compelled' by 'actual necessity' to move down the river. While some men were building stockyards, they were attacked by the Aborigines who had been working with them, and three were killed. Police were summoned, and after a search at least 12 Aborigines were killed and others taken into custody. It is apparent that no one was sure if those who attacked were the ones who were punished. Nor is it clear how many Aborigines were killed, or whether it was the men who had been working with the party who had attacked. One reason for the Aborigines' anger is clear. They had been forbidden access to the river presumably for the usual reason; it was said that they frightened the cattle (*SMH*, 24/8/1842).

The graziers' report to the legislative assembly on this matter called for effective dealing with such cases as 'the savages must be handled with authority and force used if necessary as a deterrent'(ibid.). But it was also revealed to the legislative assembly that there had been indiscriminate shooting and massacring of blacks who may not have been the actual murderers. It was pointed out that an assigned servant had been in charge of the party, which included ticket-of-leave men, and the Chief Justice said that acts of cruelty against natives are committed not by gentlemen of education but by convict servants (ibid.). It is clear that all constructions put on these events underplayed the fact that the Aborigines had been forbidden access to the water. They may have already felt retribution for disobedience to such a savage command. The legislative assembly deplored but did

---

[4]Earlier, in 1839, the border police force was formed to enable the commissioner to enforce the land legislation and ostensibly to protect the Aborigines. At this period 'Reprisals simply got out of hand' (Rowley, 1972a:38). The Native Police, set up in the 1850s, consisted of white senior officers with black troopers who were employed in areas distant from their homes to put down the attacks of the blacks (ibid., 39). They became notorious for their indiscriminate violence.

not, or could not, control such events. They too wanted the country farmed.

Attacks on Aborigines were kept secret because government policy explicitly forbad them, and also because of growing outrage in some circles at the frontier violence. The prosecution and hanging in 1838 of seven white men for the massacre of Aborigines at Myall Creek, was not forgotten by the settlers. It was suggested at one time that 'settlement must be delayed till the work of extermination is completed' (Rowley, 1972a:169). One settler asked the critics from the cities 'how else would they have us deal with the situation . . . other than by remaining out of the country altogether?' (ibid., 155).

Commandant Frederick Walker of the native police gave the squatters support when, in 1849, he:

> passed along the Darling with a newly recruited force of native police. . . . His aid was opportune in "checking the aggression of the aboriginal natives". There were "some (Aboriginal) lives lost" and two of his own party were wounded while attempting to arrest six tribesmen charged with a particularly atrocious murder (Hardy, 1981:83-4).

Hardy is reporting the parliamentary discussions. Norton, a surveyor who was in the region at the time, says that it was common rumour that the blacks had been shot down through the district without mercy during this visit of the native police (Norton, 1907:69). A contemporary newspaper of 1849, reporting the same events, described an encounter between two troopers and a group of 12 initially friendly blacks; 'one of them attempted to wrench the carbide out of Geegaw's hands and another threw a jagged spear at Lairy (who) caught the spear and immediately killed the black'. Four others were shot at once (*MM*, 9/5/1849). Such reports demonstrate the creation of a certain view of the wild Aborigines. Perhaps it is not surprising that pleasure was taken in dramatic exaggeration in the usually uneventful bush life, and when few observers were present their interpretations could not be challenged.

As in other parts of Australia, detailed local knowledge of early violence is virtually non-existent in the district, though the ignorance among whites is more profound than that among blacks. In 1944 some Aborigines personally recalled being present as children at mass killings. One was 'hiding in a log while her parents and the rest of the local group were rounded up in a stockyard and shot.' Another 'returned to the camp to find every person there dead from eating poisoned flour.' One white man lined Aborigines up by the river and shot them and another would 'round up the gins and brand them with a red-hot iron' (Reay, 1949:100). It is not clear exactly where in western NSW these events took place. Sites of such occurrences were memorials, perhaps authentic war memorials, but since then such knowledge seems to have lapsed in many Aboriginal communities. It is no accident that such events are not part of official history. Suppression and reinterpretation began almost before violence occurred, due to contemporary sensitivity and the threat of prosecution. This was accomplished by the creation of the notion of primal black savagery as well as by suppressing or reinterpreting news of events. But both in words and action, violence became accepted and habitual. Bobbie Hardy found in early documents 'hints of severity towards the Aborigines of the Darling to counterbalance protestations of benevolence'. She refers, for instance, to retaliatory mass shootings and to Aborigines being shot down like dogs (Hardy, 1981:78).

The explorers faced 'trouble with the blacks', or 'black violence', and so there was considerable preparation for violence on the part of exploring and surveying parties. Fears were fuelled by reports of violence, and not stilled by reports of peaceful passage. With no police available until after the frontier regions had been 'settled', the first squatters took measures to ensure the safety of their stock and themselves. The only visit by Commandant Walker with his native police in 1849 'found the blacks on the Darling were friendly with the exception of a few who attempted to murder two police . . . Walker came up with four of his troopers as the attempt was made and shot four of the blacks' (Jervis, 1962:389). Many such accounts purport to show the blacks 'treachery' by omitting any mention of possible motive.

Settler violence; direct and indirect

Most districts of NSW saw a bloody massacre of Aborigines. The worst single episode in the western region occurred at Hospital Creek, near Brewarrina, in the 1850s. As is usual there is not a lot of first-hand written evidence, and there are different second-hand versions. John Collins, who left a diary describing the events, recognised that the laws of the blacks in regard to their women were very strict. He goes on to say:

> Our special Walcha stockman, having taken unto himself a gin, was warned to let her go; but he was too happily situated to take

any notice. Whereupon the tribesmen speared both, and dragging their dead bodies into the open burnt the hut and the adjoining stockyards (quoted in Clune, 1952:82).

A 'corroboree' followed, the sounds of which brought the other station hands with their guns. They:

> fired into the lunatic mob. Settlers from the surrounding district reinforced the stockmen, and together they drove a mob of men, women and children (thirty in all) across the Darling. . . . There a general slaughter occurred. Nobody was so lucky as to escape. Skulls, broken or dinted, and one or two with the leaden slug embedded in the bone, are shown to this day. A second crowd of aboriginals made out to Narran Lake, only to be massacred in a ditch off the Goodooga road, known as Hospital Creek (ibid., 82-3; see also Cameron 1982:1).

A version of the story of this massacre is part of the Aborigines' oral history in the area, but is not generally known of among whites (Goodall, 1982; Mathews, 1977a:75). Another contemporary diarist said:

> The wild blacks were that bad that all the cattlemen had to deal with them old and young on the Quantambone plain and shot them. There was about 400 and that is how the creek got its name, Hospital Creek, there was only two picaninnies left, a boy and a girl (Kerrigan, 1882, quoted in Kamien, 1978:15).

A newspaper report of this massacre in 1869 accuses the black trackers from the Liverpool plains of being the instigators and says that these blacks had 'for years shot down everything black in human shape' (*MM*, 19/3/1869). Such accusations of outrageous violence by blacks, often told with apparent satisfaction, were not uncommon.

Besides that massacre, there were long drawn-out struggles that included slaughter. Violence was interpreted and mythologised by newspapers and popular historical accounts in a way which made it seem both necessary and mundane. In 1872 a bushranger, whose wife and child were 'massacred' by blacks, was given an unofficial pardon and permission to shoot as many Aborigines as he liked. He used to erect a stockade near waterholes and pick them off through the peep-holes. One billabong near a local village was known as stinking lagoon because bodies were left in it (Kamien, 1978:15). In another incident, a permit was granted to the sole survivor of a family killed by Aborigines 'to shoot any black he came in contact with, and this he did for some time until he shot a blackfellow in the street of one of the towns, which caused an uproar . . . then the permit was cancelled' (*HB*, 5:17). The accuracy of these stories is unclear, but they show an acceptance of this kind of violence.

Those who actually faced the Aborigines on the frontiers were usually the shepherds and stockmen, assigned servants or ex-convicts in the early days and later free employees, who would usually be in the bush under duress. Neither would be likely to have their master's interests at heart or that of the pastoral enterprise. Some of those who joined the punitive expeditions were also employees. Whether such men were, on average, more or less willing than their employers to use violence against Aborigines is not at all clear. A suggested defence for the men who were hung for the Myall Creek massacre was that they were assigned servants whose actions were in the course of their duties (Rowley, 1972a:36).

There were a number of stories of the murder of hutkeepers which led to reprisals such as that mentioned above. One surveyor recorded an incident in his diary when 'the hut keeper . . . thought blacks were harmless . . . was killed and mangled by them'. This incident was not included in his official report, perhaps because it was bad publicity for the country (Heathcote, 1965:106). The seriousness with which the settlers discussed the killings of white men had less to do with their affection for their fellow whites, than with the safety of their enterprises and success in the conquest of the land. The conviction that gentlemen do not murder was useful for the official view. But it seems that few early settlers in the western region would claim to be gentlemen. Those who did could claim that they also faced extreme circumstances where extreme measures were necessary.

When police arrived in a town, the violence did not so much abate as become officially sanctioned. After Sergeant Steele was stationed in a western NSW town in the 1870s he:

> decided that the (300) Aboriginals should remove to the opposite shore and gave instructions for an immediate exodus, with a supplementary order that although they might visit the village at day-time none should remain after six. Most of the poor devils crossed the river forthwith, and the few stragglers who loitered were horsewhipped through the streets by Steele himself. Every day after sunset the sergeant would begin his rounds, and on the first crack of the lash, shirt tails could be seen flying towards the river, which the blacks used to take in their stride (Collins' Diary, quoted in Clune, 1952:83).

Collins also mentions the advantages of crinoline skirts, even without the cloth on them, for the gins 'especially when Sergeant Steele's whip came racketing about' (ibid.).

The day to day interactions between Aborigines and whites often included violence. The need for secrecy also was accepted and there developed, in the late 19th century, a particular way of talking about the blacks which stressed the problems they created for the settlers and denied the validity of their motives. In fact denied that there were such things as motives among savages.

By 1860, the arguments about the treatment of the natives would have been familiar to those who were arriving in western NSW. Those who stayed in the district developed a less fearful attitude. John Edward Kelly, Dowling's major companion and head stockman, landowner and later a businessman in the town, said:

> I never fired a shot at a blackfellow in my life. On one occasion I came suddenly on an Aboriginal who, not knowing what sort of animal I was, exhausted his armaments upon me the whole of which, I being very active, dodged. . . . I could have shot the black easily as I was a true shot and had a revolver in my hand. But my common sense told me that the poor fellow conceived himself to be fighting against some unearthly monster for his bare life, and my conscience told me it would be pure murder to kill him (*T & C Journal*, 26/3/1887:634).

It is possible, given the way punishments were often meted out among Aborigines in those days, that the spears could have hit Kelly but were intended to frighten or warn him. The disparaging tone of such accounts never includes any recognition that such 'poor fellows' had rational aims or humane impulses. Once, in 1860, Kelly's party had trouble finding a camping place and decided to camp where a 'Boorah'(*sic*) was taking place. He ensured his safety by calling out the 'kings and chiefs' and forcing them under pain of death to collect all armaments in a pile.

> This done, Mr Kelly rode up, perching himself on the top of the mound of spears etc. covering the kings with his revolver till the horses were unpacked and unsaddled. The body of blacks were then allowed to fix their camp, but were given to know that on the slightest sign of any treachery the kings would be shot. The night was passed in safety, and the horses were considerably refreshed. The next party of five white men who went out to the

Paroo was to a man murdered by this same tribe of blacks' (*T & C Journal*, 26/3/1887:634).

It is unclear whether the commentator sees that Kelly's actions in humiliating the senior men during their religious ceremony could have caused the subsequent murders. A tribute to Kelly in 1873 said he was 'among the first to wrest from the blackfellow what we now call our homes, and to him and men of his stamp, civilisation is indebted for the pushing outwards of her standards (*T & C Journal*, 28/5/1873:711).

Good and bad blacks

During this early era there developed a set of notions justifying the removal of Aboriginal resistance to white enterprise. One already referred to was their innate treachery. Another differentiated between the uncivilised or Myalls that were the problem, and the station hands who had to be protected. The independence of the native police had sometimes led to the killing of station blacks which was, according to evidence given at a select committee enquiry in 1856, 'a serious matter, as it diminished the labour supply and brought disaster to Aborigines known to the settler families as persons' (Rowley, 1972a:41). Station blacks were protected, but also severely controlled. They were considered, in some sense, the property of the station owner. No one any longer expressed sympathy for the wild blacks. The view that the station owner is the possessor of the land and that the Aboriginal is the intruder, became an entrenched assumption (ibid., 155). Ward asserts that even the 'prisoners and emancipists. . . . Currency Lads and poor settlers generally shared the conviction that the new land belonged, morally to them' (Ward, 1966:59).

The contrast between good and bad blacks was to become entrenched in the ideology of race relations and is apparent today. The distinction is clear in a report of the 'justifiable murder' of one 'Black Peter' who was, 'even among his own people, a hunted fugitive'. It was asserted that he was supplied with food by his countrymen because he had them in absolute terror. The report says:

his hands were more than once reddened with white man's blood. . . . The capture and escape of this man in the first place, his recapture, attempted escape and fearful death will do much to show his people (and there are more as bad almost as himself), how sure and sleepless is the white man's wrath (*T & C Journal*, 10/2/1872:167).

There developed a system of mystification, perhaps better described as an expression of local culture, whereby stories and news items were written in a way that was meaningful locally and yet not shocking to outsiders. Thus, when a 'lesson is gently taught', or they are 'dispersed' or 'hunted away with rifle shots', all is understood (*Empire*, 8/9/1866). Violence is justified by the danger which lurks about. Reports that 'The blacks some miles up the river are slaughtering one another and the whites fear trouble' (*Empire*, 13/10/1865), is not intended to clarify the basis of the troubles. Frequently, unidentified bodies found in the bush are said to be victims of the blacks, though no evidence appears (*Empire*, 2/2/1864). A feature of all these accounts is the lack of recognition or speculation about the blacks attitudes and needs. It almost appears that such an issue could not be recognised; talk of treachery and savagery made things simpler. For example, when Vincent Dowling's brother John was killed, the story was told in such a way as to arouse sympathy for the brave white pioneers. Hardy gives this account :

> When John Dowling's body was found some weeks after his murder on the Paroo in 1865, nothing in the camp had been touched. . . . The assailant was thought to be a Wadikali tribesman . . . who was helping Dowling survey a track from Mount Murchison to the Paroo. Why he felt impelled to crash his waddy down on his master's skull was a mystery, but not one that Dowling's friends deemed worthy of much pondering. The fundamental fact was that another white man had been killed by "the niggers", and it behoved his compatriots to take their revenge (Hardy, 1981:116).

Dowling is said to have subsequently became a terror to the blacks (Maxwell, n.d.:385). The surveyor Norton, who heard of this death after he left the district, wondered whether the earlier merciless treatment meted out to Aborigines by the native police had caused such reprisals (Norton, 1907).

Vincent Dowling was admired as an upstanding man who was 'one of the few brave and hardy pioneers that helped develop many of the resources of this rich and powerful country. He was the farthest out magistrate at Thargominda' (Maxwell, n.d.:385). There is no indication, in the many tributes to Dowling's contribution to the pastoral industry, of his implacable harshness towards anything that got in his way. Few seem to have thought about the effect of the everyday harshness towards the blacks which some of his diaries reveal.

For instance, one significant and long-standing source of conflict between indigines and invaders has been dogs. The native dogs, which were valuable for hunting and also domestic pets, were a major problem to the pastoralists, scattering and killing sheep. In his first five months in the west Dowling killed 31 native dogs, recording a shooting every few days. It is clear from other comments that he knew these dogs were the companions or pets of the natives, yet he does not indicate any awareness of resentment he might have caused. Nor does he show any more respect for the blacks' inanimate property. Once, in the first few months, Dowling responded to a white workers' complaint that 40 blacks had attacked him, by taking all the goods from their camp (Dowling, 17/8/1859). Another day they found a blacks' camp and he says 'Stole some of their instruments. Left knives in return' (Dowling, 3/9/1861).

Dowling took firm precautions when he saw possible danger. 'Came on a camp at night of blacks. Took turns to watch them all night. . . . Let the Blacks go at daylight' (Dowling, 14 & 15/9/1861). One night Carpoo and Woe pestered him for rum. His tactic was 'Made them both screwed and sickened them of their desire'. The next day they are 'very seedy' but Dowling 'Made Woe ride a horse called Coon. He threw him the first time, but he managed him after.' Such casual comments about making the blacks do things for him, are common in Dowling's diaries. Not only did he make them show him the way here and there and make them ride horses, but he made them work hard at tasks which must have been somewhat meaningless to them. No wonder he occasionally returned to find 'my black boy had bolted' (Dowling, 20/8/1861).

There seems little doubt that both black and white violence would have been seen by the perpetrators as revenge for attacks or violence from the other side. It also seems clear which side was destined to win what was a violent struggle for supremacy, for in technological power the whites had immense advantages. The response of the blacks is not well understood, but it was clearly complex, and varied from continuing fierce resistance to immediate capitulation.

RESISTANCE AND MIXING

Resistance

The responses of the Aborigines to the whites had a determinant effect on the treatment they received. The pattern of resistance which developed on the frontiers was clearly a prelude to the reprisals meted out by the settlers. Subsequent responses to dispossession, station work, camp life and surveillance was an important part of the development of relations between blacks and whites. To what degree then, and at what stage did the Aborigines mount resistance to settlers? Is it valid to call all aspects of Aboriginal behaviour that created problems for the settlers 'resistance'? Is reluctance to change, or slowness to adapt, resistance? Or should resistance refer only to deliberate attempts to stop invasion and refusal to concede defeat? Even though defeated, surely it is possible to resist complete domination? It seems to me that the notion of resistance need not depend on conscious planned campaigns, but simply on denial of cooperation. If the settlers were not being accomodated, they were being resisted, regardless of motive.

While the invaders refused to recognise the legitimacy of resistance they must have known they were not welcome, for the simple existence of blacks was sufficient reason for arming. No other response to resistance appears to have been contemplated. One squatter warned others of the problems they would face on the Darling: 'Any party intending to squat here would require eighteen months supplies and plenty of ammunition, the blacks being very numerous' (*SMH*, 23/4/1850). Surveyor Charles Arthur, who was sent to lay out 200 miles of the river frontage into runs prior to its being 'thrown open' to tenderers in 1858, took a 'party of 8, well armed and prepared for any encounter with the Aborigines' (Jervis, 1956:7). There are several reports of warnings, preparation for violent defence, and then a peaceful journey of exploration. Norton, for instance, in 1859, armed himself reluctantly and, despite the fact that he travelled alone for many miles and often camped alone, only saw three blacks who would not let him approach, and they ran off. He exclaims 'And this was the country where I had been specially and repeatedly warned that the blacks were fierce and not to be trusted' (Norton, 1907:69).

Others took precautions. The surveyor White said the natives were 'very troublesome especially about the Bogan, and he never allowed them near the tents at night' (*HB*, 2:56). Another explorer came across vast numbers of Aborigines who were, he says, 'kept in check by the firm and prudent measures of Mr Ray' (Jervis, 1948:76). It appears that, in this area, any violent resistance was a matter of individual killings rather than large-scale concerted attacks or the harrassment and stealing of stock which occurred, for instance, in Queensland

(Reynolds, 1981). Lack of detailed evidence precludes our knowing the degree of conscious resistance. Clearly some Aborigines offered threats of various kinds, though the popular notion of generalised Aboriginal savagery conceals most specific examples.

A number of questions concerning the beginnings of the new social system in NSW will be raised in the context of an examination of what these events might have meant to those who are silent in the history books, but who nonetheless were most directly implicated. The question of black involvement in policing blacks and suppressing their resistance needs discussion, as does the widespread sexual interaction which has been such a significant part of 'race relations'.

First it should be recognised that Aborigines probably had little desire to emulate the behaviour of the whites. The German missionary Schmidt said 'I judged that they consider themselves superior to us.... they preferred their mode of living to ours' (ibid., 48). Further, they knew themselves to be more competent and knowlegeable especially in the bush. Darling River Aborigines told Simpson Newland that 'rain never fell without the exercise of aboriginal power, and but for them, the white man, his cattle and sheep, would perish miserably' (ibid., 49).

Unless they had heard about the invasion from those nearer the coast, Aborigines who guided the explorers had no reason to suspect that their activities would lead to disaster. With no notion of monopolisation of land for the benefit of some to the detriment of others, and no recognition of what the pastoral industry could be for, the blacks first realisation of the threat posed to them by the whites would often have been when attempts were made to keep them from the stock, from the rivers and from taking those things to which they believed they had a right. Their 'trespassing' and 'pilfering' was met with violence, often with death.

Where such conflict was absent there remained, for a time, cordial relations. Perhaps the most striking example is the experience of Eyre, explorer and pastoralist, who settled on a property in the south and was appointed Protector of Aborigines. Hardy speaks of his 'personal success among the blacks'. Eyre himself described it thus:

> I have gone almost alone among hordes of those fierce and bloodthirsty savages, as they were then considered, and have stood singly amongst them in the remote and trackless wilds, when hundreds were congregated around without ever receiving the least injury or insult. In my first visits to the more distant

tribes I found them shy, alarmed and suspicious, but soon learning that I had no wish to injure them, they met me with
readiness and confidence. My wish became their law; they con-
ceded points to me that they would not have done to their own
people. . . . Tribes that never met or heard of one another before
were brought to mingle in friendly intercourse. Single individuals traversed over immense distances and through many inter-
vening tribes, which formerly they never could have attempted
to pass, and in accomplishing this the white man's name alone
was the talisman that proved their safeguard and protection
(Hardy, 1981:58).

While elements of this account appear fanciful, Eyre clearly experienced
no hostility. He left the district after three years, in 1844, without having
experienced 'a single case of injury or aggression' (ibid.).

When the Aborigines became disillusioned with the whites, either
because of unfulfilled expectations of reciprocity or because of unjust
violence, or sometimes when they had been forewarned, they often
threatened the lives and endeavours of the settlers. Further south and
west, stations were abandoned for a time (Hardy, 1977:68). It was
then that talk of wanton ravages and treachery began.

There are individuals whose outspoken resistance to whites and
their ways is recorded. Simpson Newland wrote of several such men.
One, for instance, recognised that further resistance was futile, and
acquiesced in the submission of his kin, yet from the very first he
'refused to hold any intercourse with the hated Boree, much less work
for him, wear his clothes, or even eat his food' (Newland, 1895:43).
Newland suggested that this man, Barpoo by name, may have been
responsible for the deaths of many a poor nameless tramp in revenge
for the wrongs of his people. There was another 'warrior hero',
known to the whites as 'Baldy', who 'refused to fraternise with the
invader' (Hardy, 1981:117).

There are tales throughout Australia of explorers being saved from
death, of children found and cared for, and of tremendous acts of
courage to assist the invaders for no other reason apparently than
that they were humans who needed help. Often the protection was
from other Aborigines. Lorna Dixon, a Wanggumara woman born in
1911, told Janet Mathews that her great grandparents were amongst a
group who protected the explorers Burke and Wills from wilder
Aborigines in 1861 (Mathews, 1977b:27). The settler Mathews was
protected by his own black employees from attack by local blacks
whose land he was eyeing (*HB*, 8:278).

While it would be difficult to justify using the term collaboration for helping the explorers, what of the police trackers and that notorious band of men known as the native police? From the beginning, the police in the west used black trackers mainly for tracking lost or criminal whites. How did Aborigines get involved in such work? First it should be stressed that black police were few in number, and they usually were recruited from already defeated communities. Also, of course, some individuals during or after a war will readily join the victor just as some remain aloof. Perhaps, also, Aborigines tended to see an employer as an individual rather than as a representative of the invaders. As for the troopers in the native police, they were not employed in the area they originated from so, like mercenaries everywhere, they were simply hired men with special bush skills. The black troopers were also subjected to a harsh discipline which included floggings (Rowley 1972a:42), presumably as a way of resocialising them.

Black trackers often helped police to chase bushrangers. The rewards for tracking could be considerable as when a charge of murder against Jimmy Kerrigan was dropped when he succeeded in tracking down the bushranger Midnight (*HB*, 8:163). The diary of the Byrock police station from 1884 to 1888 reveals that a series of trackers were employed, but gives no account of how they were recruited or why they lasted so briefly at their jobs. (*HB*, 4:128-30).

Men who were apparently powerful were endowed with plates hung on a chain around the neck asserting their royal status. This practice was one of the indirect means used to placate the blacks. While the pendants were certainly worn, it is doubtful that the notion of conferred status would have been taken seriously by those who were given them or by those who were not. Like the silly names such as 'Gaspipe', they may have been meaningless to the blacks but would nonetheless be effective denoters of status to whites. In a station diary, four 'Kings' are recalled 'standing in regal silence with their brass plates proclaiming their identity waiting for rations from the store' (*HB*, 8:199). The success of such means of domesticating and resocialising people is difficult to assess.

Another way of resocialising was by befriending and interfering with those whose labour was useful. Familiarity and control are the mark of the relationship with 'our blacks'. The black 'girls' are recalled by first names (*HB*, 8:199). In the 1860s, one exploring party enjoyed friendly relations with 'black men and white living happily side by side at the same waterhole' trading ducks for flour and sugar. But inequality is apparent:

> One evening the camp's wit made 'policemen' of the tribesmen who came to call, cutting their beards into all sorts of ludicrous styles, some French, some Yankee, a few clean-shaven on one side. The Aborigines were delighted and had no idea that the operation served any other purpose than to enhance their dignity (Hardy, 1977:131).

Rowley describes a farmer who 'combined humanity and restraint', but points out that for the blacks he employed it was just 'another road to unconditional surrender'. In the long run they were no better off than those groups who stubbornly resisted (Rowley, 1972a:29).

Miscegenation

Then and now, miscegenation is a subject of great secrecy, more even than violence. Perhaps it should be made clear that Aborigines had a very different notion of sexual relations from those that prevailed among the European invaders. Rules and restrictions on sexual expression were important to both groups, but the contrast between the rules, and the context in which they operated, was marked. Accounts of common practices which typified Aboriginal society before gross invasion and adjustments took place indicate that the assumptions about sexual encounters that probably caused the severest difficulties were the apparent freedom of women to follow their own wishes, the reward expected for a woman's sexual favours, and the virtue associated with generosity of men concerning their wives' sexual availability.

White men's assumptions will be more familiar to readers. They were not necessarily rapists or inhumane, but their reaction to Aboriginal practices would almost certainly have been negative. The notion of any kind of payment to the husband of a woman, or even the notion of a husband lending his wife, would not have inspired respect among either white labourers or squatters. More important, sexual relations of whatever kind took place in a context where white men had considerable power, often of life or death, over Aborigines.

There is informality and humour discernible in some of the first sexual contacts. Sturt was amused at the temerity of the Aboriginal women in their desire for sex with the explorers. One wonders how the Aborigines explained his denial of their desires. At later periods, as towns donned a respectable facade, Aborigines began to be seen as a moral threat, for sexual rather than spiritual reasons of course. While there is mention of half-caste children from the earliest times, some presumably fathered by overlanders or having come from the earlier invaded areas, there is virtually no discussion of their origin or their fate. The more powerful citizens, usually landowners or town businessmen, were the magistrates in the late 19th century and they attempted to reduce the social and sexual interaction between blacks and whites. The penalty for frequenting the black's camp was 14 days gaol. Vincent Dowling says:

> . . . it is a great pity that something can not be done to remove the temptation from drunken and inflamed men, for at almost every corner and turn . . . are camps of gins and their friends and, at daylight and dark, their drunken orgies disturb the town from its propriety. This coupled with the yelping and rushing of scores of dogs make up a very nice opera (*MM*, 30/8/1863).

One case against an Aboriginal which was heard before the JPs Becker, Dowling, Byrnes, Hughes and Foott, was reported thus: 'among the number was an attempted rape by a sable biped of this colony. The case was very weak, and the noble savage was sent to his run rejoicing' (*MM*, 7/1/1869).

In Australia generally, the longer-term relationships between black and white were disapproved of even more than the casual ones (cf. McGrath, 1984). One of the few alluded to is that of the bushranger Frederick Ward (alias Thunderbolt), whose 'half-caste gin' was found busy planting the stolen property when the police raided the camp. 'Mrs. Thunderbolt . . . gave them a little Billingsgate and twitted them on their want of success' (*Empire*, 2/5/1865).

There were many white landholders who forbad intercourse with blacks. For instance, Mathews would not allow his men to go to the blacks camp (*HB*, 8:279). Others encouraged boundary riders to keep Aboriginal women. Charlie Phillips, who was the son of an Irish boundary rider and an Aboriginal woman from the Kullalee people, explained that 'Station managers in the old days allowed boundary riders to have a woman. It kept them satisfied' (*HB*, 7:7).

The public attitude of the whites to what they called half-castes, or half-breeds, was quite simple. The white community disowned them. There was no question of the white half being considered sufficient reason for claiming them into the racial category of whites. Their status seems to have been of an inferior kind of black. What the blacks themselves thought of their half-caste children in the early days is not clear, although there have been a number of popular views promulgated on meagre evidence. It seems probable that reactions would partly depend on the particular experiences of relations with white men, both of the group and the mother herself. The fact that Aborigines generally seem to view genetic paternity as being different from social paternity, does not mean that Aboriginal men would accept children fathered by those who for any reason were considered an enemy.

There is sufficient evidence from other parts of Australia and from individual histories to realise that in many cases the mother considered the child as hers, and the usual emotional attachment occurred. There are also cases recorded of children fathered by whites being rejected. Infanticide was a recognised practice in cases where a child was considered for some reason illegitimate, often because there was another at the breast (Cowlishaw, 1978). Thus a mother's wish to raise a particular child fathered by a white man would be likely to depend on the kind of relationship she and her kin had experienced with whites.

The fact that the names of most black families are taken from the early settlers does not imply that these settlers begat them. Nor can we assume that they did not, and in some cases we know that they did. One popular reason which has been given for the 'Aboriginal problem' is that low-class whites interbred with the originally pure and noble black and produced the worst of both races (Hardy, 1981:90). Even were such genetic theories at all meaningful, it would be difficult to demonstrate that those fathered by landholders had better prospects than the children of boundary riders! All seem to have experienced similar fates.

In 1871 a Scottish settler took up a selection of 60 acres, and later managed to get a 10,240 acre 'homestead' lease adjoining his selection. Two of his sons selected adjacent properties. One of them married an Aboriginal woman who bore a number of children, all of whom helped work the property for their stern and hard-working father. The 'half-cast' boys left home early, one at 14, and worked at other stations where they were paid. When their mother died her sister moved in and looked after the old man until he died. Then the sister as well as the remaining children left the property, and the other brother with his white wife took it over. That is, those who were only half Scottish left, taking their Aboriginal half with them. There are now two rather different lines of descendents of the original Scot.

One line owns land, and puts the stress on the second syllable of their surname. The Aboriginal line has had a rather humbler fate as itinerant workers, and seems content to comply with the differentiation by putting the stress on the first syllable of their name.

I have outlined the way the pastoral industry was established in western NSW. The Aborigines, who registered their law and land titles in their songs, found they could not enforce them. They were indeed taught a lesson as the pastoralists claimed. But the Aboriginal Protection Board, which eventually achieved almost total control of Aborigines in the state, continued to instruct them. Before following this major change in the relations between the races in the next chapter, we shall examine the process of establishing the rural workers as part of the pastoral industry. The way landholders sought to establish control over their workers shows interesting parallels and contrasts with the way control over the blacks had been achieved.

WORK AND WORKERS

Work

The harshness of the environment for those accustomed to a different way of life did not only affect landholders and their banks in the late 19th century. The work of all of the early white men — managers and labourers alike — in what they called the outback, was demanding and dangerous because of the isolation, their lack of understanding of the geographical conditions and because the land was for a time defended by its previous owners. The graziers' universal interest was to graze cattle and sheep so that they could make profits from their flesh and their wool respectively. Stock had to be herded before the days of fences, and later fences had to be built and sheep shorn. Food supplies were a constant problem for those accustomed to flour, sugar and tea.

With the road transport from the east sometimes held up for many months, and the steamers from the south likewise often stranded for long periods, self-reliant communities developed. These included large numbers of men engaged in stockwork and shearing, clearing and fencing, building, tank-sinking and doing the multitude of tasks required by a community. Little is known of the origin of the white men who did much of this work. Some were assigned servants, 'government men', who were the cheapest labour available. Because of the chronic shortage of labour, 'the outback offered something nearly approaching absolute economic security' (Ward, 1966:76). Further it offered a life free of convention and restraint that some men took to with enjoyment. However the labour force was not stable; Anthony Trollope called them the 'nomad tribe' (ibid., 73). Aborigines were also employed. The unsatisfactory nature of the labour force was considered as just one other hardship that the pioneers faced besides the isolation, lack of comfort and danger of attack. Little attention has been paid to the hardships of the employed workers, or to their struggle against the pastoralists' control.

White workers

The stations needed workers who not only provided satisfactory service but who would stay. Dowling, who liked poetry, Latin aphorisms and philosophical speculation, showed a pragmatic willingness to use the services of black and white workers to his own ends and an overwhelming conviction that those ends were of paramount importance, even justifying his own, temporary, misery.

Shepherds, so necessary to the grazing endeavours before 1870, were not recorded by name or even reputation — except for a collective one as foolish drinkers. According to Ward, shepherds were despised by other pastoral workers (ibid., 185). They lived in solitary huts scattered around the runs. Dowling describes one of the hutkeepers he came across after a long, difficult and solitary journey as 'the most filthy looking ruffian I have seen for many a long day. . . . Anything cooked by him must be rank poison' (Dowling, 29/6/ 1863). Dowling spent that same night with an Aboriginal couple and expressed satisfaction in their company. The shepherds' life was not an enviable one. Not only were their quarters poor and their work solitary, but they were held financially responsible for the sheep. Supplies were delivered to them once a month, and their pay annually, after deductions for any sheep they had lost. Such a method of control could not be applied to Aboriginal shepherds, who were paid only in kind. The white shepherds' orders to pay were taken to the nearest bush shanty, where the publican commonly took possession of it and supplied the shepherd with grog until it ran out. 'This process was known by the name of "lambing down" from the publican's point of view and "knocking down his cheque" from that of the reckless reveller' (Glover, HB, 3:124).

The isolation did not mean lack of surveillance. In 1865, one Thomas Wilson, a shepherd, was committed for trial for the killing of one sheep, the skin of which was found outside the hut by the overseer (*Empire*, 2/5/1865:5). In 1864, a shepherd 'lost' 1,500 sheep during the flood. He had been five days on an improvised raft living on dead sheep, then on live ones. He was aquitted on this charge, but was given 14 days prison under the Masters and Servant's Act for losing some of the remaining sheep which he had abandoned (*Empire*, 27/6/1864:5). While the Masters and Servant's Act gave the employers a powerful form of control over labour, the shepherds sometimes got their revenge. A local resident complained that 'A scoundrel hired as a shepherd and watchman . . . served about three or four weeks, when he drove his flock up in the middle of the night to the overseer, said he would shepherd no more, and demanded to be paid for the time done. Of course, this was refused. The scoundrel then cadges his way, not to the nearest Bench but to a Bench 360 mile from here . . . he gets a summons for the manager to appear to answer the claim for six months wages . . . a distance of 360 miles, in the middle of shearing' (*PT*, 2/5/1862). The manager did not make the journey and presumably had to pay the wages. The Masters and Servant's Act remained a powerful legally enforceable weapon in employers' hands.

The spread of wire fencing during the 1860s meant the gradual end of shepherding, though for a time fences were destroyed by the displaced shepherds in an effort to retain their means of livelihood (Cameron,1978:25). Boundary riders, who enjoyed a far higher status, replaced shepherds (Bean, 1963:29).

Shearers were also necessary when it became clear that wool was more profitable than beef or mutton. They walked for many miles in heat and flood to get to a shed in time for the roll-call, but had no guarantee of being employed. Jimmy Gibbs, a gun shearer, who left a record of his experiences and whose pride in hard work seldom allowed a complaint to appear in his diary, describes carrying his swag 180 miles to a shed, with food for the journey, and when that shed cut out, taking a coach and another 110 mile walk to another shed half way across the state for 10 weeks work in 1893 (Gibbs Diaries, *HB*, 9:184). Shearers were required in large numbers for the huge flocks of sheep. By the 1880s, flocks of 30,000 sheep were common. Torrance, a manager, complained that shearing was slow and that shearers were often off work with sore hands, and grumbling and crying out for tobacco (Currawinya Diaries, *HB*, 2:177). In the days of blade shearing shearers used to carry their swag and 'work' their shears as they walked to keep their wrists strong. Many of them suffered terribly from swollen wrists as a result of the intensive and temporary nature of shearing (*HB*, 2:10).

The hours were long and any sheep badly shorn would not be counted to the credit of the shearer and, in fact, might mean the loss of payment for a whole pen (*HB*, 2:194). Until the 1870s the sheep were washed by the shearers before shearing; shearers also had to do their own cooking, and buy their supplies from the squatter's store (Ward, 1966:101). The living conditions of the shearers were rough. In the early days they slept on chaff bags in unfloored tin huts. Even in the 1920s Lawson described their 'Thinking, eating, gambling and cooking accomodation . . . for thirty men in about 18 by 40 feet' (quoted in *HB*, 2:185).

The shearers, like the shepherds, were said to always drink their pay. In sorrowful terms an observer remarked in 1863:

> It is, no doubt, to be regretted that money so hardly earned should be so easily parted with; but such are the habits of these classes, with their long abstinence from drink, that when they receive their cheques (perhaps fifty or one hundred pounds, or more), they never stop till they get to a public house, lodge their cheques in the landlord's hands, and in a few weeks at most "knock it down", and with empty pockets and impaired health seek another flock, and wait for the next shearing to repeat the same courses. The reason given for opening these houses are that men will spend their money, however far they have to travel . . . so we save them the trouble and keep the money in the district (*Empire*, 31/3/1863:8).

Such opportunism, such profiting from the weaknesses of 'the inferior classes' has not disappeared. Publicans today similarly deplore the behaviour of those whose drinking habits they profit from. But, as Ward says, the 'fanatical improvidence' of the pastoral workers, who were said to 'earn their money like horses and spend it like asses' (quoted in Ward, 1966:188), was a response to their conditions. As the conditions changed, so did the prevalence of this self-destructive response (ibid., 191).

Besides shepherds and shearers, increasing numbers of skilled and unskilled labourers were employed in station work, fencing, ringbarking, doing stockwork and manning the new woolscours. Builders were required. Wheelwrights, carpenters and cooks were needed. The steamboats had their staff, as did the businesses in the newly sprung towns. There is little information about the lives of these workers apart from the complaints of their employers. Many were illiterate, which is one obvious reason why their views are unknown. Many were 'men almost wild', survivors of the days of convict labour, who feared 'neither God nor man unless it be a policeman' (Bean, 1963:26). The arrival of a policeman caused a wholesale decamping of the workforce from one station in 1864 (ibid., 27). In 1900 Toorale, a station of 1,500,000 acres, employed 100 men all year round plus 43 shearers, assistants and cooks during the shearing (*HB*, 1:130).

The shortage of labour sometimes meant increased wages. It was reported with alarm in 1875 that carpenters or blacksmiths could get £3 per week and the unskilled £2, and that extravagant wages of £1 per week were being offered to female servants. The newspaper comments dryly that the principle of 'women's rights' is evidently respected in the district (*HB*, 4:180). Shearing was sometimes delayed with the shortage of shearers in good seasons. £1 per hundred sheep shorn became the established price, though 22/6 per 100 and a dry ration was sometimes offered (*T & C Journal*, 26/9/1874). But, after the 1869 drought, wages were lowered to 15/- . A newspaper item reports 'Mutiny among the shearers at Beemery, who are not willing to take the new rate. . . . But they had to return to work, as they "found there was such a thing as law"' (*MM*, 12/8/1869). It is from such a background that the shearer's union developed to challenge the power of the pastoralists to use the shearer's labour as they wished. These workers faced particular problems of isolation and lack of means of communication. Unity gave them the powerful weapon of the strike; the sheep had to be shorn. This developing struggle between employers and workers became more significant for the pastoral industry after the earlier struggle with the blacks had been won.

And another kind of inhabitant became the focus of complaint as emphasis on respectability and civic pride increased. In the view of many commentators the outback was a haven for ne'er-do-wells, and many of the local's problems were put down to the activities of the criminal or lower-class element. In the years after police were appointed and court sittings held, the vast majority of the cases concerned drunkeness and bad language, with theft, destitution and exposure (presumably indecent) comprising most of the rest (*HB*, 8:165). Local business people complained of the ruffians who came to the district. There were also suggestions that some of the landowners harboured horse thieves and criminals (*MM*, 16/7/1863). However the definition of crime was somewhat flexible as cattle duffing and sheep stealing was a part of many bushmen's lives (Ward, 1966:203).

Black workers

The inhabitants of the west before 'explorers' or 'squatters' arrived, the Aborigines, as they came to be known, did not write about their experiences. No one recorded their knowledge or views. Before settlement had proceeded very far, commentators accepted that the Aborigines were primitives, with all that that term implied, but in the very early years of the first settler/explorers they were not seen as a threat to the pastoral endeavour, though possible attacks had to be guarded against. The explorer Mitchell expressed the naive hope that European settlement would not result in their destruction (HB, 1:3). Some accounts could be describing another species. One writer recalls that on the Darling in 1857:

> There were some fine tribes of blacks living along the rivers, big strong men and gins, and all as naked as the day they were born. They were very inquisitive but fairly wild and only an odd one would come near our camps. Although they did not seem anxious to fight we knew they were not to be trusted.... We always slept with loaded gun ... revolver ... and the saddle horse tied to a handy tree. ... Cattle dogs (would) warn me of anything strange approaching the camp. They had a special dislike for the wild blacks and never missed a chance of showing it (Wellington Times, 14/12/1922).

As time went on hostility, murderous intentions and other negative characteristics of Aborigines were all discussed as indications of the nature of the particular group, never as resistance. The skills of individual explorers in dealing with the blacks were considered important in determining whether they were 'troublesome'. In fact the reverse emphasis would be more accurate. European endeavours and aspirations had a great deal in common, whereas there was a range of Aboriginal responses to the arrival of Europeans. Hardy's comprehensive study of the Barkinji (Hardy, 1981) shows the tremendous variety of Aboriginal reactions to European incursions in different places, at different times and from different individuals. Aborigines provided assistance, comradeship, and heroic rescue in various situations. At other times they showed suspicion and fear, and at others were demanding, harrassing and aggressively spitting and whistling. Outright hostility, direct attacks and more sophisticated tactical warfare continued in some places for long periods, while elsewhere examples of remarkable honesty, forgiveness, forgetting and even humour, were being recorded (ibid., 48,62).

Before the settlers arrived on the Darling, the overlanding of large herds of cattle and sheep to markets in Melbourne and Adelaide had led to intense and violent conflict with Aborigines in the southwest. At least two large herds of cattle and one of sheep were completely wiped out (Hardy, 1977:31-5). The overlanders' weapons were not enough to deter the large numbers of attackers and eventually the government was prevailed on to 'send a police force to deal out justice'. This 'justice' was eventually meted out with guns (ibid., 34-6), and the route was made safe for the huge herds of sheep and cattle which for many years poured down from northwestern NSW and Queensland to Adelaide and Melbourne.

In a number of ways Aborigines were used to assist in their own disinheritance. They were commonly used as guides by the more successful explorers, both famous and local, and continually by travellers for many years to follow. In most accounts of the times there are dozens of unnamed guides mentioned as the black boys, or niggers (e.g., quotations in Jervis, 1948). Those lost in the bush relied on Aborigines to find them. Further down the river the wool teams depended on the natives and their bark canoes to make the crossing, and it was the custom of the commissioner of crown lands to 'reward the most intrepid and active by the present of a Blanket from those allowed by the Social Government for annual distribution to the Aborigines' (quoted in Hardy, 1981:82).

It appears also, that use was made from the very first of black labour for stock and station work by the squatters — when it could be obtained and made to comply (Hardy, 1977:70). During the Victorian gold rushes in the 1950s, the increased demand for meat had co-incided with the depletion of the labour supply, leaving many stations all over the country entirely dependent on black labour. Two or three whites ran properties with thousands of stock, and appreciative comments were made about the excellence of Aboriginal workers. Payment for labour was regular. 'Clothes tobacco and rations were issued twice weekly to allow for their improvidence' (Hardy, 1981:87).

Where Aborigines resisted becoming labourers, the methods used to gain compliance varied from violence to bribery, and the combination of these two methods seems to have proved irresistible! In 1871 an account of station life included this description:

Nearly all the work here is done by blacks who are transferred from one employer to another, sometimes at a very low figure indeed. They make splendid shepherds, and their rations are not very expensive as they consist of 6 or 7 pounds of flour, 2 lbs of sugar, no tea and a fig of tobacco with a sheep to the tribe once a fortnight (Jervis, 1948:167).

Dowling's diaries make very clear the usefulness of blacks as sources of information, as guides and as musterers, shepherds and bark-strippers. There is no indication of payment except in tobacco. Dowling mentions Yarry a number of times for a few weeks and then, 'Got up at daylight and found Yarry had bolted. Intend to let him go as I have no right to keep him. I am sorry to part with him though. Hired Jimmin Wilson in his place' (Dowling, 5/6/1859, *HB*, 3:14). On a property to the north, 'the black boys of Tinenburra comprised the majority of musterers and great stockmen they were too. Their wages were clothing and food . . . with a pound note in their pocket if by chance they got away to town for the races on Boxing day' (*HB*, 2:144).

Dowling frequently hired men, and frequently discharged those who were not satisfactory. He often recorded the price of labour, and clearly one advantage of black labour was that it was paid for only in tobacco and tomahawks, and later in food. During his subsequent years of exploring the rivers to the north Dowling made constant use of information from the blacks. Common are entries such as: '*25th June*. Saw an old black his son and wife. Obtained what information required.' The next day he 'Got hold of three gins and a black. They told us the creek had run a little up above' (Dowling, 25 & 26/6/ 1861, *HB*, 5:138). In these cases his two Aboriginal guides and workers, Woe and Carpoo, were probably interpreting, although their services are only mentioned in passing such as when having 'caught some blacks' he found that 'Carpoo can't understand a word they say' (ibid.,146).

Dowling shows no doubt about his right to demand these services. 'Dropped on some blacks. I am very glad of this fortunate occurrence as I intend to make them show me the way across to the Irara and show me a number of springs that I believe there are between the two places.' He succeeds in 'shepherding the blacks' and shooting game for the party and, though they 'got out of their reckoning after going some distance', Dowling got to the Irara and found the springs he hoped for (ibid., 139-40). Sometimes he seems to have been led astray. 'Self and Mr. Preston and Jacky blackfellow as a guide . . . went to Barugha . . . but black lost himself and after 40 miles we had the pleasure of camping without water and had to return' (Dowling, 28/9/1859; *HB*, 3:13). Such an event may, of course, have been a deliberate attempt to mislead. At times Dowling used sarcastic patronising terms like 'my sable guides Shirt Tails and Bowie Knife' (Dowling, 24/9/1861, *HB*, 5:148).

Dowling was not a stereotypical racist who disliked and disparaged blacks. Once, after travelling many miles in discomfort and solitude he 'met an old blackfellow and his gin . . . [who] invited me to spend the evening with them. I accepted their invitation, they made a fire and pulled some grass for my bed, were exceedingly attentive and polite. On the whole spent rather an agreeable evening. How little satisfies one if one could only believe it.' He accepted the hospitality as a nobleman might that of his vassal, and in the morning he 'Started my hostess, Kitty I find is her name, for the horses at daybreak. She brought them and received her reward in the shape of half a fig of tobacco'. He gained information from them about water sources, and extended a 'pressing invitation' for them to visit his sheep station (ibid., 169).

The 1870s diaries of the grazier Torrance show a dependence on Aboriginal shepherds to whom supplies were taken out regularly. But they were not reliable. 'Quite often they found that sheep had been let go in the open as the blacks had decided to go walkabout' (Currawinya Diaries, *HB*, 2:166). A newspaper correspondent provided an account of the situation of Aboriginal workers in the north of the region in 1885. There were, he wrote:

> On all stations . . . a certain number of black boys and gins all employed and it is difficult to see how stations could be worked without their assistance. The vast majority receive no remuneration, save tucker and clothes. They are, of course, bound by no agreements, but are talked of as my, as our, niggers, and are not free to depart when they like. It is not considered etiquette on the part of one station to employ blacks belonging to another. Cases have occurred where blacks belonging to both sexes have been followed, brought back and punished for running away from their nominal employers. For the main part they are fairly well treated, clothed and fed (quoted in Reynolds, 1981:142).

It is clear that Aboriginal workers were a necessity on these stations. They were also cheap. A further advantage was their familiarity with the country, which not only enhanced their ability as shepherds and stockmen, but meant that they were at home in a country which white labourers often saw as alien and hostile. But Aboriginal employment remained, to a large extent, confined to temporary, menial and casual work. Their place as shepherds became redundant, but they continued to be employed in the lower-status occupations, although fluctuation in the availability of other labour sometimes gave Aborigines local opportunities.

A shortage of labour is clear from this description of the method of recruitment.

The next week another search for blacks to muster horses, got Neddy, Paddy Melon and two gins . . . . Another search for blacks for the muster most on walkabout . . . half a dozen strange blacks bolted out of the camp. . . . I got hold of one with kangaroo dog but he gave me the slip while I was counting sheep. . . . Brought his blankets away and burned all the waddies and nulla nullas of the others. . . . Monkerilla not shepherding well lately and wants to go walkabout for a while.

Though busy shearing . . . the search for blacks went on . . .

2 who had bolted were run to earth . . . and spending the night locked in Mr. Salmon's bathroom before being borne triumphantly home next day (Currawinya Diaries, *HB*, 2:166-70).

Names such as Gaspipe, Bandicoot, Lucky and Hippo are indicative of the status of the Aboriginal workers. Although nicknames were endemic in the outback (Ward, 1966:78), such ridiculous ones would not be borne by white workers. In 1872 the recruitment seems to have ceased.

This year the blacks behaved reasonably well, except for Bally who speared Peter through the hand with one spear and through the knee with another and bolted, and for Topsy who was found in the camp at the station. Mr. Torrance gave her a hammering and sent her back. . . . Monkarella played up too, and was found . . . camped with another shepherd. Mr. Torrance gave him a dressing, shot one of their dogs, and took the others from them (ibid., 172).

Besides such occasional descriptions of the vicissitudes of dealing with their blacks these diaries give much detail about the stock, horses, garden and visitors.

It was not only Aboriginal men who provided labour on these early stations. While colour determined the pay, gender largely determined the work, though Aboriginal women did sometimes become stockworkers. When Henrietta Foott arrived at Fort Bourke station in 1862, she remarked that the clothes which were washed with the assistance of a black gin, were as clean as from a royal laundry (Foott, 1958:156).

The supply and then the control of labour became more problematic as the control of 'wild blackfellows' became more secure on the stations. The value of Aborigines as workers was increasingly recognised, but it did entail costs different from those for the single, white, male employees who seem to have been more numerous. The Aborigines lived in communities, and these communities could not be ignored. A 'black's camp' became a part of the largest stations, and though this was not so common as in the Northern Territory and Queensland, they remained a major feature of some of the properties in the area (Norton, 1907:69). It was clearly an advantage to the station management to have a captive labour force, especially as they were seen as able to provide for themselves and yet were available when and at what price the squatter desired (Goodall, 1982:23). Dowling evinced a certain bewilderment when a group of about 50 Aborigines turned up and camped near his camp on Fort Bourke a few months after he arrived in 1859 (Dowling, 1859, *HB*, 3:4). This group became the source of the black labour that Dowling frequently mentions. He did not of course feel any obligation to support any but those who worked for him, and even these need not be paid a wage as they apparently had an independent mode of subsistance.

Dowling thus indicates how important labour relations were to the early settlers. His diaries are mainly a record of his exploration and reshaping the land to the pastoral enterprise. They also reveal that, despite his philosophical notions of the vanity of man and the brevity of life, it was towards the economic success of his business enterprises that his energy and ambitions were directed. It is not to denigrate the man to recognise this, for his endeavour required courage and fortitude and he presumably could have chosen much easier ways to attain a comfortable life. However, his success required a certain ruthlessness. He had the power to hire and fire workers and he did so apparently without compunction. If the blacks made war on him, he won. Though an educated man he adopted the popular term 'nigger' and used the sarcastic description 'sable'. Dowling received much admiration as a brave pioneer, and was surely one of Jervis' quintessential 'bold spirits'. A short biography of Dowling says 'Although exposed to frequent attacks from the blacks he escaped without hurt — but not without some close shaves — Yet he did not retaliate and not until 1865, when his brother John was murdered by the blacks, did he ever shed a drop of blackfellow's blood'(Maxwell, n.d.:385). A newspaper report of 1865 expresses satisfaction 'that Dowling is at last rewarded. He has been opening up country for others to occupy' (*HB*, 5:95). Thus the man's reputation as a humane, generous and brave explorer and pioneer is sustained by a selective account of his relationship with the locals.

It is ironic that Aborigines' 'way of life' was only recognised when it saved the landowner money. There is further irony in the fact that these landowners, in limiting Aborigines' access to previous hunting, gathering and fishing places, were reducing the chances that the labour force would continue to exist. Perhaps the severe depopulation made this issue appear insignificant. From the 1860s previous sources of subsistence were being depleted anyway with cattle eating the grass and other game fast being squeezed out. While fishing and a few hunting skills have been retained until today, these have become largely the secret and specialised knowledge of a few men.

When the pastoralists had achieved control of Aborigines who had previously threatened the lives of men and stock, the relations with workers developed greater significance. We shall see below how the control of Aborigines was transferred to the state, and class relations became more problematic.

Chapter 2

From rags to riches and riches to rags

THE NEW CULTURE

Fluctuating fortunes

It was not only the original inhabitants who were experiencing dramatic changes in 19th century Australia. Everywhere men and women were struggling in new situations to make their fortunes, or to avoid losing them. Under such conditions the old patterns of status and style, of deference and manners, the expression of class, were shaken up. While family money and status could be of great practical assistance for those taking up grazing properties, they were neither indispensable nor a guarantee of success. Many of those who were successful in the western region had humble origins. There were others who made or lost fortunes and left. Those who made them are well remembered.

Samuel Wilson arrived in Australia in 1852, at the age of 20, with nothing. He became very wealthy and aquired many properties, including Dunlop and Toorale on the Darling. He was knighted, endowed universities and founded a powerful family line. Tyson was another who began as a farm hand and eventually held over 5,000,000 acres. He was unmarried and died intestate. Another was Kidman, who is reputed to have tried to buy New Zealand for a bull paddock! (*HB*, 2:11). He is recalled with affection by Aborigines in the west as he encouraged them to remain on his property, saying that they brought rain (Beckett, 1958a:37). Kidman's sons became 'collar and tie men'. Other very wealthy landowners such as McCaughey severed their ties with the district by removing their investments when the precarious nature of the profits was revealed. Vincent Dowling left the area in the 1880s for a more benign climate.

The stockmen originally hired by these men often 'made good with very little schooling' (*HB*, 5:101). Many young men set out with virtually nothing to seek their fortunes in the west as drovers, stockmen or sometimes skilled tradesmen. Some then became head stockmen, managers or supervisors, and subsequently took up selections, drew blocks or bought the lease from the owner. Occasionally a working hand married into the owner's family. Thus, through working for the big owners, someone with ability, luck and an eye to

the main chance, might become a landholder in the western region
and keep the land in the family. It is often not clear when or whether
the manager became the owner, and the distinction seems to have
been deliberately blurred. Often an owner became a manager after
the mortgagee took over a station (Bean, 1963:24). Such arrangments
are still made today. Sometimes the successful men went into business in the towns and stood for parliament or, more frequently,
became active in local government.

It may be that the western district, because of the isolation,
afforded more opportunity for poor white men to acquire property.
There were few 'gentlemen jackeroos', perhaps due to the isolation
and harsh conditions.[1] But though many of the local landholding
families in the outlying regions had humble origins, status differences did not become insignificant. Rather the markers of status
changed. There was a gradual smudging of the old signifiers of
superiority and a development of new ones. Many who pioneered
the land had no 'breeding' to be proud of, and a number were even
ex-convicts. Bean describes how 'the boss moved with unquestioned
authority among strong, independent, sometimes unruly men'
though he often had no 'claims of birth' to respect (ibid., 20). Bean is
developing the ideology, which came to dominate Australian society,
of the natural equality among men in the bush, where natural superiority will be recognised.

It is of course the success stories which are recorded with pride. The
local people gain reflected glory both from the qualities of the individuals involved and the period of history or the economic and
social system which allows such 'social mobility' to occur. But those
who made good are of course the minority; the stories of the failures
are rarely told, and their descendents have little reason to repeat
them. Indeed they seldom know of them. Men with large families,
those who selected poor property, those who faced drought, and
those without an aptitude for stockwork and bush life would have
had little chance of success.

A few of the early owners who lost all they had are mentioned with
sorrow. One man who 'had £10,000 in the bank and 40 square mile of
splendid country' was next seen 'at the fire of a drovers' camp eating a

---

[1]Jackeroos were the sons of British aristocrats or later of wealthy Australian landowners, sent as apprentices to other stations where they learned the station work from
scratch. Some were aristocratic weaklings and wastrels and became the butt of
bushmen's jokes (Ward, 1966:194-5). But sometimes they bought property themselves
and so extended their family holdings. An uneducated man would find it difficult to
manage a station, as literacy and some knowledge of business were needed.

begged meal'. But it was 'not all his fault either. . . . More than half of the hundreds who have lost as much and more, and have come down only not quite so low, divide their ruin partly between bad seasons and bad laws' (HB, 5:56). A once wealthy Melbourne man was buried without a service in Bourke in 1872 (T & C Journal, 20/1/1872:71). We hear even less of the fate of any women and children who experienced these disasters.

The disreputable could gain wealth through more dubious means such as cattle duffing. Ward asserts that 'all honest bushmen, more or less, were cattle duffers and sheep-stealers on occasion' (Ward, 1966:203). With the emphasis on individual initiative and a highly mobile form of capital 'the few rogues had ample scope for their activities' and the homeless flocks of the 'grass pirates . . . plundered the public stock routes and vacant grazing lands until well into the twentieth century' (Heathcote, 1965:198-9). Recent newspaper reports indicate that such activities are still common in inland Australia (Weekend Australian, 25-26/5/1985). Other rogues flourished in the lucrative liquor trade and became by-words for ruthlessness and greed (Ward, 1966:85). Two men who had grog shanties conducted a friendly rivalry over securing the big cheques from the tank-sinkers and fencers (Clune, 1952:85). The emphasis on individual initiative in an egalitarian society meant that wealth gained in these ways attracted little disapproval. It could be put to as good use as any other money.

Pubs were important in the west. In an alien land, in unaccustomed solitude, the whites needed the pubs for their gatherings. For a long time townships consisted of a store and one or two grog shanties or pubs. Bark huts gave way to weatherboard and slab shacks, and then to brick structures. Copper mining brought more people and prosperity to the region, and by the early 1890s towns were flourishing with the major banks represented, and bond stores and customs agents serving the trade. Smaller villages grew in the outback.

In 1883 one town was dubbed the Chicago of the west being 'crammed full with insurance agents, Sydney bagmen, and travelling watchmakers'. But foreboding is apparent in a comment that 'every other well dressed stranger one meets in town now is a "Rabbit Inspector"' (T & C Journal, 25/9/1886:640). By 1885, when the railway line was opened, the bubble of prosperity was beginning to burst, but already the area had been transformed utterly. The country, the people and the land were being directed to a totally different enterprise from that which prevailed before the whites arrived, an enterprise which entailed severe hardships for many and insecurity for all.

Changing Manners

Ambivalence about the display of status is evident in many newspaper reports of the times. There was fluctuating but growing prosperity, and a degree of luxury might be witnessed on some of the larger properties. Some owners built huge stone houses, offered lavish hospitality, employed retinues of servants, and rode abroad in carriages drawn by stylish well-matched teams (Hardy, 1977:184,221).

One town claimed to have 'more gentlemen . . . by birth, names and education . . . than within the same radius of any other inland town on the colony' (*T & C Journal*, 8/6/1872; *HB*, 2:98). But an 1873 newspaper report of a ball in the same town deplores those who elevate their heads too high and parade their social position with old country ideas of birth and ancestry which ought to be kept in the background (*HB*, 5:53). The labour tradition also developed and flourished among the shearers and Jack Meehan, shearer and labour man, was elected MLA for the district in 1904 (*HB*, 2:7-10).

Those who came to occupy the most prestigious social positions did so because they literally made their fortunes in Australia. Among the white population, old lines of status demarcation were severely shaken up and the distinguishing manners of the 'aristocracy' were largely obliterated. Old family connections were no longer a reliable indication of wealth or of social status. Those who did have pretentions to a 'cultured lifestyle' found that style difficult to achieve in conditions which lacked trained domestic labour — as well as most of the other material accoutrements of the gentry's manner of living. Further, because many of the squatters, or those who became the squatters, were only just becoming landowners, they had little experience of the manners of the landed gentry had they wished to follow them.

Many attempts to establish the marks of privilege were nipped in the bud by financial hardship. With the rejection of the British Toff, and widespread contempt for the 'new-chum', the 'remittance man' and the 'colonial experiencer', there grew another tradition which came to symbolise the unique characteristics of Australians. This tradition emphasised qualities common to man and master in the bush. Superiority was based on toughness, hard work and honesty, but also initiative and intelligence. Ward lists the characteristic outback virtues as being manly independence, egalitarian collectivism and mateship (Ward, 1966:2). The expression 'He was a whiteman and refused a swagman nothing' (Gibbs Diaries, *HB*, 9:189) indicates that generosity was valued, at least by the swagmen. These qualities could be found in people with no family tradition, and indeed Ward considers that 'rough and ready improvisation were convict traits . . . [and] also, in the outback, often necessary conditions of survival' (Ward, 1966:87). However, the traits of those who had survived for thousands of years in this 'outback' were not described in the same terms, and were accorded no admiration. As is the case today, status groupings among whites were made against the background of denying the blacks any status.

Kinship did not lose its significance, not the least because kin ties allowed for the development of trust in a situation of lawlessness. Connections to newly fortunate families could be used to wield influence. But inequality was masked by the egalitarian forms of interaction which were common between white man and white master in the bush.

> We drove to a big hotel by the river divided into two parts, the bushman's and the squatter's in the old colonial style. . . . There was practically no distinction of persons on the hotel balcony . . . where bronzed men lounged, smoked, drank and gossiped for a third part of the 24 hours. The boniface of the hotel was on the easiest terms with all his customers, and would slap a wool king on the back and call him by a familiar nickname with as little ceremony as he would use with a swagman (*SM*, 28/11/1896:1125).

This author, the wife of the representative of one of the great Sydney firms, was also surprised to find that a woman she had been introduced to in the drawing room was a maidservant, who was better dressed than her mistress. But she writes of this as if it were all quite original and charming.

Some old traditions were clung to for a time. One family continued to dress all the children in white, the boys in white linen suits. But such pretensions did not last. A report from the 1930s remarks on the heroism of the outback women who, 'in terrible conditions and heat, without help, without conveniences, without holidays and without a proper diet still kept their houses spotlessly clean despite the eternal blowing sand' (Bird, 1961:98). Some women cooked huge meals for the station hands, at a hot stove in the heat of 114 degrees, with thick stockings to keep off the flies. Not all women had to adapt to such work. One new bride found conditions difficult as she did not like cooking. Her husband, the station manager, asked the shearer Jimmy Gibbs whether he could cook. Gibbs' story continues: 'of course our own cook Scotty at the camp was a champion cook he said to me if you could cook for the men in the camp till I get you a cook I could bring Scotty in here to cook' (Gibbs Diaries, *HB*, 9:188). No one seems to have objected to the notion that the homestead cooking was more important than that for the shearers. Thus egalitarian manners did not of course indicate that man and master were equal.

The significance of tradition did not disappear with the shake up in the old class allegiances, but new traditions were formed and new family histories begun. It does not take long to legitimate new traditions and reject others, as the change in the status associated with convict ancestors in recent years demonstrates.

There are today a few carefully nurtured family connections with the earliest settlers in the district. Descent from the first white child born in town; the first white man to see this or that river; and the first to buy land, to get married or to die in the town is a matter of pride, or at least of record. The family stories often displayed for public view by local historical societies also indicate something of the assumptions about who is important and why. The pedigree of workers who own no land, and of Aborigines who used to have it all, warrant no mention.

Through these changes a number of themes emerge in the preoccupations of western NSW towns which are still characteristic of outback life. From the start of white settlement there has been a conviction that the character of the men who have lived in the outback is different from those who inhabit the towns 'down inside' and experience a safer and more comfortable life. Those with city ways are rejected if they challenge the ways and the thoughts of the country people. An early example is the scant sympathy shown to two teachers when they complained, in a letter in 1876, of the appalling conditions with 134 pupils in a tin shed with dirt floor (*HB*, 1:217). Parochialism is commonly expressed in admiration for the men on the land with their natural virtue, and denigration of the city slicker. The small-town shopkeepers publically side with the squatters in affirming the virtues of outback life, but so do the pastoral workers who partake of the virtue without the financial rewards or the status of their employers.

A second distinctive theme is the peculiar sense of resentment in relations with the government. Again it is the pastoralists who promulgate the view that, because the pastoral industry benefits the country as a whole, they deserve to have their interests looked after by the government and should also be compensated for living in an isolated environment. Complaints about lack of school facilities for the children of the squatters began early and continue today (Heathcote, 1965:152). In the 1890s graziers complained that 'returns from pastoral activities did not permit their families to take holidays or take part in social activities locally' (ibid.).

Drought and flood relief have been accepted by pastoralists for many years. But this same group of people are unwilling subjects of other government decisions. Baldy Davis' speech in the legislative assembly in 1901 complaining of the government not understanding the needs and requirements of the west, was just one of a long line of such complaints (*HB*, 2:8-9). The local view is that residents of the west need and deserve government support both in business and in personal life because they are subject to more difficult conditions than other people. In the early days, the arguments of those in the west were with more fortunate graziers 'down inside' who dominated the legislature. As time went by the rise of more powerful interest groups led to all graziers uniting, and today the rural industry in general tries to speak with a united voice. But throughout each period the western graziers have managed to develop personal contacts with particular government ministers because of the necessity to explain the special situation in the west. Part of that specialness stems from the presence of 'the blacks'.

There is a local independence evident in these themes. Indeed, the distance from the forces of law allowed relatively independent sources of power to be established. Local rules are made by influential townspeople whose power is derived directly from their control over local resources and their virtual monopoly of contact with the government and other outside agencies. Government legislation can thus often be either bypassed or subverted. The common forms of patronage which are evident today, were apparent in the activities of influential citizens before the turn of the century (*HB*, 1:215; *HB*, 5:50). It is through control over local government that a small group of wealthy townspeople in alliance with the landowners has been able to have its way on many local matters.

Finally, there is an unbroken history of complaints about misrepresentations in the city press and elsewhere; 'The west is misunderstood'. In the 19th century, just as today, there were cries of outrage about the *Sydney Morning Herald*'s inaccurate reporting of events in the west (*HB*, 1:237-9).

Depression

The search for grass and gold came to an end. After the prosperity of the 1880s came subdivisions, more droughts, rabbits and a de-depression caused by a fall in the wool prices. The alarm caused by changing economic conditions was accompanied by the recognition of even more intransigent pitfalls. The natural phenomenon of drought, at first believed to be an exception, showed itself to be an implacable enemy of pastoralism. Then the rabbits arrived, eating and breeding faster than the sheep and cattle. The disastrous effects of overstocking with hooved beasts, land degradation and scrub infestation, were apparent from the mid-1880s (Jervis, 1948:179-83).

The early volatility of the new industry is evident from the fact that all but one of the original 33 owners of 1851 had disappeared from one area by 1879, while the average size of holdings had more than doubled since 1866, and the number of leasees declined (Heathcote, 1965:125). Despite the legislation of 1884, closer settlement was not achieved due largely to family partnerships and to 'dummying', where a squatter would 'select' the most valuable portion of his own leasehold under a dummy name. Investors in the west country had been victims of an exaggerated idea of property values and properties sold in the 1890s would not fetch the price of the improvements (Jervis, 1948:182; Hardy, 1977:192ff.). Many suffered, but others gained a firmer hold. By 1900 companies and banks controlled almost three-quarters of the area in leaseholds (Heathcote, 1965:144).

The pastoralists saw the government and the workers as responsible for their problems because of the legislation reducing the size of holdings and the shearer's refusal to accept lower wages. But it was the 'financial crash', in particular the drop in the price of wool on the British markets, which paralysed the whole pastoral industry in 1893.

The bursting of the bubble of prosperity did not destroy the established pastoral industry or the dominance of white civilisation. People now found themselves following three kinds of calling. The townspeople were mostly engaged in commercial activities; the pastoral workers received wages for a range of jobs which were almost always physically arduous; and the station elite, usually considered the most important group, made a living from wool and beef while often working beside their employees. The second category has been continuously reduced in numbers over the last one hundred years until today there are very few wage earners in the pastoral industry.

It is not necessary to follow in detail the demographic changes that have taken place since the turn of the century, nor the economic ones.

Repeatedly, soaring prices creating boom periods and fortunes have been followed by depressed prices and further foreclosures, most frequently affecting the smaller owners. Accompanying these man-made crises are the even less predictable droughts and floods with pests, scrub infestation and land degredation as constant sources of distress. The blacks are seldom mentioned as problems after the 1880s — we shall see why.

The stories of success and failure are well enough known, but the demonstration they afford that an individual's acquisition of wealth and status are largely dependent on historical accident is not a popular one. The landowners try to create the impression that they have always owned land, and that there is something natural about the status of landowner and employee. Success is attributed to personal qualities, not to the fortune of good seasons and prices. The wealthiest owners gained enough land in the early years to remain secure in poor years, and thus social categories of wealth and status have attained a degree of rigidity despite the chance nature of their origins and the challenges mounted by members of the inferior categories. The racial categories have also rigidified in the face of change. The contingent nature of good and ill-fortune is especially evident in the groups defined by race.

Images of Aborigines

It is easy to read about the past as if the curious and quaint ways of our forebears had little to do with us. It is easy to grant moral worth or to pass censure on those whose words and works we can present selectively. But my aim is to show that the pattern that developed in the relationship between whites and blacks should be understood, not as the product of moral turpitude of individuals but, at a general but fundamental level, as a consequence of the priorities stemming from the pastoral industry. Some individuals were more eager than others to further that industry, and some cared little about the destructiveness it entailed. Others protested and bemoaned the dying of the natives.

Despite such variation in the responses of whites, destruction prevailed, and a pattern of accepted images of Aborigines began to dominate the newspapers and official reports. Some of these themes are still with us although many have been modified over the years. All depend on the reporting of 'the other' by one of 'us'.

From the beginning it is clear that the reporting of attacks by the blacks was much more popular than accounts of attacks on them. In fact, within one or two decades of the first pastoral establishments there were numerous vague, exaggerated or fanciful accounts of the treacherous and untrustworthy nature of those who were being forbidden access to their land and rivers. For instance, an 1880 newspaper gives an account of the 'massacre' of Lee's men (discussed above) who 'being taken unawares by the treacherous blacks nine were mercilessly slaughtered'. Such descriptions are not only wildly innacurate but display a general patronising denigration. The writer says that it is '. . . only 30 years since the occupation by whites and, barring some few loafers about the public houses and homesteads, not a blackfellow left in this district. Fatal to the blackfellow is the introduction of rum, syphillis and blankets' (*T & C Journal*, 14/2/ 1880:314). This author blames the annual gift of blankets for the eventual succumbing to 'his hereditary enemy — consumption'.

> Personally I am not a great admirer of the blacks, and I like them to stand to leeward of me, for they have a very fine aroma of their own . . . for as a rule a blackfellow does not wash his face, hands or body before he says his prayers of a morning, and I never knew one to do it for choice afterwards (ibid.).

Such sarcastic and knowing attempts at humour became a common theme of journalistic comment. Aborigines were no longer feared but figures of contempt and ridicule.

Popular understandings about Aborigines can be gleaned from passing comments of the settlers. The belief that there is something called 'the nature of the blacks' which can be defined by the more incisive white observer was discussed above. A natural savagery is a part of this nature. For instance, in explaining how a man who appeared at the window wielding a butcher's knife was repelled, one woman said 'My father [was] a bushman used to wild blacks methods and therefore was a light sleeper' (*HB*, 2:5). The blacks were also scapegoats for frustrations. Torrance's diaries record 'a row with the cook about the blacks as usual' (*HB*, 2:168). And when news arrives of Dowling's little girl being burned to death it is surmised that 'she must have been about the black's camp' (*HB*, 2:167). Even the blacks' suffering can be the object of contempt. They are described as subject to complaints like scurvy from which they suffer the most excruciating pains. 'They are continually asking for medicine of which castor oil is their favourite. It is wonderful to see with what gusto they drink it and how they smack their lips afterwards' (*T & C Journal*, 17/6/1871).

A new kind of observation of Aborigines began to appear after some years of settlement. The tone is of kindly interest in the quaint tourist attraction of the natives. In 1894 a tourist reported:

> we observed a bevy of black gins approaching, each laden with what we afterwards discovered to be portions of an emu they had killed. There were only 17 dogs accompanying the gins. . . . Afterwards two old blackfellows came on — one a fine stately old fellow, with full flowing grey beard and whiskers. This was the king. The queen also walked past, dressed only in half a blanket, in a most dignified and stately manner. . . . There was a camp of about 50 blacks half a mile away, but time would not permit us visiting them. . . . I have collected a good deal of information respecting the customs of the various tribes . . . (*SM*, 31/3/1894)

Another style, which remained common until comparatively recently, used extravagant compliments in irony. Jervis, for instance, gives the origin of a name; '"Milparinka" is said to mean elopement. In times gone by, one of the original lords of the soil ran away with one of the dusky beauties and settled down on this waterhole, hence the name' (Jervis, 1948:229). An account by the wife of the Sydney representative of a big company in 1896 says:

> The leisurely procession of copper coloured bushmen was often broken by a couple of lubras flaunting in European fashions of the year before last, beribboned and befeathered hats and scarlet cotton gowns. Others preferred the time honoured custom of a blanket and a possum rug. We had royalty too, in the persons of an important looking blackfellow and his lubra, who were called the king and queen of the Darling. Brass plates hung around their necks and gave their names and titles. They knew enough English to be able to beg in that language and came to me one morning with their usual request, "White monee ladee." — I set them to earn their money by plucking a wild turkey. The king begged the entrails which he roasted in a small fire and devoured. A humble request from the queen to her royal consort for a little of the feast was sternly refused (*SM*, 28/11/1896:1125).

In 1923, a newspaper reported the death of a 'typical old Australian aboriginal' well known in the district (*Western Herald*, 3/11/23). Such benign and patronising remarks were common when speaking of those who had caused no trouble. There was little serious public comment on the changing nature of the Aboriginal communities until the 1940s.

RACE AND CLASS

The Afghan case

There were races other than Aborigines and Europeans in the west. Chinese and Afghans as well as blacks and gins were common terms denoting racial categories. Seldom can a racially defined group of people have been so obviously used and then discarded when no longer profitable as the Afghans. In 1866 Sir Thomas Elder imported from India 120 camels and their drivers, all men (Hardy, 1977:108). Other large landowners on the Darling imported more, some establishing camel breeding herds. Forty years later neither camels nor cameleers were welcome.

Transport was a major and constant source of concern in the far west. If it was too expensive to send the produce out or to get the stores in, then the pastoral enterprise would cease to be profitable. Horses and carts and bullock teams were the first transport. Then for a time river steamers flourished. They were floating shops from the south, and could take out the wool at times when the bullock teams were bogged on flooded roads. However they were often interrupted, sometimes for months and even years, by low rivers.

Then the bullock teams were faced with another rival — the camel trains which were especially useful for bringing wool to the rail depots (Bean, 1911:264). Later, when other more economic forms of transport became available, the previously cheap camel transport was also superseded and the romance associated with river transport could not save the steamers. In 1885 the railway created the next challenge, but it was the internal combustion engine which finally led to the demise of the steamers and the bullock and camel teams in the 1920s. The aspect of camel transport which is of most interest here is the cameleers.

The cameleers were known as Afghans although most were from the Punjab.[2] Many came as indentured labourers with half of their first years wage deducted to pay for their passage. While they were welcomed by those for whom they represented a more economical form of transport, the camels and the Afghans who drove them faced hostility from others. The camels were said to cause horses to bolt. The camel trains had to circumnavigate the towns, and there were objections to the camels grazing on the town common. Afghans'

---

[2]In 1911 Bean said: '"Afghan" in the west is about as wide as "Dago" on the coast. It covers about one hundred and fifty wholly separate and distinct races of India not to speak of anything originating between Manchuria and about Hungary — provided it drives a camel' (Bean, 1911:212)

camps were segregated from the town and they suffered a series of attacks, both direct and oblique. For instance, to offend the Muslim's religious sensibilities, bacon was concealed in consignments of goods and once the locals put a pig's head in among the cameleers' stores causing all to be discarded.

But the worst hostility came from their rivals, the teamsters, whose livelihood was threatened. The camel teams offered cut rates on short hauls, and in drought were often the only carriers who could operate. The teamster's view was that 'hard working honest men, with large young families (were) thrown completely out of work through the carriage rates having been reduced to starvation figures' (Hardy, 1977:219). The cameleers had no union nor any means to protect themselves from exploitation. Crowthers asserts that they were 'brought over from South Australia around 1880 to lower the rates of haulage and break a carrying monopoly' (HB, 1:43). It is certain that the graziers did not complain about the camels or the low carriage rates. Nor did those who imported the camels and cameleers in the first place suffer any criticism.

Some Afghans themselves became independent operators or even breeders, and are said to have employed their countrymen at very low wages. This would have further alienated them from the local workers (Cameron, 1978:39). They merited hostility from the shearers too. When the Teamster's Union supported the shearer's strike in the 1890s and refused to bring the wool shorn by non-unionists from Queensland to the Darling, the cameleers carried it. They were escorted in 1891 by police from Cunnanulla to Barringui (HB, 2:64).

When those who had imported the cameleers had no further use for them, many were returned to the Punjab whence they had come. Afghans were never given citizenship despite many applications. While those who wished to remain were allowed to retire and die here, as several graveyards show, none were given permission to bring wives. A few who had owned a camel team developed other small businesses and married local women. One even became town clerk and mayor of a western NSW town. In time the few remaining Afghans and also the few Chinese became individual oddities, accepted as a peculiar but sometimes useful part of the town. Old residents today speak of what wonderful gardeners the Chinese were, but how they were afraid of them as children.

The hostility and violence shown towards the 'Afghans' is often described as interracial friction (e.g., Cameron, 1978:39). This implies that, had the cameleers been European, there would not have been conflict, despite the clear attribution of the tension to economic rivalry. The conflict took place at times when the pastoral industry was suffering fluctuating fortunes and when the transport industry was in decline. It was these changes which made such friction inevitable. Whenever racial conflict has become intense, it is embedded in wider conflicts, which themselves developed independently of racial mixtures.

But conflicts, whatever the underlying cause, were experienced as interracial when specific racial groups were targeted. The larrikins of Bourke beat up the Afghans (Jervis, 1948:167). Shearers refused to work beside a Hindoo or American negro although they would work readily with an Australian black or with a New Zealand Maori (Bean, 1956:186). The union did not allow the employment of Chinese cooks and there were no Chinese or Kanak shearers (*HB*, 2:197). On the other hand landholders were eager to employ Chinese labour when it was cheap (Heathcote, 1965:156). Chinese gardeners are often mentioned with admiration for their ability to grow garden produce, and, as mentioned above, an Afghan became a mayor. Thus, race cannot be seen as an independent determinant either of individual fortunes, of group identity or of social conflicts. Race is a dependent variable, a factor that is evoked as an idiom through which power relations are exercised both through institutions and in terms of everyday interactions and practices as we have seen. It is important to have established that this was so in an earlier era before going on to show in later chapters that it is still true today.

Shearers; the necessary workers

The shearers' willingness to work with Maoris or Aborigines should be seen against the unenviable conditions under which shearing took place. Anthony Trollope, a British novelist visiting in the 1870s, thought that the 'nomad tribe of pastoral labourers . . . were degraded by their customary right to receive free rations and shelter for the night in station "huts"' (Ward, 1966:9). In fact the conditions of all pastoral workers, including shearers, were from the beginning such as to be a threat to their very health.

The tally board, which recorded the number of sheep each shearer shore, was an important focus of interest in each shed. The pride and competitiveness associated with shearing ability may be seen as a way of creating status; it was also advantageous to the employers to have shearers competing to do more work in shorter periods of time. Jimmie Gibbs' diary, for instance, gives only brief accounts of the strikes which were so significant in shearing history, being more concerned with his own physical prowess in withstanding hardship, his achievements in the sheds, and the approval he gained from the bosses. He did make a mild complaint about the 600 miles he had to travel for 17/6 a 100 in 1899 (Gibbs Diaries, *HB*, 9:188).

The skill and competitiveness that the tally board symbolises may explain the shearers' comparatively high status among pastoral workers (Ward, 1966:186). The itinerant life, free from ties to one employer or one place, could seem to lend romance to the life. But more important was the fact that shearers' skills were essential if the wool was to be gathered, and because of this they were in time able to organise and demand better conditions and pay from the pastoralists.

The workers' response to technology which simultaneously re-lieves them of the hardest work and of the wages they get for doing it, was played out in the western district more than once. The shepherds' attempt to retain their niche in the labour force by destroying fences has already been mentioned. The shearers used to have to wash the sheep, but the introduction of the woolscour, which could clean 70 bales of greasy wool in 12 hours, relieved them of this task. There appears to have been no resistance from the shearers to its use. However when machine shears were first installed on the 1,400,000 acre Dunlop Stations in 1888 to shear 186,000 sheep, the shearers refused to use them (Hardy, 1977:214). They were talked around by one of the inventors after being three weeks on strike. In the following year many sheds installed the machines.

The Shearers' Union was initially formed in the 1880s not to improve their pay and conditions, but to stop them deteriorating. The rates of 21 and even 25 shillings per 100 sheep shorn, which became common on the Darling in the 1870s (ibid., 106) were threatened when the price of wool plummetted. In 1885, 2,500 bales of sound wool fetched less than 1,400 bales of inferior wool had in 1884 and the graziers asserted that the costs of shearing and shipping the wool could exceed the price paid for it (*WN*, 29/5/1886; *HB*, 9:166). The squatters decided to reduce the rate of shearer's pay. A newspaper notice, signed by managers and owners of 17 stations, stated a set of conditions including a shearing rate of 17/6 for 100 sheep (*HB*, 2:193). Whatever the economic justification, the pastoralists' action provoked such resentment that the Shearers' Union, previously con-sisting of small local branches, had 16,000 members and 500 union sheds by the end of 1887 (*HB*, 2:194).

It was at Dunlop Station in 1886 that the men refused to work for the reduced rate. The police were called to clear the mob of nearly 100 men off as trespassers (*HB*, 9:166). The men set up a camp and, supported by Shearers' Union funds, they held out for nine weeks and won their demands for one pound (20 shillings) per 100 (*HB*, 2:194; Hardy, 1977:213). This strike clarified the dramatic differences between the interests of employers and those of the workers which had been previously obscured by outback egalitarianism.

The shearers wrote an open letter to the local townspeople asking for support. They stated that the price offered for shearing of 17/6 per 100 was not acceptable. The men are:

> all determined to hold out and not shear until they get 1 pound per hundred as usual. In the event of not getting (it) ... we propose to make a camp at Honeyman's East Toorale Hotel. We write asking you to assist in getting business people to uphold us in our endeavours to hold out ... by public subscription (*WN*, 31/7/1886; *HB*, 9:166).

These honest outback battlers clearly felt that the justice of their case against the sudden cut in their wages would be apparent to all, especially the small business people in the town who probably had their own complaints about the graziers. However the editor of the newspaper that published this letter showed no sympathy. He wrote:

> Now considering (1) at the wages offered, men can earn 14 to 20 shillings per day (2) that £1 will purchase more than 25/- two years ago (3) that when work is done and they get their money they will probably be off elsewhere, and Bourke may go to the devil for all they care; we think the above circular as a piece of cool cheek stands unrivalled. If the Bourke business men depended on the shearers, they could form a camp in the insolvent court and always have it full (ibid.).

As this indicates, the business people in the towns saw their interests as firmly on the side of the landholders, and spoke of the unionists with little respect. As we shall see below, one hundred years later this is still the case.

The struggle intensified in 1891 as the Pastoralists' Union began to recruit shearers and shed hands from the unemployed in the cities. This was part of a wider move by employers to repudiate trade unionism in the face of an acceleration in the fall of world prices (Fitzpatrick, 1946:71). In response the shearers formed strike camps of several hundred men near a number of stations along the Darling.

When the strikebreakers, or free labourers, arrived by train or steamer they had a dramatic reception, with police and graziers trying to shepherd them to safety away from the shearers who tried, with considerable success, to recruit the new arrivals to their Union cause (*Australasian*, 18/7/1891:132; *HB*, 2:196-7). But with the police, the railways and the Masters and Servant's Act on the side of the pastoralists (*HB*, 2:192), the shearers were finally forced to agree to work with non-union labour. They did gain an agreement on wages and an assurance that no Chinese and Kanaka labourers would be employed.

The newly amalgamated Australian Worker's Union was then faced with further attempts to reduce wages. There were a number of violent confrontations and attempts were made to block the river boats which carried either strikebreakers or 'black' wool. Many unionists received severe prison sentences and one died of a gunshot wound received in attempts to talk to the 'scabs' in the sheds. The man who shot him was commended and given a prize (*HB*, 2:198). The value of a unionist's life seems similar to that of an Aborigine a few decades before. Mounting a threat to the pastoral industry attracts not only physical violence but calumny. After the 1891 strike the shearers were blamed for the downgrading of the district (*HB*, 1:181). Again there are echoes of an ideological battle to denigrate those who threaten the supremacy of the pastoralist's interests. This time the issue concerned the legitimacy of workers' struggles, an issue which has remained significant throughout the last hundred years.

The Union did not win this fight; they finally surrendered to the far stronger forces ranged against them. By 1897 only six branches of the AWU remained. Over the years the Union gradually built its strength again. Despite the reverses Gibbs could assert that in 1915 shearers did not know what hardship was. They no longer had to walk or cycle hundreds of miles to the sheds. 'Before we got as high as one pound a hundred we had to strike and fight the squatters to get that and those days the accomodation was rough' (Gibbs Diaries, *HB*, 9:195). The Union's strength revived. In 1945 it was demanding the right of workers to earn enough to buy a house and afford 'some of the comforts that make a home a home' (*Western Herald*, 1945; *HB*, 9:299).

With the downturn in the profitability of wool production in recent years, some of the gains shearers made during the last one hundred years are now under threat. Remarkably similar struggles have taken place in the 1980s as were fought in the 1880s. The issues now as then centre on the right of the Union to control, or in this case defend, rates of pay and conditions against the right of the employer to negotiate directly with individual workers. The fight has again come to direct attempts by pastoralists to bring in non-union labourers, and the physical attempts by shearers to stop them doing so.

It is clear that the social conditions of shearers, their pay, and the circumstances of their work, have been negotiated over the years on the basis of their crucial importance to the pastoral industry. The same is true of other pastoral workers. The difficulties they have in commanding better wages or conditions is related to such factors as the frequent oversupply of labour, the personalised relations with the employer which are common in the outback, and the lack of ability to organise due to isolation. One group of workers had even less power to determine the conditions under which they existed.

The native's niche

The popular images of the foreign, quaint and slightly sinister Afghans, as contrasted with the dinkum Aussie shearer, disguises the fact that they shared one basic attribute. The fate of both has been largely determined by their usefulness to pastoralists. Camels and Afghans outlived their usefulness, but the shearers' skills remain essential to the pastoral industry. How did Aborigines fit into this scheme of things?

The place of Aborigines in the pastoral economy is significant in a number of ways. As a group within the colonial and contemporary society they have always been poor, as they are today. This fact must be considered in relation to their access to wages. Further, the work of any group of people who depend on selling their labour is a major determinant of their lifestyle. This is not just because it determines their income, but because of the repercussions of the physical and social circumstances of that work. Beckett found, in 1957, that the only contact Aborigines in western NSW had with whites — other than police and Protection Board officers — was through the men's work, with bosses or fellow workers. Even this contact was not available to those who worked in 'coloured gangs', that is, on contract work with an Aboriginal contractor. Nor was it available to women, most of whom had no paid work (Beckett, 1964:35).

Ward asserted that the character of the convicts sent to the colony improved as a result of the opportunities they were given to become workers due to the perennial shortage of labour (Ward, 1966:33-4). It might be asserted that the character of the Aborigines, as assessed from their public image, has fluctuated according to *their* opportunities in the new regime. It is clear that, from the arrival of the first stock in the west, Aborigines were of considerable value as workers in a labour-hungry region. Most Aboriginal men became pastoral workers of one kind or another. It remained possible for several decades to leave the station and live on wild foods. Beckett found that, 'Up to a generation ago there were some who would periodically take to the bush, to live for a while on wild meat. Emu, kangaroo, possum, goanna etc., are still eaten, and everyone enjoys the excellent fish that abound in the rivers' (Beckett, 1958a:190; see also Reay, 1945:313).

In a rare Aboriginal biographical account Eliza Kennedy, who was born in 1902, recalls her childhood when whites were avoided because of the fear of being shot (Kennedy & Donaldson, 1982:7). Later, when such fears had abated somewhat, the 'shame' or shyness which was an appropriate and expected reaction in many social circumstances and a matter of normal propriety among Aborigines, did not make dealing with the new regime easy. As Eliza grew up it was increasingly clear that the skills she had learnt from her mother and other relatives were insufficient. She had to learn another language and other skills as well as how to be at ease among strangers without feeling 'shameless' (ibid., 12). Eliza did work for whites, but never liked to do so. She was aware of exploitation and refused to work for one family because 'They wanted me for a bit of a slave, I suppose, but I wouldn't be in it' (ibid., 13).

Eliza Kennedy's husband was one of the very few Aborigines to draw a soldier settler's block after the first world war, but with drought and lack of capital he, like many others, was forced off the land (ibid., 15). In the late 1920s their wandering began again 'its scope no longer dictated by the availability of wild food and water supplies, and collection points for government rations, but by the search for wage work on pastoral stations' (ibid.). That work has not led to great riches. Eliza now lives with 'ten grandchildren in the ricketty old house at Lake Cargelligo with its single outside tap' (ibid., 26).

Goodall, in a detailed study of western NSW between 1909 and 1939, has described the captive conditions of the Aboriginal labour force in the 'black's camp'. Food was poor and rations meagre, so modified subsistence continued. Aborigines hunted rabbits and kangaroos (Goodall, 1982:51), at once relieving the pastoralists of pests and of the need to feed their black workers. There is meagre evidence concerning the degree of dependence on Aboriginal labour but Goodall shows that, on three pastoral stations, 25 to 30 per cent of the employees were Aborigines. In each case Aborigines formed a small percentage of the permanent workforce, some in senior positions and some as shearers, but most were boundary riders and casual labourers engaged in scrub-cutting and lamb marking, mustering and general shed work at shearing time. *Most* of these more casual and lower-status jobs were done by Aborigines. 'Mari' (the local Aboriginal self-appelation) women were domestics and launderers. The station ledgers have entries for 1914-17 such as 'Gin; 5 weeks washing 7/- per week.' There was no award for NSW pastoral or agricultural workers before 1921 (ibid., 53) but there were customary rates. Some stations paid Aborigines the same rate as whites and some lower, but they were cheaper employees anyway as accommodation was not supplied (ibid., 54).

Many of the largest properties in the northwestern region had an Aboriginal 'stock camp' at least until 1905 (ibid., 49). The Aboriginal Protection Board (APB) also issued rations on a number of northwestern pastoral properties or remitted the cost of the rations to the pastoralist, thus subsidising the pastoral workforce (ibid., 39). There was less demand for Aborigines' labour in the west with the break up of the great properties after the first world war, and they were no longer allowed to camp around the homestead (Beckett, 1958c:93-4). The use of Aboriginal women as house servants gradually became rarer, presumably with the break up of the stock camps on the properties. There is little information available to trace this process.

The Aborigines did not apparently suffer from the rivalry of other pastoral workers, although information about workers' personal relationships is virtually non-existent. Bean asserts that 'The Australian worker of his own accord regularly recognises his obligations to the blacks' (Bean 1911:264). Perhaps partly because of their small numbers Aborigines were never excluded from union membership and award rates. However, they were still liable to exploitation not suffered by more educated and experienced workers. Not only were they paid in rations and blankets in the early days, but they often remained unaware of their entitlement. Beckett records one example of deliberate cheating when the employer paid his Aboriginal workers in silver coins, trying to convince them that it was great riches (ibid., 1958a:125). There was a legacy of bitterness left by such cheating. 'None of that "Jacky" stuff for me' said one. However others seemed not to care so long as they could earn some cash and such men were still being defrauded (ibid., 126).

In one area Aborigines vividly recalled the scanty rations of tea, tobacco and flour for rural work during the depression years (Reay, 1949:100-1). A shortage of labour in 1944, in one area at least, led to Aborigines demanding the same wages as white employees. This was grudgingly given, but sometimes liquor was used to entice Aborigines to work. Some rural employers expressed disapproval of laws 'which forbid the regular thrashing of aboriginal employees' (Reay, 1945:299). Reay's Aboriginal informants believed that if the local white people had their way all the old Aborigines would be killed and the young ones conscripted to work without pay (Reay, 1949:101).

Beckett gives some indication of the place of Aborigines in the pastoral industry as it had developed by 1957-8. The pastoral west no longer employed Aboriginal women. The Aboriginal men could usually find work as stockmen or station hands. Even shearing, the most highly unionised and most highly paid pastoral work, was not closed to them (1964:34). Of 116 men in Beckett's 1958 survey, 85 were directly employed in the pastoral industry mainly as fencers, station hands, drovers and boundary riders, as well as shearers (1958a:195).

However Beckett says that many Aborigines did not want to work long hours over long periods, but rather wanted to earn a certain amount of cash and then stop (ibid., 193). It should be recognised that pastoral work such as fencing, droving or shearing, usually entails working away from home for continuous, sometimes long periods, thus entailing a radical break from Aborigine's practices. Shyness with strangers meant that many Aborigines would stick to a previous employer or even prefer to stay at home (ibid., 194-6). Aboriginal communities did not put earning cash as the top priority, though not all Aborigines adopted the values that prevailed on the reserves. Much of the work Aborigines did was seasonal or occasional, and they revealed a liking for pastoral work (ibid., 193; see also Reay, 1949:114). While there were a number of gun shearers among the Aborigines, a few employers claimed to not hire Aboriginal workers because of their unreliability and disinclination to work regularly (Beckett, 1964:34). One hospital matron would not employ any Aborigines on the wards because they were too dirty but another matron had several ward maids and trainee nurses (Beckett, 1958a:192).

Such variation among employers made it difficult for Aborigines to develop any systematic counter measures to discriminatory practices.

It was the casual nature of their work pattern, rather than different wages, which led to the very low average income which Beckett calculated (ibid., 206). 'Aborigines appear more impoverished because they have larger families than Europeans, work less regularly, and spend their money in such a way that they have nothing to show for it' (Beckett, 1964:34). Another contribution to low incomes was the fact that contract work, especially in isolated situations, gives opportunity for underpayment. It is clear that values which had been formed under pre-existing conditions were a significant part of the reason for Aborigines' reluctance to take advantage of those things the new system had to offer. However, as we shall see below, there were grim external forces which continued to ensure that Aborigines' common attitude to work and to other aspects of life were markedly different from those prevailing among whites.

In rare accounts of the more informal social interaction between black and white we can gain a glimpse of occasional friendliness, but also of the inequalities that have been such a significant part of these 'race relations'. The apparently friendly rivalry Dowling describes in diving or in a foot race between a black tracker and a stockman (Dowling, *HB*, 3:69), barely conceals a marked lack of fellowship. It is only with the workers or the poorer rural populations that we glimpse a more equitable relationship, although even here the black employees often experienced being fed separately outside (Beckett, 1958c:100). Jimmy Gibbs' humble family lived in a bark house on the river where the blacks were very plentiful. He says, 'My mother used to give them flour tea and sugar and I tell you my mother lost nothing in doing so, as the blacks used to catch wild ducks and fish and give to mother' (Gibbs Diaries, *HB*, 9:178)

In 1958 Beckett predicted that 'In the event of a recession the aborigines would be particularly vulnerable, because of their almost exclusive dependence on the one industry and because they have few skills, little experience and no contacts that would enable them to move smoothly and quickly into other industries' (Beckett, 1958a:223). In later chapters the accuracy of this prediction and the consequences of the loss of work will be discussed. However it is first necessary to look at the other determinants of Aboriginal social existence in the years preceding the loss of pastoral work.

PROTECTING ABORIGINES
Protective legislation?

Colonial governors in the British colonies had instructions from the earliest days of settlement to protect the natives. A House of Commons select committee on the means of achieving this protection recommended in 1837 that missionaries, protectors, reservations, schooling and special codes of law be established until the Australians (a term at that time meaning aboriginal Australians)[3] learned to live in a civilised and Christian manner (Rowley, 1972a:20).

In the colony of New South Wales, however, the problems were apprehended somewhat differently from at 'home'. In 1856 'No member of the select committee (on Aborigines) questioned the philosophy at which NSW settler democracy had finally arrived: that of the one good bloody lesson as the basis for peace in frontier negotiations' (ibid., 42). Indeed that committee recommended greater military efficiency. But when the war seemed to have been won, and the challenges to the landholder's dominion had abated, protection policies were developed. The relations between Aborigines and Europeans on the pastoral frontier were replaced by specific forms of intervention by the state.

Under the invader's laws, Aborigines have never been the same as other people in Australia. Until 1876 Aboriginal evidence was inadmissable in court because they could not take the oath on the bible. This must have saved the hide of many murderers. The Commonwealth Constitution of 1901 stated that 'In reckoning the numbers of the people. ... Aboriginal natives shall not be counted' (Gumbert, 1984:35). It also stated that the Commonwealth government could legislate for any race except Aborigines. The states retained their power to legislate for Aborigines independently until the late 1960s.

Prohibition was the earliest protective legislation. From 1838 to 1862 the Publican's Licencing Act forbad the sale of alcohol to Aborigines. The outcry that followed the repeal of this law led to the

---

[3]When the natives had ceased to be called 'Australians', no alternative proper name had developed or been suggested by those who coherently argued that 'aboriginal' should not be capitalised on the grounds that it was not a proper noun (Reay, 1964:167). However, as proper names often originate in descriptive terms, that argument seems somewhat specious. Further, it was not within the power of Aborigines to make the public or officialdom accept the proper names they conferred on themselves, as Reay suggested should happen. In 1970 the Commonwealth government decreed that the capitalised term Aboriginal should be used.

passing of the Supply of Liquor to Aborigines Prevention Act in NSW
in 1868 (Curthoys, 1973:164). However with the lack of police in the
outback 'there were few Aborigines who did not get to know the taste
of rum' (Beckett, 1964:38-9). New South Wales appointed a Protector
in 1881 whose job was to oversee police, report on conditions and
supervise the distribution of rations and blankets. The Aborigines
Protection Board (APB) was established in 1883, but had no specific
statutory powers until 1909 when the Aborigines Protection Act was
passed. The APB was to supervise this Act.

Their task was at first thought to be a temporary one, as it then only
dealt with the dwindling population of full-bloods. This notion of the
APBs task being temporary is echoed in the later assimilation policy
which, if successful, would also become redundant. In fact the Acts
which directly curtailed the freedom of NSW Aborigines remained in
place until 1962, and the Board retained some of its powers until it
was replaced by Commonwealth government's Office for Aboriginal
Affairs after the 1967 referendum (Rowley, 1972b:406). The Protection Act was designed to control rather than simply protect. Aborigines were to be segregated from white society rather than left in the
wild hinterland, or wandering unchecked through the towns. The
new legislation sought to alter their behaviour by encouraging them
to do work that would be of use in the wider society. To this end the
APB established reserves, separate areas for the use or confinement
of Aborigines. Some reserves remained areas simply set aside for
Aborigines where they had the right to live and farm or fish. Those
classed as 'stations' were commonly known as 'missions' and a
manager, a matron and sometimes school teachers were appointed
by the Board. Such staff required no specialist training. It was thought
that the characteristic of being European was sufficient qualification
for teaching Aborigines, an ironic comment on the reverse argument
often made today. There were no missionary run institutions in the
west although, according to Donaldson, the Aboriginal inland
mission influenced most western NSW communities during the
1920s and 1930s (Kennedy & Donaldson, 1982:13).

While life on an unstaffed reserve was free of the daily surveillance practiced by managers and matrons, the police or a local
school teacher were employed by the Board to fulfil the same role.
Wherever Aborigines lived they were subject to the Protection Act.
The Board's local officers could visit a camp or unstaffed reserve at
any time. While the 1909 Act excluded part-Aborigines from the

missions and reserves, after 1918 they were included in the category Aboriginal and made subject to the same limitation on their rights. It was recognised that there were large numbers of such people who required, it was believed, close supervision and retraining (Morris, 1985:100).

The Protection Act gave the APB considerable powers over Aborigines. Residents had to report their comings and goings to the manager, who could exclude residents from the station and their homes (Rowley, 1972b:69). On a station Aborigines were required to 'obey all reasonable instructions and commands of the manager or other responsible officer of the Board' (Beckett, 1958a:66). Gambling and liquor were forbidden, and both of these became the focus of defiant habits. It was an indictable offence for a white person, other than a police officer or Board official, to enter a reserve or consort with Aborigines (ibid., 67). The protection legislation was amended in 1915 and 1918 giving the Board greater powers to remove children for training as domestic servants.

Through later amendments and the Board's change of title to the NSW Aborigines Welfare Board (AWB) in 1943, the invigilation continued. Many regulations ensured that a station manager held sway in all matters. The Board could withdraw an Aborigine from employment for reasons to do with his well-being. Medical examinations and hospitalisation could be ordered. The manager could take charge of a ward's wages. Livestock could not be kept without permission (ibid., 63ff.). Although the Welfare Board was supposed to include two Aborigines, one to be a full-blood, there were never nominations for the latter position (ibid., 65). The senior public servants and one anthropologist took decisions unaided by Aboriginal wisdom.

There were changes over time in the stated policy, mainly towards a more precise pedogogy through the rewarding of the 'good people'. In 1942 the Board aimed 'to give assistance to deserving families to enable them to secure homes of their own. . . . A further aim was to inculcate into the aborigines the habit of self-help, to develop agricultural possibilities on stations and to develop pride of possession' (ibid., 69). Prohibition sat ill with the assimilation policy, so in 1943 an amendment to the Aborigines Protection Act allowed the APB 'to exempt from the liquor restrictions those whose behaviour had proved exemplary . . . in practice those who did not drink' (Beckett, 1964:39). Such people were given a certificate which is still bitterly recalled as a 'dog tag' by Aborigines. The holder of an exemption certificate was in a different legal category from relatives who would none the less expect to be supplied with liquor. Further, the Board could cancel the certificate at any time (Beckett, 1958a:64). Of course these laws were ineffective in stopping Aborigines from drinking, but they did exclude them from hotel bars and they did allow them to be hounded by police.

Those Aborigines who lived in states where they could register on the electoral roll were thereby constitutionally eligible to vote in federal elections before they gained the federal franchise in 1961 (Rowley, 1972b:403). However they were not compelled to enrol, and many did not do so. In 1958 Beckett could assert of western NSW, 'In many respects (Aborigines) enjoy a legal status no different from that of other residents . . . they have the franchise for both state and federal elections, they are liable to the penalties and protection of the law, they pay taxes, receive free education and can claim Unemployment, Sickness and Maternity benefits, Child endowment and, if not resident on a government reserve, Old Age Pensions. . . . However in other respects they are subject to special provisions in both state and federal law' (Beckett, 1958a:63). These 'other respects' in fact made every facet of life under the Act quite different from other citizens until it was repealed in 1968.

Fear and loathing under the Act

Aborigines moved into the towns in the early part of the century as they continued to be forced off the land. Drought and depression as well as changing ownership and the process of selection affected the Aborigines' 'stock camps' on the properties, although some camps remained at least until 1913 (Goodall, 1982:44,76). In the towns Aborigines became 'fringe dwellers' and were identified as a 'problem' by the increasingly respectable townspeople. 'What appeared to ordinary townsfolk as a threat to public hygiene, morality and civility, was a charge on the conscience of the philanthropically inclined. Thus, from various quarters came the clamour for segregation of Aborigines, whether for their own good or the Europeans' (Beckett, 1983:7).

The reserves and missions were a solution to that problem. Aborigines could be put out of sight and still be available as pools of labour for local farmers and pastoralists (Rowley, 1972b:66ff.). Sometimes these priorities were in conflict. For instance one camp which was at a convenient spot for employers to locate a worker was moved by the AWB to new houses half a mile from the village. This meant a loss of employment opportunity for these pastoral workers (ibid., 294). Townspeople continuously tried to distance Aboriginal camps from the town, despite the extreme inconveniences this caused people (e.g., Reay, 1945:303-4). Often, as well as a government reserve, an unsupervised town camp existed under some duress.

Charity was generally frowned upon as it was thought to cause pauperisation (Goodall, 1982:45). The reserves were encouraged to be economically independent as farms, and the residents were expected to work on them. Young people were trained to become servants or rural workers. In some areas of NSW Aborigines farmed successfully, and they were assured that the reserves were given to them in perpetuity. They were told that it was the Queen's land to give them as long as they stayed there. However the farms were taken and the reserves were gradually reduced in size (Morris, 1985; Goodall, 1982:35,39,192; Rowley, 1972b:67; Barwick, 1972).

From the start, Aborigines had been unable to resist the savage and personal forms of colonial frontier oppression discussed earlier. However the kind of control exercised under the Protection Act was far more intrusive, and though we cannot here trace the details of the policy and practice since the turn of the century until it was repealed in 1969 (Wilkie, 1985:8), the major effects of the policy on those still alive needs to be considered.[4]

The work of Jimmie Barker provides us with one of the rare accounts of life under the Board by those that endured it. His life history reveals clearly the personal aspects of domination. Managers on the stations were sometimes despotic and even sadistic men. He says, 'The managers were armed with a baton, handcuffs and a revolver. These were supposed to be used if there was trouble, but Evans used them for his own amusement. This applied to most of the managers. They did not give the Aborigines a chance, and we were always in trouble' (Mathews, 1977a:64). Barker describes direct violence done to children and adults. He continues; 'They did very little for us, and we all needed help, education and a better way of life. . . . Very often they were under the influence of liquor; but drunk or sober, their treatment of both adults and children was always unpleasant' (ibid., 82).

---

[4]The evidence concerning the earlier era in western NSW comes mainly from recently published Aborigines accounts (Mathews, 1977a; Kennedy & Donaldson, 1982; Edwards, 1982), some published articles (Reay, 1945,1949; Fink, 1957; Read, 1982), and two unpublished theses (Beckett, 1958a; Goodall, 1982) as well as from my fieldwork in the area.

Another form of coercion destined to cause anguish was the up-rooting of whole groups of people when the APB decided to close one reserve or open another. Such decisions were made on a variety of grounds, but seem to have invariably been carried out with harassment and inhumanity. Sometimes no warning was given and possessions were left behind (Kennedy & Donaldson, 1982:16-17). Some groups were moved several times. One woman in Brindleton has inherited her deceased father's desire to find his brother who was put on a truck heading for South Australia when the rest of the family was being taken east. The Aborigines all knew that the Board had the power to move them to any place in the state (Mathews, 1977a:82). After a second uprooting of one group, women as well as men and school-aged children began to drink (Kennedy & Donaldson, 1982:20).

The taking of children was perhaps the most inhumane form of intrusion. The criteria for the removal of children by the APB was, from 1909 to 1915, on the same grounds as that applied to white children; that is, if a magistrate found them 'neglected'. Many white children have suffered the experience of being declared state wards and the years of virtual slavery it entailed (Barbalet, 1983). The misery experienced by such children, whether white or black, was often extreme, but Aborigines as a group were more liable to lose their children and less able to regain contact with them. After 1915 the APB did not require a magistrate's ruling to take Aboriginal children. Between 1883 and 1969 approximately 5,625 Aboriginal children in NSW were removed from their parents' care and placed in homes. The Board's report of 1921 said, 'the continuation of this policy of disassociating the children from camp life must eventually solve the Aboriginal problem' (Read, 1982:2). To this end communication between parents and children was discouraged, so that many children believed themselves unwanted. Parents saw the situation as tantamount to kidnapping. Many never found their children after they were taken, though stories drifted back of brutality and interference with personal freedom (Reay, 1949:100). The plaintive song 'My brown skin baby, they take 'im away' depicts a common Aboriginal experience.

The terrible distress caused by these draconian measures has only recently been recorded (Read, 1982; Edwards, 1982). Many victims of these policies — whether those children brought up in institutions dedicated to assimilating them, or the helpless parents who were deemed unworthy to even know their children — are still suffering the effects. The provisions in the Act concerning custody of Aboriginal children and the control of state wards remained after other restricive policies had been abandoned (Rowley, 1972b:407). As recently as 1964 Rowley found two separate grandparents on one reserve who were gradually buying enough new iron, without nail holes, to roof their shacks in a waterproof manner so that they could apply to the Welfare Board to 'get their children out of pawn' (Rowley, 1972b:296, 299).

Lack of knowledge of the Board's functioning precluded any effective measures to counter its power. While the residents of a reserve might know when the inspector was coming, they could not know what names were on his list, or that the local police, the committal procedures and even the homes to which children were to be sent had all been prepared in advance (Read, 1982:3). There are many stories of attempts to hide from the inspectors, but the manager or the local police could not be avoided forever. Eliza Kennedy said that the people protested about conditions when they could, complaining to 'the head fellow down from Sydney' but with no result (Kennedy & Donaldson, 1982:20). The Act always allowed for much discretion on the part of managers and police, so that Aborigines in one area or at one time might be comparatively well-off and in another be suffering extreme distress. Acceptance of Aborigines by the local population varied also, as the reaction to Aboriginal children in the schools will show. Thus it was more common for Aborigines to merely hope for a good policeman or manager, than to mount concerted resistance to distant authorities. However some forms of resistance were also endemic as we shall see below.

The prohibition of liquor seems to have led to close surveillance of the camps, but not to prevention of the supply of liquor. Police rarely charged Europeans with supplying liquor to Aborigines (Reay, 1945:300), but they regularly arrested Aborigines for drunkenness, sometimes waking them to do so. Beckett describes the chilling experience of having police patrol the reserve six times a day (1965:41). They would break into houses if they believed a drunk Aborigine to be there. Under these conditions there was little point in trying to escape and Aborigines were not deterred by the fines, prison sentences and beatings allegedly inflicted on them. Beckett says 'I have seen men drunk again within half an hour of release from jail' (1964:40).

Drink thus attained enormous significance in the lives of Aborigines. Beckett sees drinking as the major focus of conflict which is given expression in 'the continued cycle of defiance, arrest and re-newed defiance. They bitterly resent the political domination that denied to them what it unrestrictedly allowed to Europeans'. One old man told Beckett 'These darkies have got no right to go fighting for the whites that stole their country. Now they wont let 'em into the hotel. They've got to gulp down plonk in the piss-house' (ibid., 40). Thus the removal of children, prohibition and the invigilation of personal lives made life for many a running battle. The farcical nature of the exercise is apparent from its consequences.

Assimilation

To understand what these apparently irrational and destructive poli-cies were about, it is necessary to recognise that the programmes developed at government level were explicitly based on lack of understanding, not only of Aborigines but of their relations with the wider society. However, implicitly the policies were intended to, and did achieve, the control of a population which posed a challenge and an embarrassment to the dominant society.

There were obvious contradictions embedded in the assimilation policy itself. The measures used could have been designed to achieve exclusion rather than assimilation as they made the Aborigines re-markably dissimilar from their would-be fellow citizens. If nothing else the draconion methods used ensured failure. Who would want to side with brutal oppressors? In general relationships with whites have taught Aborigines mistrust and bitterness.

The physical conditions were not designed to promote assimi-lation. Where houses were provided for Aborigines on the reserves they were, for many years, two-roomed, unfloored tin huts. Later concrete floors created even unhealthier conditions (Kennedy & Donaldson, 1982:17). Once skeletons were found on the reserve site which caused great anxiety (ibid.). Being subject to a matron's inspec-tion of one's house; being liable to lose one's children, or even one's right to go home to the reserve; not being allowed to fraternise with whites and perhaps above all not being allowed to drink in pubs; all these experiences were so different from all that outback Australians hold dear that the notion that such treatment would lead to 'assimi-lation' sounds ludicrous to say the least.

Another aspect of the contradictory nature of assimilation ideology is the assumption about the attitude of whites. In a country where 'The smallholder's grinding poverty ... gave rise to the pastoral worker's contempt' (Ward, 1966:199), the even poorer Aborigines had little chance for respect. As Beckett says, 'racism expressed itself in contradiction, for while officialdom insisted that their white ancestry would enable them to enter the ranks of Australian society, white prejudice ensured that few did' (Beckett, 1983:9). Assimilation theory said that Aborigines were to be changed so that they would be acceptable to whites. They could then become economically self-sufficient and there would be no need for the APB or the reserves. In other words, the Aborigines would disappear. To this end the Board claimed to make 'particular efforts to raise the standards of housing, home-making, hygiene and education ... and ... to correct drunkeness and what is considered sexual immorality' (cited in Beckett, 1958a:72).

Many whites did not want to mix with Aborigines and made that fact quite clear (Kelly, 1943; Reay, 1949; Fink, 1957). But the legacy of separation which is still so apparent today is not simply the result of some traditional dislike. Those who did wish to mix were not allowed to. Reay describes the peculiar tensions created among fellow pastoral workers when the inclination to drink together is thwarted by a law which makes one socially superior to the other. The result is indignation and hostility between them (Reay, 1945:297). It is no wonder that for most Aborigines 'contacts with Europeans are impersonal, ephemeral, and limited to the business in hand' (Beckett, 1964:35). The AWB did not allow Aborigines to consort with those whites who wanted to mix with them because such whites were of undesirable character (Beckett, 1958a:73). Aborigines were presumably unable to judge whether such men were exploiting them. But Aborigines were to join the lower orders of society, as is made clear in a number of the Board's pronouncements, and thus would presumably eventually come into contact with the people they were being protected from.

While no formal colour bar existed, this did not mean that no barring occurred. For instance Rowley talks of the 'hygiene barrier'. 'The matron ... reserved the right to reject a "dirty" Aboriginal from the ward and to put him on the verandah; could she have similarly rejected a non-Aboriginal instead of having him washed?' (Rowley, 1972b:262).

The Welfare Board's report in 1942 said that the aim was 'To assimilate the aborigines particularly those of lighter casts, into the general community' (Beckett 1958a:59). Such concern with shading was embedded in all the ideas about Aborigines, although it was in the form of assumptions rather than explicit theory. One widely recommended policy was that of breeding out the colour from the part Aborigines (Rowley, 1972a:139; McGrath, 1984:274-5). This was based on a notion that *the* differences between Aborigines and whites were directly related to that physical sign of difference which was constantly emphasised, skin colour. A notion that the gradual dilution of the 'blood' would lighten the colour and solve the Aboriginal problem is echoed in many statements. It was not made clear how the 'gradual and beneficial mingling and absorption' (cited in Curthoys, 1973:118) would be achieved, because relationships between black women and white men were not given social approval. McGrath points out that while casual sex or prostitution with black women could be seen as simply a result of male sexual imperatives, it was the long-term relationship implying emotional attachment to an Aboriginal woman that was treated with scorn and attracted sanctions. 'White men were forced to suffer guilt complexes because of their supposedly "dirty" and sinful relationships with black women' (McGrath, 1984:238-9; see also Reay, 1945:298).

Because of these preoccupations among whites, skin colour became significant for Aborigines, especially those who were lighter skinned and either eager to assimilate or unwilling to remain marginal. One woman hoped her child would not have blue eyes because she wanted to keep her baby. A fair man claimed to have married a dark woman so that his children would not suffer as he had from being a half-caste (Kelly, 1944:143). Fink also asserted that the motives for marriage included colour, though she believed that the upwardly mobile women tended to marry lighter coloured men to enhance their status. 'When babies are born the women all go to the hospital to see the colour of the child' (Fink, 1957:104-5). However the acceptance of children of any hue seems more common among the majority who are not trying to alter their identification (Beckett, 1958c:97; Fink, 1957:109).

The reluctance of many Aborigines to assimilate was occasionally recognised. The Board's report in 1944 said that the 'present clinging together' even by the 'light castes', ensures friendship in 'a somewhat cold world' and that this practice would continue 'until colour prejudice towards the aboriginal mixed blood has been eradicated' (cited in Beckett, 1958a:69). But the colour spectrum had a different meaning to those whose ancestry meant that their families were of various shades. An elderly Brindleton Aboriginal man recalls, 'We couldn't drink in the old days. Had to get a card. In one pub they served one brother and not the other. My brother Charlie couldn't get served. His colour was against him I suppose.'

The usual tension between a remote community and the city authorities was present in the relations between the APB and its employees. The Board's deliberations were far removed from the communities they ruled, but they saw themselves, and were seen by the local whites, as sympathetic supporters of Aborigines. However the Board seems to have neither controlled nor supported its staff on the reserves. The manager had power over the residents' everyday lives, but he was unable to influence the Board, and some managers did not have copies of the regulations they were supposed to administer (Rowley, 1972b:69). Eliza Kennedy said 'They didn't like the manager that done too much for the blacks. They'd sack them fellows' (Kennedy & Donaldson, 1982:20). Also local people did not necessarily cooperate with the Board or its employees. At a meeting of the Australian Council for Native Welfare in 1951 a minister representing a state with large number of Aborigines said that most criticism was coming from 'people in the southern parts of Australia. Many of these people would not know a nigger if they saw one' (Rowley, 1972a:39). Such deriding of outsiders' concern and denigrating references to Aborigines is as familiar in rural Australia today as it was then and in the 1880s.

Access to public education demonstrates something of these tensions between local people and the decisions taken by authorities in the cities. The Board of National Education provided what public education was available in NSW from 1848 to 1866. It held that it was impracticable to provide education for the 'children of the blacks' (Harris, 1976:1). The Department of Education began in 1880, but no policy was developed towards the scattering of Aboriginal children who were attending the schools until, in 1883, white parents in Yass objected to the attendance of about 15 Aboriginal children at the public school. The Minister for Education's response opened the way to excluding Aboriginal children from NSW schools. 'No child, whatever its creed or colour or circumstances ought to be excluded from a public school. But cases may arise, especially amongst the Aboriginal tribes, where the admission of a child or children may be prejudicial to the whole school' (ibid., 2). The department's policy was not to exclude Aboriginal children if they were 'habitually clean, decently clad, and that they conduct themselves with propriety, both in and out of school' (ibid., 2).

When the Aboriginal Protection Board was formed in 1883, it recognised the importance of education 'in order to lead the aboriginal people to a proper understanding and appreciation of the mental processes involved in Australian civilisation and life' (cited in Beckett, 1858a:75). Both the Board of National Education and the APB supported the education of Aborigines in principle, but their practices led to a varied situation for Aboriginal people. In some areas they were welcomed into the school, while in others they were excluded because of a parental campaign. This sometimes resulted in a special classroom being established for Aborigines. In other places schools were opened on the reserves, providing a special limited course of instruction for Aborigines taught by untrained teachers. For some, exclusion from the local school meant exclusion from the opportunity for any schooling. Even in the 1940s, parental lobbying led the government to make Aboriginal children in one area travel to a distant Aboriginal school despite objections from other parents, including the RSL, that the fathers of excluded children were soldiers in Australia's second world war forces (Harris, 1976:5).

The settlement schools were intended to assist the boys to become capable farm or station labourers and the girls useful domestic servants. 'Instructive trips into the bush were recommended'! (cited in Beckett, 1958a:75). In 1938 the curriculum was expanded and by 1940 the Board thought that 'some of the pupils with an admixture of white blood frequently exhibit an intelligence that permits them under good school conditions to proceed at the normal rate' (ibid., 76). Not until 1952 was it recommended that the normal primary school curriculum be followed in Aboriginal schools. Only in 1949 did the Department of Education provide official support for the entry of Aboriginal children to schools where local opposition occurred.

In some cases Aboriginal pupils were useful. In 1914 one western NSW school was threatened with closure because of too few children. The attendance figures were boosted by the enrolment of itinerant Aboriginal workers' children. When the parents of the white children objected to their presence because 'morally, mentally and physically the blacks are not fit to associate with the children', the Department of Education upheld its principles of equal opportunities of education for all by promising 'strict supervision by the teacher during play hours and separate seats in the school' (HB, 3:92). In one town Aboriginal pupils were admitted to the public school but not to the Convent. Many white parents in this town gave their children a Catholic education as a result (Reay, 1945:298).

Exclusion on health grounds continued for some years in particular areas. There are a few Aboriginal schools still in existence, now properly staffed as other public schools. 'They exist for geographical reasons or at the request of the Aboriginal community' (Harris, 1976:6fn.). Until 1972 the NSW teachers handbook still contained the regulation requiring principals to defer or refuse enrolment of Aboriginal children on the grounds of 'home conditions' or 'substantial (community) opposition' (ibid., 6).

CHANGING ABORIGINAL CULTURE

The vanished mobs

Accounts of the lives of Aborigines in rural New South Wales are so rare that the popular notions of 'dispirited remnants' and 'detribalised blacks' are difficult to challenge. They call forth a picture of dirt and misery which has little room for a real and varied group of people living their lives out, sometimes with great courage and an awareness of their historical tragedy and sometimes in bitterness. I want here to try to depict, from the meagre evidence available and from personal accounts, the cultural responses of Aborigines to their lives under the Act. While depression and destructive drinking have been common, there has also been humour and warmth, and a sharp cynical intelligence which sees clearly the nature of the perpetual harassment. The memories of Aborigines in the west are at once more varied and more poignant than popular imagery allows, but some common and continuing themes can be detected.

A sense of loss which may have been widespread in earlier days is evident in recent autobiographical accounts such as that of Jimmie Barker and Eliza Kennedy. Barker remembers his intense sorrow when, in 1908, his family left the camp on the Culgoa where a group of Muruwari people lived speaking their language, hunting and fishing and telling the old stories (Mathews, 1977a, Chapter 1). In the 1940s Kennedy's travels revealed only 'reminders of the vanished Marfield mob . . . little miamias everywhere' (Kennedy & Donaldson, 1982:20-1). George Dutton, an initiated leader in the west, wept when he heard a traditional song recounting names and places (Beckett, 1958c:102).

Aborigines in NSW ceased many cultural practices. While the tribal groups have tended to stay together, there are indications that in some situations the old people refused to teach the younger ones either the specific esoteric knowledge of ritual and religion or the

kinship rules and language. In some cases the younger people refused to learn them. In 1957 Beckett said you could:

> still get a few to show you what the dance steps were like; they
> facetiously call it the "blackfellers' Charleston", which is as close
> a description as one could want. Men . . . can still sing the old
> songs, tapping out the rhythm on a couple of boomerangs and a
> pillow. But the younger generation don't like to hear these songs.
> They giggle and say it makes them feel "shamed". "We're like
> white folks, now," they say. (Beckett, 1958b:37).

A decade earlier Reay found knowledge of Aboriginal song cycles which
were performed 'only in the presence of a few old men for whom the
songs have not lost their meaning. Younger mixed bloods scoff at these
songs, which have many obscene elements, mimic them in their
drinking parties, and treat them as an obscene jest' (Reay, 1949:96).

In 1944 Reay found that the 'native dialect' was spoken 'in the
individual family' but 'Because of white people's contempt for and
prohibition on the use of aboriginal dialects . . . aborigines are
ashamed and confused if one of their number uses a native dialect in
the presence of unsympathetic white people' (Reay, 1949:91; see also
Fink, 1957:110). However there was also a conscious attempt by
some to retain what was left of the language, and people were still
attached to their own country and desired to return there to die (Reay,
1949:92,106). Wailing at funerals was disapproved of or forbidden
because whites found it distressing (ibid., 105). Reay describes the
suffering caused by a manager insisting on the solemnisation of a
marriage which was 'illegal' in kinship terms (ibid., 312).

It seems that traditional sentiments, ideas and practices were the
focus of much wider conflicts than those caused by such direct
attempts to suppress them. Conflicting attitudes were evident in
response to the performance of 'corroborees'. These sometimes
caused deep rifts in the community, particularly between those who
are 'not ashamed of being a blackfeller' and those for whom it means
that the participants were still ignorant 'old timers' (Reay, 1949:111).

Thus the reluctance to teach or to learn definitively Aboriginal
practices may have been the result of experiences of ridicule, or a
belief that such forms of knowledge were inappropriate under the
new conditions. As in some remote regions today, Aborigines, particularly the young, must have felt considerable conflict about those
traditions which were overtly despised by Europeans. A measure of
ambivalence is not surprising in the relationships of the young to old
people, to the ritual life and to the kinship and marriage systems (cf.

Cowlishaw, 1983:67). The judgements about whether to teach or use the language and about whether to perform the rituals or tell the stories, were conscious rational judgements made under extremely oppressive social conditions. The overt and more external expressions of culture, such as language and rituals, were a mark of inferiority in the eyes of those who dominated Aboriginal social life. They also represented the different meaning the world held for Aborigines. Sometimes they became the focus of resistance and of a continuing struggle to retain such meanings and to defy the new order (Morris, 1985). Reay's account shows that in the 1940s traditional marriage rules were also the focus of a struggle within the Aboriginal community with some people fighting to retain their validity while others claimed ignorance of them (Reay, 1949:106-7).

It seems then that there has been no single simple rejection or retention of tradition, but a complex history of changes in the context of a political struggle for survival in which different and contradictory strategies were being adopted. One obvious if minor example of the use of cultural practices to resist harassment is what Reay calls gibberish words. 'There is an element of possessiveness in the use of camp slang' which is partly to do with its function. For instance the words for 'policeman' and 'white people' are signals for dispersing when 'gambling' and 'drinking' are in progress (Reay, 1949:92).

There were other more subtle and pervasive understandings of the world that continued to flourish in the new conditions. For instance the interdependence of kin remained of more importance than the privacy of the nuclear family in its own house, the common preoccupation of the whites. The European way of life, involving 'making a home' and 'getting on in the world', conflicts with the system of sharing and borrowing which operates among people 'of their own colour' (ibid., 114). Reay mentions the 'genealogists of the camp' who can trace the relationships of everyone in the camp (ibid., 106). Possessive and protective affection are part of the ideal of good maternal care (ibid., 115). Beckett remarked that Aboriginal women lived like the men except for drinking. The women were genuinely shocked by neglect of children (Beckett, 1958a:42,158) and

> The inhabitants of a camp or government settlement have been acquainted with one another and one another's affairs for most, if not all, of their lives. Many are related. The most intimate and permanent relationships of their lives are maintained with neighbours and kin, whose behaviour is highly predictable. No one expects from any other a high degree of economic effort or

strict observance of any moral code. There is a general assurance that neighbours and kinsfolk are ready to give food, clothing, or whatever is needed to tide over a temporary shortage (Beckett, 1964:34-5).

Given the conditions of the invasion and the Act, there is cruelty in blaming Aborigines for the loss of their traditions. Beckett says 'People who had learned to respect and even admire the traditional culture of the Australian aborigine shake their heads when they see how low contact with whites has brought them. . . . Is this all that the white man, so convinced of his cultural superiority, has been able to give the black?' (1958b:41). Just as cruel is the fact that prejudice was reinforced by the conditions which had been imposed on Aborigines. 'They (whites) are offended by the unsightly camps on the edge of town and regard their coloured neighbours as a dirty, feckless, drunken and immoral people who "give the district a bad name". They consider "the abos" an unregenerately delinquent group on whom government assistance paid out of the taxpayer's pocket is simply wasted' (Beckett, 1964:36).

Aborigines have always been aware of the way their camps and their habits were seen by whites. The citizens of the large and small outback towns have often tried to exclude their dark neighbours from its churches, swimming baths, schools and hotels. The Protection Act and the Protection Board did nothing to protect Aborigines from such discrimination. It is not therefore surprising that many Aborigines who might have been eligible for 'citizen's rights', or who could have 'passed' as whites, chose not to do so for it would entail identifying with those who despised ones' kin. Rewards for those who did join the whites were sufficient to seduce some into applying, though the 'cast barrier' was usually such as to preclude real acceptance except of some individuals. Those who did aim for higher status earned the resentment of others (Reay & Sitlington, 1948). Individuals had to reject anything concerning their dark relatives if they were to join the whites (Fink, 1957:101).

Virtually nothing is known of Aborigines' ideological responses to the multifarious and involuntary adaptations that were taking place except for the explicitly political activities of Ferguson, Patton and others (Horner, 1974). Tamsin Donaldson attempts to describe the ambivalence concerning the sense of progress or status attached by Eliza Kennedy to the learning of white ways. Eliza refers to 'Growing up in the ashes', 'coming up out of the fallen leaves' which Donalson says express the notion of rising from low or humble beginnings. 'But they manage also to deflect the pejorative associations of metaphorical "lowliness". The ashes (and fallen leaves) . . . are vividly evocative of a childhood hearth and home that were quite literally close to the ground' (Kennedy & Donaldson, 1982:11fn., my parenthesis).

Aquiescence and anger

Acceptance of the new regime may have seemed to necessitate the rejection of the old. One elderly Brindleton woman's account of her father's life indicates his aquiescence in the changed rules of social life. He was a police tracker at a tiny settlement for years.

> He would not talk about the past or teach the kids the language. He said we had to learn to live the white way. Perhaps it was because of the killings. He knew about one massacre. He was working on a station when he was ten years old and one night got a message on the "mulga wire" to get up and go to the fence and his people came and picked him up. He often got "mulga wires". He was strict with us kids. We had to take back oranges we picked from a tree. He was decorated for tracking lost people and criminals as well as sheep thieves.

Such aquiescence can be contrasted with the resentment of a Brindleton man of about 35 whose family nurses a bitterness and stubborn determination to survive. He says,

> Mum came from Tibooburra and before that from Coopers Creek. When gold was found there the Aboriginal people were got out and our family was moved in a truck. Mum was 7 or 8. She dont talk about it often but when she do you know it wasn't a pretty sight to see Aboriginal people shoved in trucks and moved onto reserves all over NSW and the people didn't take care of who they grabbed and families were split up.

Defiance is a common response. For instance Aboriginal groups sometimes moved from where they had been forcibly settled (Beckett, 1958c:131). On one occassion 200 people swam the Darling to listen to a speaker who was banned from the mission by the manager (*Western Herald*, 3/11/39). Anger is apparent in the response to the Protection Board's decision in 1951 to charge rent for the often inferior housing. The payment of rent was intended 'to awaken in the residents a sense of responsibility and a pride in their own houses'. The Aborigines on some stations refused to pay rent. The Board was concerned because of the 'psychological reaction it has caused in the reasoning of the defiant minority'. Less than one-third of the rent owing was paid in 1956 (Beckett, 1958a:70). Finally in 1957 the Board threatened legal action, and in one case took it.

Underlying such overt defiance was the blacks' very different style of living. Such differences are often treated as givens or as a matter of choice, and the consequences for their relationship with the white population is discussed. But this very relationship has determined much of the Aboriginal response. Based as it was on inequality in every realm, the relationship with whites has been crucially import-ant in the creation of Aboriginal culture. As indicated in the previous section, Aborigines were hardly able to ignore white people. The marked differences in available resources, and dramatically different histories of the two groups, has created differing values and priorities.

The rebellious display of disreputable behaviour is one distinctive response to oppressive conditions. Fink observed that 'such activities as gambling, drinking in excess, wasting money and neglecting homes and personal appearance all have the effect of emphasising their difference from white people. . . . This type of reaction is an agressive assertion of low status; it seems to say "Look at me . . . I'm coloured and I'm dirty, drunken, lazy, irresponsible like they all say . . . that's my privelege because I'm coloured . . . I can do as I like because that's what they expect of me anyway"'' (Fink, 1957:103). Reay also found drunkenness conferred prestige. Her account of two Aborigines boasting competitively about having the most convictions for drunkenness indicates their contempt for an unjust law and the lack of shame associated with imprisonment (Reay, 1945:300-1).

Beckett's description of the music that Aborigines made in western NSW in the late 1950s is perhaps the most definitive account of the nature of Aboriginal ideology in these conditions .

> They would make up a song about anything — rainmaking, catching porcupine, a lost child. When the white man appeared they made up songs about him. When the white station manager sent his aboriginal workers off to a distant paddock, while he returned to fornicate with their women, there was a song about it. There was a song about the government man who, coming to inspect rabbit infested stations, was taken into the parlour and plied with whiskey (Beckett, 1958b:37).

Many songs concerned the practice of drinking.

The demon drink

The only drug in pre-18th century Australia was the mild Pitcheri (Watson, 1983). Rum, which was the common spirit of the frontier, caused devastation, particularly as there were no conventions to control unfamiliar reactions or to regulate consumption (Beckett, 1964:37). The taste for strong drink and the bouts of drunkenness which Beckett says are common to the old time bushman and Aborigines may be to do with their conditions of living; harsh and despised. But it was the fact that alcohol was illegal for Aborigines that gave their drinking practices their most distinctive features.

Aborigines were denied entry to that shrine of mateship, the pub, except as mendicants at the back door or begging from a workmate, someone with 'citizen's rights' or a relation whose pallor allowed them entry. Even to be in possession of liquor placed them outside the law. Surveillance of camps and harassment was a constant experience, and the only alternative was for the whole community to comply with the law and cease to drink. The police felt themselves obliged to attempt to enforce the law, probably under pressure from the townspeople. The ludicrousness of the situation is evident in Beckett's story of one man 'in flight from the police, who drained his bottle of port as he ran; when he had emptied it he stopped and, throwing the bottle aside, said "Alright, now you can take me!"' (Beckett, 1958b:39).

A defiant style of drinking developed which entailed 'the excitement of getting the liquor, running the police blockade, risking goal and sneaking out into the bush to consume it with a great deal of noise and flourish. Memorable sprees are celebrated in song and story and the whole business described in an elaborate set of cant terms and catch phrases' (Beckett, 1958b:42). The preference for strong liquor rather than beer is not surprising given the surreptitious nature of the supply. 'Even when drinkers are quite free from the fear of interruption they gulp down large quantities with ostentatious abandon. . . . a positive value is placed on inebriation' (Beckett, 1964:41). Beckett went so far as to assert that drinking activities 'provided a core around which a new and consciously distinctive aboriginal folklore is developing' (ibid., 46).

Such conditions of existence affect the children as well as adults in a community. James Baldwin has articulated the way experiences of this kind can affect a growing child:

When I was little I despised myself, I did not know any better. And this meant albeit unconsciously, or against my will, or in great pain, that I also despised my father. *And* my mother. *And* my brothers. *And* my sisters. Black people were killing themselves every Saturday night ... when I was growing up (Baldwin, 1971:178)

Kevin Gilbert writes of 'Grandfather Koorie', an old Aboriginal man who challenges angry young Aborigines with their depression, destructiveness and lack of self-esteem, which is produced in the same way as Baldwin's feelings about black people (Gilbert, 1978). One Brindleton resident recalls his early introduction to the forces of law:

We had some strict welfares out here. Mum and Dad had to go away to Dubbo once. The older ones in the family had to stay home to look after the little ones and we had only spent two days at home and the welfare came down and we found ourselves sitting down in the police station and a date was set for us to go to court and later on when the court case came up a member of our family passed away and by the time Mum and Dad got back from the funeral we was already tried and convicted. Because our parents weren't there they were thought not to care. So we were sent for two years to an institution. I was nine and my brother was ten. Two years for truancy. Also we had to wait 14 days in the Brindleton jail waiting for an escort, not knowing what happened.

Aboriginal folk songs from western NSW give a unique insight into the realities of Aboriginal life and into the spirit of their response which is at once cynical and defiant. The pleasures of drinking, even of drinking metho are described, as is the release from pain which comes from having a spree, or cutting a rug.

It ain't no dice until you've got the price,
And then you give your mate a tug,
You'll be smiling again as you walk down the lane,
Because you're going to cut a rug.

'The aborigine is determined that he will drink and it is the duty of the police to see that he does not and to arrest him when he gets drunk. The result is an utterly futile fight between the two, in which neither gains any ground' (Beckett, 1958b:39). Many songs, such as those quoted below (ibid., 40, from D. Young, Wilcannia Folk Songs), depict this running battle and the suffering of the police cells.

No sweets no sugar in your tea, no smokes to ease your mind,

You're camping on an old floor mat, the concrete for your bed,
You feel your belly pinching and you wish that you were dead.

Beckett says the Aborigines accept that the price they must pay for getting drunk is this treatment by the police. 'Self-pity is not an aboriginal vice' (ibid.), as is illustrated in another song (quoted in ibid., 42):

The people in town just run us down,
They say we live on wine and beer,
But if they'd stop and think, if we didn't drink,
There'd be no fun around here.

Just the other day I heard a women say,
We're nothing but a bunch of mugs,
Although we fight and drink and end up in the clink,
We're going to cut a rug.

The awareness of the disapproval of the whites is accompanied by a defiant refusal to comply, or to even pay lip service to their judgements. One man indicated his preference for a syrup tin to drink from as a statement of loyalty to Aboriginal standards (Beckett, 1965:40). Beckett wrote of his difficulties in trying to 'describe a situation which my Aboriginal friends took for granted but which my white readers would find shocking, while I hung uncertainly between the two' (ibid., 38). This dilemma faces many liberal-minded observers when they confront the horrors of destructive drinking (Shepherd, 1976). For Aborigines the dilemma is more painful (cf. Gilbert, 1978).

'Black Velvet'

Circumspection and secrecy have dominated the sexual aspect of 'contact'. A silence remains around the possible ambivalent attitudes of Aboriginal men and about the reasons why Aboriginal women had liaisons with white men. Whether the majority of white men involved were fellow workers, landowners or officials remains unknown. The immediate circumstances of these dalliances are only occasionally hinted at. The wider questions of how they affected gender relations in the Aboriginal communities at different periods, and the degree to which they reflect gender relationships in the society dominated by white males, can be considered only in a speculative fashion.

In the main the 'half-caste' population originated in less than felicitous circumstances. The men in the outback were not all violent sexual exploiters of Aboriginal women, as some accounts of the frontier imply (Sykes, 1975), but sexual exploitation was an intrinisic part of the colonial enterprise. One frontier man has described the situation thus; 'What then? Walk around among the budding belles in a fit of sexual repression, when all the while they laugh at the "good one" as a stupid fool. Not on your life. The pioneer makes the country by using the gifts within it to his needs' (Harney, quoted in McGrath, 1984:233). Aborigines are seldom so explicitly classed with the natural resources of the country. Such a view allowed white men to absolve themselves of guilt for taking advantage of Aborgines' powerlessness and for fathering offspring for whom they took no responsibility. As these men came from a society where paternity has considerable significance, such abandoning would seem to indicate a widespread contempt for Aboriginal women.

Virtually nothing is known of any systematic Aboriginal ideology concerning this matter. Sometimes sexual intercourse may have been part of attempts by Aborigines to achieve some control of white invaders as has occurred more recently in the Northern Territory (ibid., 258). It seems that Aboriginal views of miscegenation were not fraught with the kind of moral judgements and status meanings which abounded in the dominant society. Kelly reports that 'the natives themselves do not discriminate about half-castes as we do; in fact, the native "stepfather" . . . is usually most proud of his wife's child by a white man' (Kelly, 1944:147). Such an attitude may reflect the extreme marginal position of Aboriginal men at this period. Kelly also recorded an old man's statement referring to an earlier era; 'This stranger, he come among us, much better we send him a woman old enough to have sense than we let him prowl after our young girls' (ibid., 147). However there are also glimpses of a direct anger concerning fraternising with the enemy which may have been common in some areas (e.g., Eyre, 1845:324).

Such variation would surely depend on local experiences over a period of time and, as we have seen earlier, in many areas Aborigines' experience of whites was oppressive in the extreme. If Aborigines were opposed to miscegenation itself there seems little reason to believe that they had negative reactions to the progeny which resulted and which came to form many Aboriginal communities. With virtually all contemporary Aborigines in NSW having some white ancestry, miscegenation could hardly be a subject for shame. Among Brindleton Aborigines today — who recognise the status meanings for whites and are aware of the sexual and social dynamics involved

— 'miscegenation' is at times a subject for humour and cynical comment.

None of the studies in western NSW (e.g., Reay, 1945; Fink, 1957; Beckett, 1964) analysed the process of miscegenation, although they could hardly ignore it. There were various summary statements about the attitudes of one or another group towards marriages between whites and Aborigines, usually referred to as full-bloods, mixed-bloods or half-castes. The contrast between Fink's finding that a group of 'Upper' part Aborigines try to marry whites (1957:104), and Kelly's finding that light-coloured people want to resolve their identity by marrying dark-skinned people (1944:147), is not as contradictory as it appears. While both authors present over-simplified motives for marriage, the stated preferences of their informants reflect different strategies in a situation where skin colour seems to determine one's social place, and therefore has overriding importance in everyone's life.

One common misunderstanding is that miscegenation which occurred in the early years created a 'mixed race' community which then ceased to marry outside itself. While the extent of exogamy will certainly have varied over time, the situation in Brindleton today suggests that mating and marriages continue to cross the barriers of race as they have always done. The fact that children of such unions are raised in the Aboriginal community means that their social world is defined accordingly.

The popular notion of 'breeding out the colour' stands in rather dramatic contrast to the disapproval of miscegenation. The former 'solution' seems to have been promulgated by those community leaders associated with the APB, who were referring to the 'stolen generation' (Read, 1982), those young people in institutions who would be trained to menial tasks and marry good working-class lads and lasses of a lighter hue. But in the towns of western NSW such a project was unlikely to catch on. In 1944 Reay said 'The middle class whites are unanimous in the opinion that the aborigines should not be encouraged to marry whites. White men who have married or openly live with aboriginal women are regarded as weaklings and traitors to their race' (Reay, 1945:298). It appears that the possibility of marrying Aborigines was only a 'danger' for what Reay calls the poor whites, mainly their fellow pastoral workers. Reay's study shows that in 1944 Aboriginal and white pastoral workers were equally excluded from middle-class society.

Both Barker and Kennedy mention the subject in passing. Kennedy says that the Keewong people had been 'a little mixed-breed mob' since 'our grandmothers were taken advantage of' but the children of 'white' fathers rarely knew anything of them; they used to hide from the station hands (Kennedy & Donaldson, 1982:8). There were, however, two exceptional outsiders who married into the 'Kewong mob', one New Zealander and one Indian Sikh (ibid.). These men became a part of Kennedy's family. Describing his various black and white forbears Jimmie Barker says '. . . many white men lived with dark girls in these country places at that time' (Mathews, 1977a:1).

George Dutton's father was a nomadic white stockman who 'drifted away up into Queensland soon after, where he died. He left the boy a legacy but George says he was never able to lay his hands on the money' (Beckett, 1958c:97). Stories of such legacies are quite common. The legacy of names also gives a clue to the social process which kept the races apart while they were getting together in the most intimate fashion. In one valley 'there live to-day descendents of earlier Australians, both black and white. . . . men distinguish one family from another by speaking of the white or black Smiths, Joneses or Hogans' (Ward, 1966:201).

There has been an almost universal reluctance to discuss miscegenation in Australia, partly because of embarrassment all round. The origin of the term is as peculiar as its meaning. Though having a precise meaning (interbreeding of races, esp. of whites with non-whites; OED), albeit one based on an erroneous notion of race, miscegenation came to imply immorality and sexual delinquency on the one hand, and on the other hand it was considered to be the means of solving the racial problems. However all sexual interaction took place in a situation where Aborigines had little power to determine their most intimate behaviour. While long-term, affectionate and loyal relationships sometimes occurred between whites and Aborigines, the social context made such a familys' group identity problematic. In most cases such relationships necessitated a degree of social isolation unless the family joined the Aboriginal community.

PART TWO

INTRODUCTION
TO THE PRESENT:
BRINDLETON

Introduction

There was until recently little in the way of scholarly interest in NSW Aborigines by sociologists, historians or any other branch of the social sciences. A brief spurt of anthropological research in the 1940s and 1950s had long faded before the period I call 'the enlightenment', that period beginning in the late 1960s, when legislation which discriminated against Aborigines was replaced by legislation intended to favour them. The new era was the preserve of the bureaucrats, and no critical outsider's eye was there to predict or record the effect of the policies on the Aborigines or on the community they were part of.

Why were the dramatic social processes of change of little interest to those whose speciality was the study of different societies? How was it that the academics allowed their studies to be dominated by the popular notions of full-bloods and part-Aborigines thus giving unintentional legitimacy to the notion that the latter were somehow less important? How was it that anthropologists, previously the experts on the subject of race and of Aborigines, ignored the whole subject of miscegenation which was altering the basis of their previous categories? A brief historical outline of the development of anthropology may shed some light on these questions.

Anthropology in the 19th century was the study of primitive peoples by those who lived in the more developed societies. There was then no shame attached to European claims of superiority. Even when no such claims were made, colonial relations bespoke the reality of the superior power of the invaders and, like it or not, anthropologists were part of that power. The search for the definitive qualities of the various races, their relative positions on the evolutionary ladder and how they had got there were the main subjects of investigation. Concern with grand schemes of human history, or with explanations of the nature of human beings in all their social and physical variability, were all a part of the anthropological endeavour. But specialisation developed and by the turn of the century anthropologists were dividing themselves into physical and social anthropologists. The methods and aims of these branches of study increasingly diverged.

By the middle of the 20th century social anthropologists were emphasising that the essential differences between races were cultural. The search for physical origins had become irrelevant to defining racial characteristics. That is, it was the culture of Aborigines which made them distinct and unique. School textbooks described the nomadic hunter-gatherers, the cleverness of their artefacts and the exotic nature of their religious beliefs. Intellectuals went to talks on totemism and moieties.

Australian social anthropologists, especially A. P. Elkin, increasingly accepted the task of defining who Aborigines were and how their special characteristics were to be described and explained. As these characteristics were comprised of the traditional culture, it followed that Aborigines were in the northern and central parts of Australia. There, because the invaders had not wanted the land, they had been left alone and continued to live largely as they had previously. That is, they had 'retained their culture'. The anthropologists sought them out and began to provide an exhaustive account of some of the complexities and subtleties of traditional Aboriginal society.

The large Aboriginal minorities in NSW held virtually no interest for the anthropological fieldworker with the important exceptions of Reay, Fink, Beckett and a few others in between. Were these people to pursue a career in anthropology it was imperative that they do major research somewhere else. Elkin wrote a good deal on the misunderstandings about Aborigines which were rife, and attempted to advise governments about the way various kinds of Aborigines, (half-cast, civilised or full-blood), should be treated. But despite his interest in culture and racial characteristics he showed little interest in documenting or analysing the cultural or biological changes taking place in the Aboriginal population.

Besides Beckett's work, there was virtually no critical interest in the active part Aborigines were taking in adjusting (or adapting) to the situation they found themselves in. Most anthropologists would have rejected the suggestion that Aboriginal culture was being reworked into a different pattern because culture was viewed as exotic and unchanging. These NSW Aborigines had 'lost' their culture. The relationship between 'race' and 'culture' was not discussed. The use of the terms half-cast, part-Aborigine and mixed-blood imply a causal connection between the dilution of the blood and the loss of Aboriginal, that is, traditional practices. The relevance of 'cast' and 'blood' to what were supposedly studies of culture was not spelt out.

In some cases there were references to these matters, but no analysis was attempted. These studies in NSW did not continue and little of the research was published. One reason was that the research concerning such groups had low status in the academic world. One researcher said that those who worked with half-casts were considered not yet ready for the important anthropological work among *real* natives.

Such judgements were due to two factors. First, anthropologists attach a great deal of importance to fieldwork, which consists of working for at least a year with people very isolated from one's homeland, in a foreign language and where nothing of day to day life is initially understood. This participant observation is considered to be the best way to come to an understanding of the society. Aboriginal groups in NSW who spoke English and no longer had esoteric rituals did not appear the proper subject for such fieldwork. The second reason is related to this. The actual content of the culture, that is, the nature of the lives of such groups, was uninteresting. Few 'traditional elements' remained, and the people lived in ways that appeared depressing and destructive. Why this should be so was not a question anthropologists felt either interested or competent to study. I suspect that they felt that it was well understood anyway, and documenting the depressing tale of racism and domination did not have any appeal. For these reasons the work of Beckett in particular, and others who did research in this unpopular field, is the more to be valued.

When in the late 1960s a series of legislative changes were made by the Commonwealth government and a new deal for Aborigines was instituted, those consulted as experts by the government were the anthropologists who had worked with traditional communities. Those who were charged with implementing the enlightenment policies were neither trained in social engineering nor experienced in the field of poverty and discrimination. The policy of Aboriginal self-management may have been supported in theory by the white personnel involved, but such people had little idea of the nature and dynamics of the Aboriginal minorities in NSW. They were unlikely to be in sympathy with aspirations that seemed inimical to their 'advancement' in the given order of society. It may be the case that such aspirations cannot be achieved, but they are seldom given full expression let alone discussed. Housing cooperatives have always excited bureaucrats more than land rights or even permission to go fishing in the Darling.

The reader may have a suspicion that my use of the term 'enlightenment' for the pro-Aboriginal policies has an ironic note to it. They would be correct, and this irony is a comment on the assumptions which dominate the common understanding of our own society. Presuppositions about a civilised society, human rights and democratic freedoms, allow us the illusion that, with a little clever social engineering, those who we know as disadvantaged can be given the advantages the rest have. Such notions hide from us the essentially violent nature of our society, in which some suffer chronic poverty and ill-health and are despised for these qualities, while those born to comfort will defend their privileges with care. In urban environments particularly, the oppressors and oppressed may never meet one another. Further, such people as will read this book may never come across those who advocate that Aborigines be punished more severely for their transgressions. But in a small town such as Brindleton one can catch the occasional glimpse of the blunt instrument of cruelty landing, an echo of the clash of the chains which bind, or one's scalp can tingle at the intensity of the hatred and violence peeping out from the mundane and parochial daily lives of the little town. Only a part of this violence is recognised; only one kind deplored.

Langton says social scientists have failed to explain how black people themselves perceive and understand their conditions. I would argue that a more serious failing is the lack of attention to the nature of white perceptions and understandings of racism. There is now a substantial literature showing that blacks have been victims of violence and of legislative and economic discrimination, but the people who lived near and interacted with blacks have not been the subject of enquiry. It has been assumed they were ignorant country folk, red-necks, whose social existence was determined by their backward attitudes.

The rest of this book is intended to illuminate the processes of racial differentiation in their contemporary complexity. As the writing progressed I was aware continually that my understanding of the depth of feeling and the private thoughts of many of the townspeople was incomplete. Further, my own formulation of the dynamics of the town and my theoretical treatment of the forces that are operating have developed during the writing, and will no doubt develop further.

Before analysing the contemporary era I will map the surface contours of the town for the reader. In later chapters the underlying structure will be revealed. In fact this separation of surface and deep structure is somewhat arbitrary. There are different ways the surface could be described. The familiar institutions and idiom with which I shall begin are really those of the prevailing language and culture. The critique of this idiom which develops in later chapters may create a certain conceptual confusion, especially in relation to the notion of race and the ways Aborgines are referred to. I shall try to head off such confusion here with a brief discussion of the concept of race.

Race is a culturally constructed category, which means that the categories are not an automatic consequence of genetic or of cultural characteristics. It is the significance given to such characteristics which creates such categories as race. In this case skin colour is a major variable; those who identify as Aboriginal and have light skins will often explain and stress to outsiders that they are Aboriginal. The veracity of their claim is likely to be questioned. Those who have dark skins and reject their identity of interest with other Aborigines, are applauded by some and reviled by others, and again will explain to whites how their skin colour fits with their identity. That is, everyone recognises that there is a process of classification going on which takes skin colour as a major sign and demands identification in one or another category. Though the categories are constructed by whites, their power is apparent to Aborigines. However the Aboriginal community does not include or exclude members on the basis of skin colour.

This cultural process of constructing categories or, more accurately, reproducing and maintaining them, is ubiqitous in human society. The process of construction of racial categories is not different in kind from the process of construction of the categories associated with age, sex, place of birth, religion, occupation or any other phenomena which can be lent   meaning and potency, negative or positive. But the most distinctive aspect of racial categorisation is that particular differences become the focus for legitimising domination. Together with categories constructed around age and sex, racial categorisation attributes inferiority to natural causality.

There are struggles about the meanings and values associated with alleged racial attributes largely stemming from the inequality of power between those belonging to different categories. Old-age pensioners (grey-power), the feminists and blacks have, at particular periods in history, mobilised to challenge the evaluation of their characteristics and sometimes to challenge the categorisation process that has separated them. These are, I would argue, political and cultural responses. It is not the categories themselves which create the struggle, but the inequalities of power that the categories serve.

For a substantial minority of people in Brindleton, identity is not an automatic consequence of their biological and cultural characteristics. Many are ambivalent about their position in the binary system of classification. The ambivalence is often the consequence of cultural and biological divergence. On the one hand, a person who is identified with regular work, a stable nuclear family and participation in clubs and associations in the town will, whatever their colour, culturally have more in common with the majority of whites than with the most distinguishable black sector of the population. On the other hand, those who are part of a large family network most of whom are unemployed and some of whom are familiar with the lock-up, who have trouble keeping up the rent payments and who are to be seen sometimes joining the crowd of drinkers in the front bar of the central hotel, these people may be fair skinned and still be blacks. Thus a set of social and behavioural traits, which also have class significance, are attributed to blacks.

The main thing to be kept in mind is that the categories Aboriginal and European, black and white are real but very imprecise. The concept of race is embedded in the town, and I want to reveal something of the way its normal use and the descriptive terms that are used to reify it come up against contradictions and manage to stay intact.

The processes analysed here are not confined to western NSW although the contemporary field research was carried out in four towns in that area. The processes that are highlighted are ones that have been found in some form in more than one place. Individuals quoted and incidents described are all real and as accurate as is possible, though the significance of events is a matter of my interpretation. It is difficult to maintain a cool and neutral distance from some of this material, though I hope all my comments are informed by compassion for those who are involuntarily caught up in this process of classification into black and white.

The ideological process of classification is only one part of the social dynamics which have political and economic dimensions. While the major external forces which affect the town are discussed where necessary, my aim here, as in earlier chapters, is to reveal the way the politics and economics of a small town enmeshes the people in a particular historical process which each tries to shape in their own way. Many see their aims involved with others and so, at particular periods, groups are formed which struggle to achieve certain aspirations. Other groupings reflect more passive alignments. It is these social groupings that much of the analysis will be concerned.

Chapter 3

The structure of Brindleton

THE SURFACE CONTOURS

The population; its colour and categories[1]

Residents make a loose division of the town into locals and blow-ins, the latter group consisting of that transient population associated with jobs in government institutions, banks and some other industries, though not with shearers and other itinerant workers. The term blow-in is used widely, and appears to have lost its negative connotations. The largest single group of these is the school teachers. Blow-ins assume they will leave the town within two to five years of arriving. Ten to 15 per cent of the population is in this category, although their visibility and influence makes their numbers appear more substantial. Of course a few blow-ins have, over the years, settled down and so the other category 'local' does not only refer to those born and bred in the town. However the majority of residents have lived all their lives in the small town of Brindleton.

The other distinguishable group is the Aborigines who are virtually all local or from other parts of western NSW. In a town of between 3,000 and 4,000 people, estimates of the number of Aborigines varies from a fifth to a third. Because the populations of western NSW towns are not large, and there are seasonal and temporary changes in population (for instance with construction works in the vicinity), demographic trends are difficult to estimate. The various complications of the 'racial' identification compound the problem.

There are quite specific official changes of policy which have led to great swings in the Aboriginal numbers. For instance, as mentioned earlier, the census questions concerning race or ethnicity changed in each of the last three censuses. There have also been changes in the official definition of who is an Aboriginal. Aborigines commonly try to avoid official scrutiny, and the local census takers do not know the Aboriginal population well enough to counter this. Further, the census relies heavily on the notion of a 'household' as the basic unit for counting. But perhaps more significant for this study are the changed

---

[1] Research was conducted in four towns with populations from 2,000 — 8,000. All have substantial Aboriginal minorities of one-quarter to one-half. Particular features of one town are used as illustrations in some places.

consequences, many positive, of identifying as Aboriginal in the last 15 years. Some of these consequences are financial, but there are also manifold social effects which are not always immediately apparent.

Bureaucrats working in the town estimate the number of Aborigines to be higher than does the census. In 1981 one Department of Aboriginal Affairs (DAA) officer's estimate of the Aboriginal population was one-fifth higher than the official count. The non-Aboriginal population seems to have been slowly declining for many years, and it appears that the Aboriginal population is growing. Thus it seems certain that the proportion of people who see themselves and are seen by others as Aborigines is increasing.

A large minority of people in the town could claim to be in either category depending on what criteria is used, and the number of people with some Aboriginal ancestry is much larger than the number anyone would identify as Aboriginal. That is, many 'whites' have some Aboriginal ancestry; many 'Aborigines' do not identify with the Aboriginal community, to mention only two aspects of the problem. An official definition of who is Aboriginal was developed to determine eligibility for education grants, housing benefits and voting for representatives in various contexts. The definition, which was developed in 1970 by the Commonwealth Office for Aboriginal Affairs, has three elements; descent, self-identification and acceptance. 'An Aboriginal or Torres Straight Islander is a person of Aboriginal or Islander descent, who identifies as an Aboriginal or Islander, and is accepted as such by the community with which he or she is associated' (Gale & Brookman, 1975:103). Such a definition allows for a degree of self-identification by people who have suffered the definition of others for two centuries as full-bloods, mixed-bloods, half-castes, quadroons, and in the contemporary vernacular, those with a splash.

But there are serious problems created for some people by the new definition. On the one hand Aboriginal children who were adopted or fostered into white homes cannot easily fulfil the identification criteria. Further some 'up-town blacks' who obediently tried to assimilate in an earlier era are resented and not accepted by reserve dwellers as deserving of recent benefits. On the other hand the descent criterion allows for the retention of a biological component in the definition of race that does not fit well with contemporary biological or social theory. A person not of known Aboriginal descent who marries or is adopted into an Aboriginal family cannot become an Aboriginal. However biology performs an important social function. Individuals can be included or excluded at will, while the categorisation has a veneer of being involuntary. Thus someone can be denigrated for claiming inclusion in the category when not sufficiently dark and for trying to remain outside it when a shade too dark. This flexibility is used differently by different groups and in different contexts.

An example will illustrate the peculiar effect that the descent or biological criterion can have. Amy is a white woman of 67. As a girl on a large cattle station she liked to play at the black's camp. That was where her friends were. She was 14 when her father died and, as she was no longer allowed to go to the camp she ran away with her Aboriginal girlfiend and got a job as housemaid on a station near Brindleton. She married an Aboriginal station hand, and vividly recalls the occasion when she defied custom to eat outside with her husband and the other black workers. She subsequently bore eight children and lived on the Aboriginal reserve for years. In 1968 the family was allocated a small two-bedroomed house by the Aboriginal Lands Trust, where she continued to raise her large and boisterous children. Amy is now widowed, and with only occasional grandchildren to stay she is not formally entitled to live in the house which is now owned by the Aboriginal Housing Cooperative. The cooperative will not evict her, but the issue is one Amy and others are aware of.

Two of her older children are strongly involved with supporting Aboriginal identity in the town. A younger girl (who is fair skinned) has a number of white friends and there have been bitter accusations by her elder siblings that she is rejecting her loyalty to the blacks.

Such accusations are neither uncommon nor ill-founded. There are many examples of people who have seized an opportunity to sever personal ties with the Aboriginal community, though often the price of trying to be acceptable to whites is a considerable degree of self-imposed isolation. However others repudiate any connections, and disavow any sympathy, with the bulk of the Aboriginal community while affirming that they are Aboriginal by, for instance, attending meetings in that capacity. Such people, as we shall see, are a boon to certain interests in the town. There are those with 'a splash' who clearly intend the 'splash' to remain invisible and others who are dark but are accepted as honorary whites in some circumstances. One or two who are fair are fully identified as Aborigines and even as leaders. Some dark people are known as Islanders, thus enabling them a degree of freedom. If they do not conform to a stereotype, their different origins can provide an explanation. Thus the position on the colour spectrum does not determine whether one is Aboriginal.

The statistical categories of Aboriginal and non-Aboriginal can therefore reflect a number of different kinds of criteria. The categories are maintained despite constant interpenetration of the groups. The fuzziness of the boundaries has not meant a breaking down of the dichotomising ideology which is a crucial part of a common sense understanding of the town and its processes. Rather the boundaries are themselves the site of a struggle over group identity. This is not just a matter of individual attempts to determine identity, or of a group's attempts to enlarge its boundaries or effect closure. It also reflects a process of seeking adherence to certain ideas and aims.

A complex and often derogatory terminology referring to those not clearly and easily identified with either of the categories is used by both whites and blacks, though the terms differ as well as the context and meaning. 'Coconut' (black outside and white inside) and 'up-town nigger' are used by blacks to disparage those who are seen as disloyal because their ties with the Aboriginal community are being put at risk by involvement with whites. By contrast these categories do not reflect recruitment to the white community. Indeed having a 'splash' (of Aboriginal heritage) is a reason for exclusion by whites. A 'splash' or a 'touch of the tar-brush' are derogatory references by whites to a genetic heritage that the person is accused of concealing. Conversely those who are too diligent in asserting Aboriginal identity are often said to be erring in the other direction for nefarious political reasons or for financial gain; such accusations are often made by whites and sometimes by blacks.

The boundaries and characteristics of these groups are regularly breached intentionally or unintentionally and are contested daily, consciously or unconsciously. Examples of such breaches and contests will feature as a part of the events to be discussed in the rest of this work. The relationship of various interest groups in the town to these categories are complex and changing. I use the vernacular terms Aboriginal and European, white and black to refer to the way an individual would be usually identified in Brindleton and to the generally accepted social groupings in the town. The multi-meanings embedded in such terms and their contested nature should be kept in mind.

The contrast in material circumstances of the Aboriginal and white populations is marked. The geographical arrangements of the town provide a clue to these contrasts. About 10 per cent of the Aborigines live on the reserve in galvanised-iron shacks with dirt floors and minimal amenities. In those towns where the government policy allowed housing to be built on the reserve, there was also a riverbank or mallee camp which provided a rent-free environment. The 'Aboriginal end of town' is where during the late 1960s the Welfare Board and later the Lands Trust and the Aboriginal Housing Cooperative built houses for those who wanted to move from the reserve or camp. Forty to 60 per cent of the Aborigines now live in this area. Since the mid-1980s there has been a relaxing of the embargo on reserve building and some reserves are now being developed. The so-called 'pepper and salt' policy has seen Aborigines increasingly housed in other parts of town. Wherever they are, the dwellings regularly contain more people than they were intended for. There is not much in the way of consumer durables in the houses, and those that do exist are used constantly. Kin networks provide a means for sharing resources, so washing machines and cars have a short lifespan.

The material situation of whites appears universally to be much more affluent. While only a few could be called wealthy, the majority have jobs and virtually all live in solid and uncrowded houses. The blow-ins form a substantial group of well-off citizens. There is also a large minority of whites who are on government benefits, but few of these are part of large families. One or two white families live in chaotic and crowded homes. They do not form any kind of a group and are publicly invisible, individually coping with the situation and, unlike the Aborigines, 'decently ashamed of their circumstances'!

The category of Aborigines who live up-town could be expanded were all those with some Aboriginal ancestry to be included. There are some of these who have increasingly lived in the way other working-class whites in the town live and, while not denying their Aboriginal ancestry, and having some relations who are more overtly identified as Aborigines, still have little to do with the Aboriginal organisations, formal or informal, and are never to be seen mixing with the blacks. The daughter of one such family works as a barmaid at one of the clubs and recently reprimanded someone who was making 'coon jokes'. This was a brave act in such circumstances, and one that is only possible because of recent strengthening of the public identity of Aborigines.

The most pervasive image of Aborigines in the town relies on those Aborigines most often seen in public. Many members of the white population of Brindleton only interact with Aborigines on the public street. Outside the town's one supermarket there is a meeting place where a small proportion of blacks regularly sit, drink, talk and stand about. There are clear status meanings among whites attached to this behaviour. Although occasionally one or two white 'bushies' sit or squat on the pavement, for most it would be a difficult thing to do, mainly because of an assumption that either abnormality or destitution is implied by sitting or drinking in the street. These people simply do not adhere to the 'proper' rules of behaviour, and most white shoppers try to ignore them. The older white male residents often greet an old black workmate or employee with patronising joviality. One woman made a point of stopping to talk, partly at least because of her professional involvement with Aborigines. She was derided by whites as a show-off, who was demonstrating publicly to try to impress them with how non-racist she was.

It is interesting to discover why the town council removed the seats that were once provided in the main street. The reason given to me by a councillor was that Aborigines sat on them. This explanation was quickly amended to 'Too many sat on them, lounged all over them. It did not look nice for the tourists.' Some of the Aborigines appear unkempt, hesitant or drunk, and are treated with open impatience or disdain in shops and other public places. It seems that this is the image of Aborigines that is dominant in the minds of many of the whites, but it is supplemented by stories of delinquency and vandalism that form a major part of social small-talk.

There is little other familiarity between whites and Aborigines in the town, so that the impression of Aborigines gained in the street or from gossip remains the dominant one for many white people. Members of some organisations do know the active and often more assimilated blacks. The older white residents' knowledge is of ex-employees or ex-workmates. The police are familiar with the more rebellious or disruptive individuals and tell stories of the violence they see as Aboriginal violence. The school teachers know certain of the more ambitious parents, as well as those considered a problem. But few whites really know anything of the day to day lives of the bulk of the Aboriginal population.

Social life

The pubs and clubs are generally clearly demarcated in terms of clientele and style. Besides their role of providing sports facilites, the clubs provide restaurant facilities, bar services and poker machines, as well as occasional entertainment. The membership of the clubs overlaps a good deal, but the graziers are to be found in one only, and there will be few wage earners in the bar that caters for the salaried blow-ins and the younger businessmen. The clubs are also a haven for older white alcoholics, who mostly remain fairly unobtrusive even when very drunk. While predominantly patronised by whites, they have one or two Aboriginal members, but have so far managed to keep out those who are likely to invite their friends.

One club shows striking changes taking place in its clientele which is a response to financial hardship. The story is simple. The club was nearing bankruptcy. The committee decided that a Friday night disco would attract enough custom to save the day. Just at this time a complaint was made to the Anti-Discrimination Board (ADB) that the club had refused someone membership on grounds of race. This made the club liable to a large fine, and the ADB visited the town to make enquiries. Some Aboriginal members were accepted into the club, perhaps to prove their non-discriminatory practices and avoid a fine. The Friday disco began to attract many young Aborigines who, even if not members, could usually find a friend to sign them in. Consequently the club finances are in a healthier state.

Friday night at this disco is marked by a clear spatial continuum from the mostly male, all white, carpeted and well-lighted bar, through a more motley section with some female and some Aboriginal people, to the darker area near the dance floor where the clientele is mostly Aboriginal. One Aboriginal woman who has a white boyfriend gave me a perceptive and funny account not only of these divisions and the disapproving looks if they are breached, but also of the way the arrangements become confused in the early hours of the morning. As the result of a fight in the car park one Aborigine's membership was revoked. He considered this unfair because the usual practice in the pubs is ejection for fighting, and only if an individual offends again is he or she barred. Where is one to fight if not in the car park? Taking the fight outside is a well-known way of avoiding the risk of being barred.

The social demarcations in one hotel in the centre of town reflects an earlier era. The back bar caters for the graziers and their friends. In the front bar and front lounge the blacks are to be found in large numbers. They spill out onto the street and talk through the open window while the proprietor keeps watch, apparently in a constant state of anxiety. An Aboriginal woman who manages an Aboriginal organisation and has some authority in the town, and who prides herself on being well dressed, sometimes goes into the back bar for a drink. One day two of her relatives came to talk to her in there.

Subsequently the proprietor came in to say to her confidentially, 'Look Carol, I don't mind if you are in here but I don't want those others to think they can come in here too. Could you just tell them to stay out there.' Clearly the same function as club membership is achieved. Those who want to drink without contact with citizens who have different mores are being accomodated.

The blow-ins go to the clubs and to one pub. Difficulty is experienced by people such as police and school teachers in a small town, because their position of authority is not protected by anonymity as it would be in a city. They are aware that they will be discussed and may be disliked. They are thrown together in those places that become a haven for them, and many come to depend on a measure of unity and support within this group. In general their relationship with the main Aboriginal population is not different from that of other whites.

The features of Aborigines' behaviour that arouse complaints in such settings are asking for money, swearing and abusing, and being drunk and uncontrolled. There are a few individuals who regularly behave in such a manner, and those who drink in the front bar have well-developed ways of countering the demands for money and for avoiding fights. But there are regular fisticuffs or fights which sometimes erupt onto the pavement, and these can cause distress to the passers by. One liberal-minded blow-in confessed that she felt a raging hatred for drunken blacks when her small daughter, who had wandered away along the quiet pavement, was almost embroiled in such a fight. The fact that two Aboriginal women onlookers did not rescue the child incensed her still further.

Two of the other pubs provide venues for a large number of Aborigines who are mostly moderate drinkers. The publicans exert strict control over violent or disruptive behaviour. One of these is frequented by those who I will call interstitial. This is a very loose grouping consisting of some who partially reject Aboriginal identification, others who are active leaders in Aboriginal organisations and 'mixed' couples. Some of these people will complain about the way Aborigines will not take advantage of the opportunities they have. They will also bemoan or laugh about the way they are shunned or stigmatised by whites. One man told me there was no racism in this town, but sometime later the same evening he described occasions of deliberate humiliation he had suffered. This pattern of denial of the problem in general terms, combined with descriptions of particular instances of racism, is not uncommon. Another feature of this interstitial group is that people sometimes call each other coconuts and up-town niggers in fun and in anger. This is also a working-class pub, where the shearers discuss union business and no graziers are to be seen.

The racial separation in pubs and clubs is achieved in a number of formal and informal ways. The club membership system is one way the town whites can avoid mixing with the disreputable blacks. It is denied that judgements about membership applications are made on the basis of race. A criminal record precludes membership, and so does a bad reputation. When I enquired of one club manager whether his club had Aboriginal members, he asserted with a self-righteous air that he did not know because he did not look at the colour of a person's skin. But the club where Aborigines know themselves to be unwelcome is the one where I heard open and public discussions at the bar of the peculiar and inferior characteristics of the blacks and the ruinous way they are being treated. The latest stories of Aboriginal outrages in the town, or of government excesses, are related in such places with keen enjoyment.

Voluntary associations

There is a large number of service and special interest clubs from the businessmen's Apex clubs to the lacemakers. Most are intended to cater for one section of the white population. Some are well-known organisations such as Red Cross, Country Women's Association and Rotary, which are affiliated with wider state bodies. As well, there are the ratepayers and water users associations which were formed in an attempt to control the shire council's rates. Several are for women, and a recently formed VIEW (Voices, Interests, Education for Women) club, affiliated with the state body and with the purpose of providing a lively venue for conservative younger women, has attracted many members.

The major Aboriginal organisations have some different features from most of the clubs as they have been formed to achieve particular ends which are somewhat different from service, hobby or recreational organisations. They include the housing cooperative which will be discussed in some detail below. Members join for a small fee in order to be eligible for a house. Ostensibly it has no social functions but, by virtue of the resouces available to its three employees, it fulfils an important organisational and communication function. That is, the telephone is used for inter-town communication, and the car is used to disseminate information within the town. The Aboriginal Education Consultative Group (AECG) emerged after the collapse of an earlier organisation which was formed in 1980, and which organised a protest concerning the school. A quiescent period ensued and then a branch of the state-wide AECG was formed. It is a moderate organisation which sees itself as making legitimate demands on the school system in cooperation with some supportive teachers. It has a core of a few women who are Aboriginal Teacher Aids and a wider membership of some parents who regularly go to meetings. It can also call on the support of a much larger group of parents in the community.

More recently formed are the land council and the Aboriginal medical service group. Two active members of the latter group have travelled to Sydney and elsewhere to attend meetings and consultations. The NSW Aboriginal Land Rights Act was passed in 1983 making all Aborigines members of the local land council if they enrol. Money was provided directly to land councils, by-passing both bureaucratic control and accountability. The amounts provided to local councils are insufficient for the purchase of land. A land council meeting was called in Brindleton at which a husband and wife team were elected as chair and deputy. They immediately bought equipment to begin cleaning up the houses now owned by the land council. However all land council funds were frozen by the state government in September 1985 as it was asserted that they were being used improperly. This is the most direct example of many where the practice belies the government's policy of self-determination.

Religious affiliation in the towns of western NSW varies according to particular historical circumstances. Brindleton has 40 per cent Catholic, 30 per cent Church of England, 7 per cent Presbyterian, and a small following for Baptist, Methodist and several other nonconformist churches (Census 1981). The Catholic church has a large Aboriginal following and two churches, one at each end of town. Mass is said weekly in both churches. There is also a Catholic primary school with about one-third Aboriginal pupils, which is at the Aboriginal end of town. There is one priest and several nuns at the convent school. A further small group of 'Indian nuns' runs a home for old men, a pre-school and other charitable works outside the government institutional structures. They also live at the Aboriginal end of town, and have very little contact with other townspeople. This predominance of Catholics among the Christian churches is not usual, but is due to a particularly enthusiatic ministry in an earlier era.

The Church of England membership is virtually all white and has apparently in the past regarded itself as ministering to that section of the population. There are a number of small but very active fundamentalist Christian groups, none of which have much of an Aboriginal following. They run several radio programmes, write regular columns in the local paper and one intermittently runs a drop-in coffee shop where Christian guitar music is played and Aboriginal youth congregates in somewhat impious noisiness. Another group runs a farm which is worked by resident students training as evangelists. They believe that civilisation grew out of self-discipline, and that material success is a sign of being on the right path. Socialism is evil and they assert that this is evident in the Aboriginal problems being exacerbated by government's social welfare provisions. Another group has begun a school using the Accelerated Christian Education programme imported from the USA. The school is flourishing under the guidance of a family from South Africa and other converts. No Aborigines are involved. The school is registered and subsidised. Thus none of the churches, with the partial exception of the Catholic church, now provides alternative views or practices in relation to the racial division in Brindleton.

Sports clubs

Some of these clubs are exclusively for one section of the community, and others attempt to get as many people involved as possible whether they are black, white or brindle. Four kinds of sports clubs can be distinguished. First there are the larger clubs for adults, where team sports such as basketball, cricket and rugby are played. Blow-ins, especially school teachers, are often involved in organising these clubs, though the football is dominated by locals. Usually about 50 to 60 per cent of members are local and a substantial minority are Aboriginal. In no cases are Aborigines in management positions, though there have been moves to form an all Aboriginal rugby team to counter the control by Gubbs, as whites are known.

The second kind of sports club is for children and youths, run by white adults, usually school teachers, which often includes 30 to 40 per cent Aboriginal members. Cricket and hockey are branches of the adult clubs, as is minor league. The pony club is an exception in that it has no members who would claim to be Aboriginal. Third, there are the larger clubs for social interaction and individual sport, including the horsey ones. The Digger's and Jockey clubs are for the racing fraternity; all members are local, and Aborigines are not welcome. The golf and bowling clubs in their sporting aspect are slightly less exclusive, with a number of blow-ins and boasting two or three dark members who are 'a credit to their race'. Squash and tennis, which have more blow-ins participating, also have a few Aboriginal members.

The fourth kind of club is smaller, with either an expensive or special interest, such as the pistol club and the flying club. These are predominantly local in membership and management and have no Aboriginal members. An exception is the boxing club which may belong in the second category as it is mainly run by white adults for young Aboriginal boxers. However it has almost entirely local membership and is a rather different type of club from all the others. One of its members has had success as a state bantam weight champion, but the club has much difficulty raising money to send the boxers to tournaments (cf. Broome, 1980).

Two other recreational venues are the bingo games and the Community Youth Support Scheme (CYSS). Bingo is attended entirely by Aborigines, mostly women but many men and children. It takes place sometimes in the Hall in recent times, but traditionally outside, near the edge of the Aboriginal end of town. Up to 250 people, many of them spectators, congregate most afternoons of the week, and by putting in 20 to 60 cents, can win $30 to $100. Home-made boards and makeshift counters are usual. The scene is lively and informal with children running about, older children and non-players moving among groups, and players sitting on the ground, often using pinches of dirt for counters. This group ran a funeral fund for some time which assisted those who needed help with funeral expenses. Once the money disappeared, and there were accusations of stealing. The conflict was allowed to die down and the funeral fund revived a few months later.

CYSS is a government-funded agency run by a town committee which employs a social worker to provide a venue for young people. It is intended to allay the worst effects of unemployment by providing some training or useful life skills. Because the young Aboriginal men make up the bulk of the clients at CYSS, it has come to operate as an informal club. Few whites attend. The social workers appointed to run CYSS have until 1986 always been from outside the town, often from the city with little or no experience of a country town with a large minority of Aborigines. At various times there have been Aboriginal assistants appointed whose position has been particularly difficult.

Other social events, such as legacy balls and club annual parties, tend to be dominated by formality and by whites, and they contrast in style with Aboriginal events which are informal and appear chaotic by contrast. These cultural differences, and the social separation they reflect, need to be seen in relation to employment patterns which in turn need to be seen in their historical context. We will now turn to the pattern of work.

WORK

Changes in rural labour

The reduction in the number of people employed by landowners has been an ongoing process, with some temporary reversals since the heyday of the large holdings in the 19th century when station employees could number over 100. Now few properties employ anyone at all besides the seasonal shearers. A married couple can run a large property of grazing stock on their own. A few have an aged retainer and temporary or contract workers are hired for particular jobs. That is, the properties are no longer labour intensive but capital intensive as machines have replaced men.

It was the rural recession of the late 1960s that many rural workers recall as having deprived them of the opportunity to work. Relief work was provided by the shire council for three years and in many cases whites and blacks worked on the same jobs, thus continuing for a time their previous common work experience on the land. One task that these workers completed was the curbing and guttering at the more privileged end of town.

Graziers in the west have adopted labour-saving devices with alacrity. Only 9 per cent of their expenditure is on wages and some of that is paid to family members. The Western Lands Commission report (1982:20,14) states that 'Less than one quarter of properties in the sample population employ one full-time workman while over three quarters have no full-time employees.... between 1963 and 1975 there was a sixty-one percent reduction in the number of "paid male employees" ... these men have never been re-employed.... Slightly more use is made of part-time employees'. About 40 per cent reported the use of part-time labour which is partly that of other graziers earning extra income (Western Lands Commission, 1982:102-3).

The graziers attribute the reduction of their use of hired labour to high wages and the reduced profits of the pastoral industry. The availability of technology that reduces costs underlies the change.

The post-war petrol revolution brought with it more efficient methods of transport which have replaced many jobs — from the early bullock teams and camel trains to droving, which continued as a major form of employment until the 1960s. The trucking of stock has now led to a virtual disappearance of the drovers. Most pastoralists have motorbikes to muster their own stock and check fences. As well helicopter mustering, which costs about a thousand dollars a day, can do in that day the work that it would take eight men on horses many days to do. There are a few contract fencers and tank-sinkers to be found and even the occasional local droving job is available. Landholders usually know a couple of fellows in town who will take a job fencing or repairing the stockyards for a payment in cash that will not interfere with their unemployment benefit or pension.

The beliefs of employers that the Aborigines are less reliable workers ensures that they get little of any work that is available. For instance the new but highly mechanised cotton industry is in a position to expect from their employees loyalty and very long hours of work. Nevertheless the managers complain about the lack of commitment from workers. Aborigines are lumped together as a category of unemployable people because the owners 'know' that Aborigines do not like to work long hours. In fact of course that judgement applies to quite a range of people, only some of whom are Aboriginal. Thus, to these newcomers in the role of employer in the outback, class and race characteristics are similar.

Besides the mechanisation of primary production, post-war development of retailing through large-scale corporations in the form of chain stores has destroyed local secondary industry and therefore reduced employment opportunities in Brindleton. Many services which once were supplied by small businesses in the district have closed or put off their employees. The supermarket is part of a chain that finds it more profitable to bring in fruit and vegetables from their regular suppliers than buy from the local growers. In a town that had five bakers 20 years ago, the one baker is having trouble surviving in competition with the suppliers from outside. One butcher supplies the supermarket and runs his own shop, severely reducing the profitabilty of the others. A few businesses such as trucking firms and motor mechanics are substantial still, and five major oil companies have depots in the town.

Some shops face decreasing profits because the more affluent residents, who can afford to travel, do much of their shopping in the larger centres. One such group organises a shopping bus for that purpose once a month, much to the vocal disapproval of the town shopkeepers. The latter group, through the Chamber of Commerce, mounted a campaign against a discount clothing stall which set up in the town once a fortnight and was well patronised by the less affluent residents. The council was asked to refuse them a licence as they were undermining the local business houses and taking profits out of the town. Thus are the contradictions of capitalism expressed in a country town.

There has been, during the lifetime of adults in Brindleton, an overall contraction of work opportunities, a reduced variety of jobs and a heavier reliance on a few industries. There is greater competition between workers, and few jobs entail personal ties with the bosses as did pastoral work and work in small local industries.

White workers

While the major enterprise in the region remains pastoral production, the work carried out as part of that enterprise has altered radically. What happened then to the men who used to do the stockwork, the teamsters and carriers, the railway men and tradesmen on the stations, the labourers and small business families who serviced the district? To answer this question I have collected genealogical material from the bulk of the black families and a large proportion of the white working-class families, that is, those families who have lived mainly from wage or contract labour.

What follows is a summary of the employment history of the descendents of 56 white men who arrived in the west before 1930 (some in 1890), who themselves stayed all their lives in one town or district, and who had at least one descendent in the district in 1984. Table 3.3 giving employment statistics will make some of these observations more meaningful (see p.127).

The main conclusions from a close scrutiny of these men's families and their hundreds of descendents are as follows:

1. Of the descendents of these men who are still in the district, almost all are employees on wages, either unskilled or tradesmen. These are the men who work in the meatworks, for the shire or as storemen (Table 3.3). Some are truckies or shearers. A few, mostly women, work as shop assistants or clerical workers. A few are unemployed.

2. A substantial number of the descendents of these families have departed the town altogether. As the number of descendents of those

Table 3.1: *Forebears of working-class whites occupations on arrival* [2]

Teamsters	4	
Carriers	7	
Tradesmen	5	(Initially on stations)
Station work/drovers	13	
Labourers	9	
Railway workers	4	
Small businesses	10	(3 publicans,4 shops, market garden, newspaper, cordial manufacturer)
Punt operators	3	
Shearing contractor	1	
Total	56	

who left cannot be ascertained, and as the departures have taken place at different stages of the family cycle, it is impossible to quantify this process. In a few families almost all have departed at each generation. In other families most have remained. I estimate, on average, that over half of the offspring at each generation have left either before or during the period when they were producing offspring. The fortunes of those who left cannot be ascertained. The ones mentioned have usually succeeded in some skilled occupation, but the frequency of such success cannot be quantified. A minority return as to a refuge, some when they are widowed or deserted, some as drunks and some to retire.

3. Some of the descendents are now on grazing properties acquired at different stages and by different means. For instance three of the teamsters themselves ended up with land, one through buying a lease with others which he later owned alone; his son lost it. Another

---

[2]Much of this information was obtained from a working-class couple both in their late 70s who have lived all of their lives in one town and who have a large number of descendents in the town. Other sources filled in and confimed most of the material. My aim was to obtain a broad picture of the fortunes of working-class families rather than a detailed picture of individual families. Arrival dates span quite a long period because my informants knew the origins of some men that had arrived when they were children or before they were born. Dating was not possible. Women not represented. The genealogies on which the above findings are based are virtually complete records of the descendents who remained in the town. Each family differs on several criteria, and in many cases the information is not complete for the early period. The summary conclusions necessarily use simplified categories. Exact and even relative dating was often difficult so it was not possible with much of the sample to correlate the family fortunes with the exact period and thus with other families or with other events.

teamster 'drew a block' in a government ballot and became a wealthy landowner. His son inherited his land and his daughters married graziers. Another's family moved to properties elsewhere and the only local descendents are wage labourers. Fifteen of the 56 men in all have some descendents on the land. Eight of these were obtained by drawing a block and five are the result of a daughter or grand-daughter marrying a grazier or someone who drew a block.[3]

4. A few of the descendents of these men own small businesses or have skilled jobs in the town though it is probable that many more of those who left may be in this category. Of the seven men who were carriers, two began family trucking companies which have been successful and employ a number of family members. Three of the original small businesses remain, two owned by descendents of the original owner, but they have only been able to continue to support one nuclear family. Several descendents of the original small business men are shop owners or managers.

5. One descendent of a station worker and one from a town family have government jobs in the town. Conversely those who have left the town for specialised training or higher education have virtually all stayed away.

6. After losing their rural jobs many men stayed in the town picking up casual work and eventually drawing unemployment benefits or the pension. Some have managed to retire with a modicum of comfort. The older rural workers recall the hard and ill-paid work of their youth. One resoundingly rejected the notion of 'the good old days', saying he had to get out of bed at 5a.m. to scrub milk cans when he was a child of 11-years-old. He remarked that 'machinery has taken the work out of work' and 'In those days you never dreamed you'd own a house.' Yet some of those men did manage to buy a house, often small and built of fibro, with a section of land, and have kept them. Others live in rooming houses and, like many of their black fellow-workers, have become depressed and sometimes drunken.

Thus with the changing economic structure of the pastoral industry involving a decrease in local job opportunities, the option of leaving town has been taken by a large number of people to pursue further employment or business opportunities, whether successfully or not.

---

[3]I use the terms grazier and block-owner to distinguish the owners of smaller properties which have often failed as profitable enterprises from the large, stable owners. The categories are not precise as blocks could be added to and become lucrative in good seasons while some properties support a family in meagre conditions for generations. In most cases 'grazier' refers to the situation where a family has a series of holdings.

The wage-earning families of 60 to 80 years ago have remained workers in the main, but the white workers have not suffered the main burden of the last decade's unemployment in the local area. Their erstwhile 'equality' with their bosses has been shown to be spurious and their movement out of the district has increased the social distance between landowners and workers in the district.

Black workers

Genealogical information was more readily available from the black population because the community is more close knit in terms of kinship and information.[4] Also there is far less mobility of the kind so common among the white population. Movement between western NSW towns does not lead to the severing of ties. It is significant that the consequences of the changed labour market are much simpler and more direct in this section of the population. They simply became unemployed.

Table 3.2   *Occupations of Aboriginal men born before approximately 1955*

Past occupation	No.	If still employed in past occupation
Fencers/station hands	32	1 is a caretaker, 2 get regular casual work
Drovers/stockmen	28	2 have had casual work in the last 2 years
Shearers	16	Several working in local teams
Other (meatworks, DMR)	19	11 still employed
Total	95	

Note: Two men have been trained for other work and have obtained better paid jobs. Two or three others are involved in such business as land rights. Most are unemployed.

It is clear from a comparison of the family histories that the Aboriginal and the white populations were affected very differently by reduced rural employment. Black workers were more likely to be fencers and rouseabouts, casually employed and therefore the first to go. Many white rural workers moved away from the town to take up different work in the larger towns or cities, or moved into the industry that had displaced them by becoming truckies, either self-employed or with friends and relations. The blacks did not have this option.

[4] I had two Aboriginal research assistants for a period of two months. The Aboriginal population sample was of a different kind from that of the whites, as it included all those men now over 30 whose previous work was known.

Those who moved did so in different circumstances. A few families moved to other country towns where they had relatives, and their location is known at least by their kin. There are two who moved away when young and through educational opportunities have gained well-paid permanent employment. Movement to the large urban centres was the main response of whites to contracting opportunities in rural employment. But the reason for many of the blacks moving in the last 10 years is quite different: the government offered them housing and work in another town under the 'resettlement scheme'. This is a scheme designed in the early 1970s to enable Aborigines to move out of their community to a new life in towns where employment is available. Housing is provided (Eckermann, 1984).

In most cases the Aboriginal workers did not have the opportunity to change their place of residence and, in the fierce competition for the jobs that were available in the transport industry, they were handicapped by lacking nepotistic ties. In a small competitive community where there is a shortage of jobs it is not surprising that the employer favours those with whom he has some personal connections, whether economic or affectionate. Thus since the days when rural work was plentiful and black and white stockmen, shearers and fencers worked together, there has been a separating of white and black workers.

Unemployment is most commonly seen by employers as a result of high wages, generous unemployment benefits and laziness. The influential citizens of Brindleton apply their explanation of unemployment particularly to Aborigines, because they are generally equated with the unemployed. This may be a faulty generalisation, but is based on observations of the local scene.

Though history provides useful legitimation of privilege there is a rejection of any historical reasons for Aboriginal disadvantage. For instance there is a popular belief that the provision of government handouts has relieved the Aborigines of the need to work and has created laziness. One woman recalled with outrage how her husband's employee 'Old Charlie', had one day asked for more money because 'some *stirrer*' had told him he was entitled to equal wages. This was described to me as the first of the bad effects of the government 'doing everything for them'. Of course he was dismissed. 'My husband could not afford to pay him all that and he was not worth it anyway.' The fact that he could not get another job and was subsequently seen drunk in the street is seen as confirmation of the deleterious effect of government policies.

The popular notion that the Aborigines will not work is supported by at least two Aborigines, one of whom had just lost his job due to a downturn in the industry which employed him. Despite this experience he argues that those fellows (meaning other Aboriginal men) will not try hard enough, and really do not want work. Such comments are not to be dismissed simply as misapprehensions, fabrications or racist attempts to denigrate one section of the population in order to excuse the failure of the economy to provide jobs. Of course lack of motivation is a consequence, not a cause of unemployment.

It has been frequently observed that 'the unemployed' come to terms with a lifestyle which does not involve daily wage labour and this process has nothing to do with being Aboriginal. However when a substantial group of people, defined as a separate category from the majority, are largely unemployed, the pattern of life in the community militates against the necessary regularity and alacrity in the mornings which is involved in holding down a job. Further some Aborigines, though wanting wage labour, will not take just any job. For instance the seasonal picking in the region is unreliable and intermittent. It requires a very early start to a very long day and yet may only last a few days. This means trouble with the dole office and back-breaking work which is painful when the body is unaccustomed to it. Often there are no friends about. There is however one large family group which has for many years set off for the seasonal fruit picking for two to three months in the south of the state.

Another painful aspect of some jobs is the joking by white workmates about Aborigines. One man found that he was expected to join in the joking. His refusal was a challenge, and the men continued to try to upset him. An angry reaction would have meant a fight and loss of the job which he held for over a year. He said that he knew others who would 'joke against their own colour' just for a bit of peace. As this man said, 'they have got you whichever way you go'. Finally, not working and expressing negative attitudes to jobs has become generally associated with the defiant attitude characteristic of the 'oppositional culture' of Aborigines to be discussed below.

Current employment

Government and public sector jobs provided 45 per cent of employment (Table 3.3). The 28 per cent of these recruited outside the town hold the senior positions. Most of those recruited locally are support staff in the schools, nursing and domestic staff in the hospital, and outside labourers in the Department of Main Roads, Telecom and the shire council. Most of the Aborigines are employed either in jobs recently created and designated for Aborigines, in areas where 'Aboriginalisation' is policy (such as the DAA), or in traineeships which last only one year. Of the full-time jobs, the 32 per cent which require training that is not available locally are virtually closed to local people. Were they to go away for training there is no guarantee that they would be appointed to such jobs, as they are widely advertised.

Table 3.3: *Profile of employment opportunities*

	Public sector jobs	Private sector jobs	Total jobs
Total	506	613	1,119 *
%	45% of jobs	55% of jobs	100%
From outside	142	24	166
	28% of above	4% of above	16%
Full-time	446	539	985
Part-time	60	74	134
Aboriginal employees**	48 9%	15	63

Source: Figures collected 1983-4.
* According to the 1981 Census, public sector employment accounts for 40% and private sector for 55% of employment, 5% are not stated.
** This is a loose definition according to public identification.

The 4 per cent of jobs in private industry that were recruited from outside the town are management positions in banks and stock and station agents. Information about Aborigines employed was very difficult to obtain from private employers. This is partly because of the confused categories. Many who have an Aboriginal heritage are not defined by themselves or others as Aboriginal. No one wants to mention this, yet there is obvious awareness of it. Virtually no Aborigines who identify themselves as such, work in the shops and other small businesses in the town. The 15 Aborigines identified in Table 3.3 are employed in the meatworks. There is one small shop funded by DAA which two Aborigines run.

Table 3.4: *Private industries*

	No. of firms	Employees			Additional part-time
		< 2	3-5	> 5	
Oil companies, service stations & motor mechanics	14	3	10	1	10
Transport & carriers, taxis	19	14	3	2	—
Services (building, panel beating)	16	14	1	1	—
Retail & wholesale supply	34	19	9	6	10
Manufacturing & primary prod. (Meatworks, cotton, orchards, not graziers)	10	5	2	3	21
Hotel & catering	20	9	9	2	31
Professional (excl. doctors)	5	5	0	0	1
Banks, stock & station agents	7	1	2	4	—
Total	125	70	36	19	

Source: Information collected 1983-4.

The vast majority of private businesses are very small family affairs. Of those employing over five people only two employ more than ten. One of these is the meatworks, which is only about one-fifth of its previous size. The killing of beef ceased in the 1970s due to rationalisation of the industry, and now only horses are killed for export. The more expert and long-term employees retained some regular work, but most of the 600 who had been employed in earlier years have either become welfare recipients or have gone to other jobs or other places. While the meatworks still employs over 100 people, the amount of work fluctuates a great deal with demand and during much of 1983-4 men were often working only two or three days a week. With recent confirmation of the product being acceptable to EEC buyers there is more work available and some younger men in the town have obtained this casual work without retaining the conditions of previous employees.

The other large private employer is the newly developing cotton industry which both grows and processes cotton. It is highly mechanised, but the one major company had 67 people on the payroll in mid-1983. Many of these work in both the cottonfields and on the gin as the season requires. The gin has been built by a USA company in half shares with the major local cotton-growing company which owns 149,000 acres. Five thousand acres in the irrigation area are planted in cotton. While expensive to grow because of the cost of irrigation and machinery and the associated labour, the returns are excellent in a good season and good in an indifferent one. This company demands total commitment from management and workers alike and it is their policy to sack anyone who is late or who does not wish to work long hours. According to one manager, no Aborigines and few of the local whites could fulfil these requirements. In late 1983 workers were recruited from interstate because the locals were not sufficiently dedicated. Rumours abound about the way the company treats its workers, but loyal employees speak highly of their bosses, the managers, who work very long hours themselves. Thus the initiatives of corporate capitalism from far outside are affecting outback Australia, with only faint grumbles from a few. Most locals whose voices are heard applaud 'development' of any kind. They could hardly do otherwise (cf. Eipper,1985).

Table 3.5: *Income profile of Brindleton*

	Individuals	No. of families Head & spouse incomes	Households
			All incomes
	(*n* 2,312)	(*n* 975)	(*n* 909)
Under $ 8,000	53.6%	33.8%	21.5%
Under $10,000	65.9%	43.3%	28.8%
Under $12,000	76.1%	53.0%	37.0%

Source: 1981 Census.

It is clear from the level of these incomes that a large proportion of the people in Brindleton depend on the social security department rather than an employer for their income. The census information says that 58 per cent of the adult population are employed, 7 per cent unemployed and 36 per cent are not in the workforce. The CES officer gave a much higher figure of 14 per cent registered unemployed. From personal observation it seems that a minority of Aborigines have regular employment, and those that do are mainly the younger men and those in government jobs where being Aboriginal is a necessary qualification. Some of the consequences of the heavy dependence on welfare will be discussed in a later section.

There is a widely recognised stagnation of the town businesses and lack of work for many people. There are constant complaints and bitter blaming of the government for the lack of moral fibre in today's society. The CES oversees government schemes to train and employ young people and retrain older ones and the Department of Employment and Industry encourages the employment of Aborigines. Some success has been achieved as employers are quite willing to take advantage of the subsidies available. In the midst of what is seen as hard times the new deal for Aborigines strikes a sour note for many.

THE ENLIGHTENMENT

The new legislation

From a past which consisted of confinement on reserves and subjection to intrusive laws the new federal legislation, enacted in the late 1960s and early 1970s, seemed to promise an era of liberty and equality for the Aborigines of Australia. Many people with liberal views welcomed this promise of Aboriginal self-determination, though others viewed the developments with alarm. Those who supported the initiatives recognised that discriminatory practices and racist ideology were still prevalent, but it was widely believed that they would become less important as Aboriginal groups gained more power.

Changes in what is called the 'political climate' allowed this to occur. Such forces as international opinion and the upsurge of protest are alluded to as explanations (Stevens, 1980:vii; Lippmann, 1981). The flourishing of political protest in turn may be seen partly as a consequence of changes in the economic order (Beckett, 1983). Aboriginal political organisations had become increasingly vocal and independent of their white supporters. The freedom ride of 1965, when busloads of white and Aboriginal students visited some NSW country towns and insisted that Aborigines be allowed to use the town facilities (Perkins, 1975), had gained a good deal of publicity. Twelve years later the Aboriginal tent embassy on the lawns of parliament house in Canberra achieved national and international attention for weeks (Broome, 1982:176,184). There were a few frustrating attempts to mobilise the rural population, but the political activists had come together in urban centres and retained little direct connection with the bulk of the black population of the country towns. They did mobilise a response from the politicians. The attempts to set up representative organisations and advisory bodies met with considerable problems, partly because of the lack of political sophistication in the rural areas and the absence of any Australia-wide organisation among Aborigines (Weaver, 1983).

I will not attempt to develop a more adequate explanation for the enlightenment policies here, but it seems to me that Brindleton's dynamics and the dynamics of 'world opinion' are part of the same process. Perhaps the change is not as profound as it appears. Rather than the dawn of enlightenment, the changes might be better seen as a readjustment to a somewhat different form of inequality by the development of a new set of terms and a new bureaucratic apparatus. In other words the insistent demands for liberty in the 1960s in various parts of the world have been contained rather than satisfied. The Aboriginal tent embassy, perhaps the most dramatic example of black protest in Australia, asked for Aboriginal independence and received something quite different.

Nearly two decades on it has been increasingly recognised that the legislative and funding changes have not solved the medical, legal, educational and economic disadvantages of Aborigines (cf. Gale & Wundersitz, 1982). Initial euphoria among those fighting for Aboriginal rights has died. There are bouts of anger, resignations, accusations of bad faith, of lack of commitment and of various forms of selfishness. Whites are accused of not understanding black needs; blacks of selling out to whites. But the difficulties are not caused by the individuals who have been implementing policy, or by the blacks who have responded. Rather, while there has been a shift in the arena and the rules have changed, the fundamental struggle continues from when it began over 100 years ago in western NSW. The new policies were incapable of letting the blacks in, especially since they were wanting inclusion on their own terms.

In this section I will examine some of the immediate reasons for disillusionment with government policies. We have seen that changes came about in the 1960s normalising the legal status of Aborigines. In NSW no laws discriminating against Aborigines remained after 1968, but thereafter another kind of law that appealed to racial categories began to be implemented. These policies are ostensibly designed to normalise Aborigines still further by removing informal barriers to equality of opportunity with white Australians. Special access to resources could only be arranged by targeting Aborigines for particular benefits. Thus education, housing, health and welfare policies were developed for Aborigines. Further these were to be implemented under the rubric of local decision-making by Aborigines, or self-management as the policy came to be known.

The new era of self-management began with the appointment of H.C. 'Nugget' Coombs in 1967 as the head of the new Council for Aboriginal Affairs. A dedicated reformer, Coombs got together a dynamic little group led by himself and Barry Dexter with W.E.H. Stanner, an anthropologist, as the third member of the council which was to run the Office for Aboriginal Affairs (OAA), the precursor of the Department of Aboriginal Affairs. The council had a hand-picked staff of 20 including four Aborigines. Coombs was determined they would be effective and he used unconventional means to ensure freedom from the problems that usually beset bureaucracies. Each of the staff was to take up an area of interest and lobby, consult and apply to the Minister for funds in a fairly independent manner. Coombs strongly believed in local decision-making. Cooper (1976) has shown how beset this whole excercise was with resistance from outside and also with certain biases which were hidden behind a generalising verbiage. For instance in establishing this policy Coombs, like most white advisors on Aboriginal affairs, had the traditional Aboriginal groups of the more isolated areas of the Northern Territory primarily in mind. While the policies did not necessarily work as planned among those isolated communities (Thiele, 1982; Cowlishaw, 1983), they were even less likely to be successful in urban centres, large rural towns or in more closely settled areas with histories of forcible protection and assimilation.[5]

A major area of difficulty was Aboriginal representation. Aboriginal organisations were asked to elect representatives but many country towns did not have formal Aboriginal organisations. Few individuals had any knowledge or experience of being consulted by white bureaucrats. In NSW those Aborigines elected as representatives were usually those few who had taken part in the basically white-run 'Advancement Associations'. The problems of Aboriginal representation were obvious to Aborigines, and in fact the notion itself is rejected by many (see Sackett, 1978). Mr Bruce McGuiness said at a Darwin meeting 'We must excercise some bravado and pretend to represent our people' (Cooper, 1976:58). While the problem might appear more severe in the NT where the literacy rate among Aborigines is lower, in NSW the alienation of most Aborigines from government is also profound. Kevin Gilbert said 'These communities are so fractured, so fragmented, so messed up that the entire concept

---

[5]This is still a common bias with Lippmann's popular book (1981) treating remote Aborigines as *the* Aborigines although the author intends to do otherwise.

of representation is nonsense. Only action, action that involves them, can possibly have any meaning' (ibid., 48).

A big conference was held in each state to which 'community leaders' were invited. These became forums for demands which focussed on living conditions and housing as well as complaints about the police. The officials used the meetings to make the OAAs views known, to drum up belief in the new deal and to collect information on what Aborigines wanted, as ammunition to gain funds. Small-scale conferences with state advisory bodies supplemented the big conferences. By the second year voluntary organisations were being funded. The council 'increasingly sought to make grants to Aboriginal organisations as a mechanism for Aborigines "managing their own affairs" and sometimes to stimulate state departments to action and to express federal policy' (ibid., 27). As a result there was a proliferation of Aboriginal organisations.

But the council remained attuned more to events in the Northern Territory than in New South Wales and the earlier settled regions of Australia. This was partly due to Coombs' interest in 'tribal' people but also because resistance to the new deal was coming from officers of the old Northern Territory Welfare Branch. They continued to be obstructive until the council was upgraded in 1972 into the Department of Aboriginal Affairs (DAA) which could ignore them.

The voices of other Aboriginal groups were being heard quite independently of the OAA. The National Aboriginal Consultative Council and later the National Aboriginal Congress had been set up in a half-hearted attempt by the federal government to 'enhance the political organisational capacities of Aboriginals and to improve their access to and influence on, the political system' (Weaver, 1983:106). But more significant were the direct demands for more radical application of a 'land rights' policy intensified through the medium of the Federal Council for the Advancement of Aborigines and Torres Strait Islanders (FCAATSI), Aboriginal publications (e.g., the journal *Identity*) and with urban groups adopting 'black power' styles and slogans. This activity culminated in the tent embassy in 1972, the same year that the new Labor government formed the DAA. At the last meeting convened by the OAA in August 1972, NSW outspoken 'radicals' joined the meeting and made themselves heard. A Northern Territory delegate complained that the southerners had dominated the meeting and that the NT delegates could not discuss or understand (Cooper, 1976:36). This issue of the divergence of interests and tactics among different Aboriginal groups is of considerable political significance and will be discussed further in Chapter 6.

The policy of Aborigines managing their own affairs as individuals or as groups, and of the government assisting to equalise standards of health and housing, employment and welfare, developed during the Coombs era. But it did not arise from consultation. It was not grass roots Aborigines who formulated and implemented these policies. Rather they came from 'progressive thinking by the individuals in the Council' (ibid., 35). As time went by, needs and wishes were expressed by those Aborigines who became spokespersons. However the schemes to meet them were formulated by the OAA and thus the bureaucracy retained control and policies did not change very much when Aboriginal groups began to formulate their views. Housing was requested by Aborigines, but not the particular housing scheme devised by the OAA.

Examples of these schemes are educational scholarships, subsidies for employers providing training, and funding of housing cooperatives. The purposes for which loans or grants to Aboriginal organisations were made included welfare activities, funeral funds, sport, arts and crafts, purchase of properties, business enterprises, housing societies, medical services, legal services and breakfast programmes. Though there were many such schemes, the coverage of the Aboriginal population was small, and the proportion of finance spent on these activities compared to that spent by government departments, or white non-government bodies, was also small. Cooper has estimated that of $61.4 million spent in 1973 on 'Aboriginal Affairs' no more than $3 million was spent on organisations which could be considered 'Aboriginal' (ibid., 36, 43fn.). With the accession of the DAA, even more money had to be spent on administration. Policies continued to focus on housing, health and welfare, and some general underlying notion of self-management remained the oft-repeated theme.

During the 1970s DAA offices were established in many country towns, and regional officers were appointed. The attempts to set up Aboriginal organisations to give money to continued, but now the DAA was there in the field to hand the money over and to see that it was accounted for.

Later I will describe how bizarre many of the events of this period appeared to some sections of the Brindleton population. But the officials in charge of implementing the policies have also found that they had some curious, unintended and negative effects. Few of these have been made public because it is feared that disclosure of misunderstandings, inefficiencies and misspending will provide ammunition to those conservative whites who disapprove of welfare spending or special provisions for Aborigines. The attention of DAA officers in country towns has been thus to some degree diverted to their conflicts with the white population which dominates the town.

Self-determination

Before describing the provisions of the new deal for Aborigines I want to indicate the fundamental misunderstandings which have bedevilled the enlightened initiatives. Perhaps the most pervasive notion in the new deal was that of self-determination, which became self-management under the Liberal government. A number of issues were confused.

First, some poorly thought-out notion of self-determination or independence underlay the new policy. There was no clear consideration of the limits which existed to self-determination in the wider society. Aborigines were going to 'make their own decisions' just as white people do. It is not clear which white people and which decisions were alluded to. In the earlier Protection Board era Aborigines had often had even the most personal decisions made for them, but the Board had long been disbanded. Perhaps the bureaucrats involved feel *they* make their own decisions, and indeed they often do. They make decisions for others too. But the limits of 'self-determination' are fairly clear for people who are unemployed or rely on pensions and reside in public housing. The intentions were further confused by notions of community. It seems to have been assumed that Aborigines form natural homogeneous and harmonious communities which can be given resources to determine their own future. Thus 'communities' were to make their own decisions. One might wonder what model was considered as a precedent for such a cooperativè community.

The claim that Aboriginal groups were to ask for and get what they wanted disguised the obvious fact that only certain things could be requested. It is not within the power of the bureacrats to deliver a diminution of hostility from whites for instance, or a reduction of alcoholism or any number of dreams of freedom that members of an Aboriginal community might have. But the limitations of what could be provided by the bureaucracy has not been spelt out.

Further, despite protestations of support for Aboriginal self-management, many of the white personnel involved in implementing the new Aboriginal policies are not sympathetic towards those black viewpoints which are radically at odds with dominant cultural practices or political and economic structures. This is not so much to do with personal limitations of intolerance or lack of imagination but rather with the belief that only realistic aspirations can be achieved. Few radical alternatives have been given expression, let alone discussed, and they may seem trivial to the bureaucrats involved in dispensing large sums of money.

For instance in discussion in Brindleton of ways to combat vandalism, Aborigines have suggested they might teach the young to use the land. But they have no access to land. A legal provision to allow and enable Aborigines to fish and hunt wild game freely could have significant consequences; at the least its significance to some of the local Aborigines is far greater than to the bureaucrats. The call for land rights has not been applauded by the bureaucracy. Other less tangible desires are also outside the bureaucratic arena.

The unspoken limitations to what could be delivered under the new policies relates to a more fundamental and more controversial problem. Did the people *know* what they want or need to solve what the government specified as their problems? Many of course were aware of certain frustrations, and some were angry about certain injustices, but most did not consider themselves a social problem. I will come back to this question when discussing the nature of deprivation.

The sharp contrasts between those whites involved with new government initiatives, and the older residents of the towns where Aborigines were to be found in substantial numbers, is another barrier to the new policies. The enlightened bureaucrats are often too conscious of their own and Aboriginal conflicts with the 'racist whites' to notice that the Aborigines really are at odds with the enlightenment. The government officials try to show the black groups how to formulate 'realistic goals', but in some cases they seem unaware of the social reality with which they are dealing. People who have lived their lives in dirt-floored shacks or humpies, cooking on an open fire, do not necessarily long for a suburban bungalow for which they have to pay rent. I am not arguing here that better housing was not wanted. Indeed housing has become the focus of desire in a situation where few material desires were ever satisfied. However those who have developed such aspirations may find they feel uncomfortable in such an environment and may not use it in the conventional manner. Further, the presentation of educational achievement as the key to all good things may not convince those who have no familiarity with books and schooling. There has been little serious consideration in the bureaucracy of how government intitiatives fitted with the aspirations and the political aims of those being encouraged to higher education.

Finally it is not clear whether the slogans of the new era meant the same thing to the bureaucrats and the Aboriginal leaders. For instance does independence for Aborigines refer to economic or political independence? Is funding supposed to reduce the worst material deprivation? If so what will that achieve in the longer term? There has been little analysis of the basis of deprivation. Close consultation and local decision-making were seen as answering these questions by answering the needs as felt at the grass roots, but it has transpired that the policy makers did not recognise what was occurring at the grass roots. One example of misunderstanding concerns the payment of rent and electricity bills which has made Aboriginal tenants poorer by increasing their financial responsibilities. Less money is left for daily requirements. These new demands were sometimes not understood as concomittant with gaining a house. Even if the new tenants were told about these responsibilities, the practice of paying bills out of an inadequate pension or unemployment benefit is a difficult habit to acquire and the consequences of not doing so are even more difficult to deal with. Tenants soon learned that they were allowed to renegue occasionally.

The delivery of the new largesse in many cases turned out to have much in common with the blind leading the blind. Thus self-determination seems to mask what is really a realignment of Aborigines towards a new form of inequality characterised by dependence on, and therefore direction by, government departments. The dependence stems essentially from the lack of ability of Aborigines to sell their labour power. They are now not even able to be exploited as workers. This structural position was earlier determined by the pastoral industry reducing its labour costs. But now any direct connection with rural industry appears to be broken. The Aboriginal population in town is controlled most directly by the institutions of government, and Aborigines have their greatest impact on the town economy through their limited spending power.

The way this change from an exploited to a welfare-dependent community has affected Aboriginal culture in Brindleton will be the subject of a later chapter. Here we will follow the policy changes and
their limitations.

The local bureaucracy

The public servants at the local level are caught between the conflicting demands of the communities they are supposedly serving and
the higher levels of the bureaucracy. A system of patronage has developed in the towns (cf. Collmann, 1979) which may contradict the
working of the rationalistic bureaucracy but which enables the system to function. The problems associated with obeying and accounting to the senior bureaucrats creates disillusion for the local officers.
The Aboriginalisation of the bureaucracy sometimes compounds the
problems. It is easier to blame a white than a black senior officer for
ignorance of the local situation. An example of the frustration associated with bureaucratic functioning comes from one dedicated public
servant who had to spend half a million dollars on housing in the
short time before the end of the financial year. Somewhat against his
better judgement, but with no time to develop a new project, he
pushed for a housing project on the Aboriginal reserve. The Aborigines on the housing cooperative, ex-reserve dwellers themselves,
had accepted the DAA policy of letting the reserve run down. They
opposed his scheme, which nonetheless had had the funds committed to it. While the officer did not see the scheme as ideal it would
considerably benefit the reserve dwellers who naturally supported
him. He was thus caught between factions among the Aborigines,
having to explain and justify to them the peculiar funding practices
which led to the urgent spending of large sums of money, and having
to justify his scheme to his superiors, an uncomfortable position for
any individual.

Even more distressing for this same officer was the resistance from
his senior officer to a comprehensive training scheme that he had put
a great deal of thought into developing. He was allocated too little
money to allow the project to work. When he pointed this out to his
superiors he was told that he had been given more than they had
originally intended because he had written such a good submission.

Sudden windfalls to be spent before the financial year ends can
have positive outcomes. In the late 1970s, $27,000 had to be spent on
recreation within two months. A large hall was begun, with a
galvanised-iron shed of generous proportions being ordered and

erected by the Aboriginal building team after rather brief discussions with the housing cooperative. Subsequently the cost of the internal structures and the safety regulations which had to be obeyed made the completion of the hall a seven-year task. This was partly because it was competing for funds with the shire council's community centre, as we shall see below. The hall quickly became an important part of Aboriginal life in Brindleton.

One of Coombs' original staff who wanted to get away from those who sat around and talked about Aborigines, came to Brindleton as the first DAA officer where he could see and hear what the people wanted. It was not hard to get the isolated country posts, and a number of the more dedicated public servants are in the west. He tried to remain an uncommitted bureaucrat, separate both from the Aboriginal factional groups and from the little group of whites in the town who are the Aboriginal supporters. He believed strongly in self-management, but soon recognised that the Aborigines in the town did not have one self with one mind. Much less did they cleave to the same notions of rationality which dominated the bureaucracy. He was distressed by the kin-based factions which formed and fought and which precluded group decisions being taken. One faction would not allow a decision to be taken in the interests of some other long-term goal, either because they did not recognise such a goal, or because to give in was to lose face. It was normal practice to try to win to the end. Notions of compromise and cooperation only operated within certain spheres, as with any community.

The DAA officer decided after a time that factions were necessary, and that one faction would be ousted if they were too greedy. Enough people knew the mechanisms for changing the leadership to provide a safeguard against too much power accruing to one family. When this officer resigned it was not due to disillusion with the local organisations but with frustration at the dependence on senior officers who, far removed from the local scene, were obsessed with accounting, programming and winning their own political battles in Sydney and Canberra. They also showed jealousy and suspicion of the regional officers whose geographical remoteness gave them a certain independence and opportunity for disloyalty.

Some of the disillusionment among those implementing the enlightenment policies did come from the local situation. There are characteristics of the small town which make social conflict — in the usual sense of differences of values and opinions about what is and should be done — more intense and personal than in a city. Implementing government policies can come up against vocal local opposition while other individuals will want to offer or receive patronage. One can neither get away from those with whom one is in conflict, nor from one's supporters. The job tends to follow a person around the town.

For those individuals who like to be well known and influential within the context of the local population, the experience is satisfying. As a president of a sports club or as senior officer in a local government office, one will be known by a large proportion of the townspeople. One's own life and actions will be of interest to many and one's disagreements with others will be of public interest. Conflicts become closely identified with the protagonists on each side. In the Aboriginal community the level of intimacy is high. Among the older white residents familiarity and gossip is taken for granted. For the blow-ins it becomes necessary to adjust to the new high profile that they are likely to gain if taking a stand on any issue. Thus the era of enlightened Aboriginal policies has created situations which affect the town of Brindleton in a series of unexpected ways.

ENLIGHTENMENT IN BRINDLETON

The first houses

Most of the finance directed at Aborigines in the 1970s which did reach its target went into housing. Through an examination of the history of Aboriginal housing in Brindleton we can see what occurred when government policies were processed through officials appointed from outside, but located in the town. There had been a few small houses built by the AWB in 1968 which were handed over to the meagrely funded Aboriginal Lands Trust, a body run from Sydney. In 1969 in Brindleton, Aboriginal community development was eagerly being pursued by a group led by two white men who were professionally involved in such activities, though both far exceeded what others would have considered their professional duty. With the encouragement of these people the Aboriginal Advancement Association (AAA) was very active, with two particularly enthusiastic and able Aboriginal leaders. In those days, one of the involved whites told me, there was a strong commitment by such blacks to 'helping your people'.

The way was not smooth. The first housing initiatives came with commonwealth funding, gained in 1974 through the DAA, to employ an architect and builders to design and construct houses suitable for the specific needs of local Aborigines. The architect came from Sydney for short visits. In consultation with Aborigines he produced a design which involved, among other unusual features, moveable walls. Aborigines were to be employed to do the building. It is not surprising that people with little experience of complex technology would have trouble both building and living with moveable walls. Though intended to suit the Aboriginal lifestyle, especially a fluctuating family size, the design appears to have suited no one.

At this time two students, who claimed some expertise in architecture and building skills, came to help. There are various views of the conflicts and incompetence which troubled this project. Two or three houses were finally built at the Aboriginal end of town after many complications concerning who was to be employed, who was in charge of organising the work and who was to choose and order the materials. In line with their progressive views the two students did not like to give orders, yet assumed that they were obeying the dictates of Aboriginal needs. In fact there was disagreement among Aborigines. Not only did the type of house not particularly appeal to those doing the building, but there was intense rivalry concerning who the houses were for. This issue was paramount to the Aborigines in the AAA.

The whole project became notorious in the town, and the two students are still spoken of with amusement or disgust by the whites — some of whom like to describe the events as if they were a show put on for their derision. The houses lasted less than six years as they were not well built. The students, who left town after about 18 months when the tensions became intense, have since come to typify what is wrong with do-gooding, which of course is different from doing good.

The housing cooperative

Like the students, the newly appointed DAA personnel who were charged with implementing the new policies usually had no experiences of country towns, of Aboriginal communities or of poverty.

What they did have were firmly anti-racist views, ideals of Aboriginal self-determination and knowledge of the bureaucracy.

From 1974 government grants had to go to incorporated groups, so an Aboriginal Housing Cooperative was created in place of the Advancement Association. The cooperative decided to scrap the architect's designs and get the local builder to build 'ordinary houses', which was what most people who made their views known seemed to want. They were to be built of fibro using a team of Aboriginal labourers who would thus acquire building skills. This method was cheap but slow, which caused a further spate of complaints. No one knew what the future policy and funding would be, though the DAA officer assured the members of the cooperative that houses would continue to be built. For the next few years houses were slowly constructed and the cooperative handled the money with the help of the DAA officers and accountant. The building team remained active for 10 years, although there were problems with a fairly fast turnover of members of the team and some conflicts between the builder and the housing cooperative due to the requirement that the rules laid down by the DAA be followed.

The housing cooperative advertised for a bookkeeper and the wife of a public servant answered the advertisement. With her knowledge both of bookkeeping and of the town, and an expressed keen interest in the work, she seemed a suitable appointee. It turned out that she knew exactly what the Aborigines wanted and did not need to have meetings to ask them! She believed initiative should be rewarded, and did not see the point of long explanations of government policy concerning community responsibility and self-management. Thus she decided to fund the cooperative manager to establish his own garden. This manager and a trainee formed the core of a conservative faction operating under the accountant's patronage.

One of the active more long-term blow-ins in town, who had become an advisor to the cooperative, was incensed at this misapplication of self-management policy just when substantial housing funds were beginning to flow. She organised what she called the 'good' people, the other faction of those blacks who supported the concept of 'doing something for our people', to sack the bookkeeper at the next annual general meeting. The grounds were her lack of response to 'the Aboriginal people'. The meeting then elected another Aboriginal manager of the housing cooperative. Another white advisor resigned in the face of this factionalism, seeing it as outside her role to take sides. It is now asserted, with what accuracy I do not know, that

that first bookkeeper robbed the housing cooperative of thousands. Such accusations are common accompaniments of departures, Aboriginal or white.

The new DAA officer, who arrived in 1976, was almost a casualty of this struggle. When the DAA regional officer came to the town to consult with the Aboriginal Housing Cooperative, he was told by the bookkeeper's faction that the new DAA appointee was not doing the right thing. This led to the threat of dismissal, but the bookkeeper's dismissal was achieved first. The DAA officer's vision of her role as facilitator of Aboriginal initiatives was thus rudely shaken up from the start. If Aborigines are so divided how could she serve 'the Aboriginal community'? Such conflicts are endemic. Their emotional intensity can leave smouldering personal hostilities among people who live in the same social sphere.

The very obvious problem remained that virtually no Aborigines had much experience or knowledge of formal meetings, of managing an office, of dealing with whites (other than policemen), or any knowledge of how government funding was allocated and accounted for. Community organisations had existed previously, but these relied on loose networks of communication and flexible patterns of interaction with only informal pressures to participate or remain. Such ignorance and lack of experience inevitably meant a reliance on whites. Though certain procedures   could be quickly learned, an understanding of bureaucratic tactics remains very difficult for small-town people. There was also a heavy burden on those 'leaders' who were forced to try to represent everybody.

One of the active Aborigines from the AAA became the first member of the DAA staff, and the first DAA office in the town was the front verandah of his own house. As the office expanded he remained a key figure, but resigned when it became clear that he would always be second in command as the new DAA officers came and went. Another 'leader' left the housing cooperative because there were 'too many pressures'. As the pressures are contradictory, such a response is not surprising. Those who learned the techniques of being responsible for community money, such as by collecting rents or dues, come into conflict with people who do not have the necessary money and do not think of such payments as the top priority. The rent collector, in obeying the dictates of self-management, would perhaps be described as a coconut, or an Uncle Tom, and the cooperative could support the complainant by dismissing the rent collector from the job.

But it was essential for the government to have Aborigines to consult with, and those whites dedicated to helping blacks, either professionally or personally, had to have representatives and organisations to deal with. The two or three Aborigines who had some experience and sufficient confidence to interact with sympathetic whites became representatives of the town without realising the consequences. They were asked to carry the frustrations and confusions of implementing a government policy that was new and in some ways unworkable. No wonder many resigned because of the pressure. There was also a good deal of disillusionment because the DAA officers kept trying to enthuse people to take part in their own community initiative. Those who complied faced changes in policy as well as demands to account for money and to learn bookkeeping. Also nothing seemed to happen for long periods except long explanations of why what had been explained last month had altered (cf. Kamien, 1978, Ch.2 for another account of local initiatives in a western NSW town).

Aboriginal organisations were also needed to allocate money to. If the policy said that an architect and builders could be employed, who was there in these country town Aboriginal populations that could receive the large amounts of money and dispense them? Who was able to fill in all the necessary forms, attach the receipts, report on progress, apply for the continuation of funding, and explain to the Aborigines at the meetings what was required of them as a part of this process? The DAA in fact did most of this work, providing expertise where it was lacking both in formal and informal ways. It is still the case that the public servants are the crucial link between Aborigines and government policies. They also serve to protect the system of funding from demands which it cannot fulfil.

The contradictions

There were immediate problems that were never resolved because they were embedded in the contradictions between the operations of government and the community's situation. While funding was generous by comparison with past years, it was pitifully inadequate to provide for all those throughout NSW who were seen to be in desperate need of houses. Only a few houses could be built at any one time. Sometimes 30 applications were in for three houses. This led to jealousy towards those that got them and towards the manager of the housing cooperative who was seen as favouring certain people.

To minimise suggestions of favouritism, one tactic in the early days was to allocate houses by drawing the names out of a hat. Clearly this made it difficult to suit the house to the family, and for those in a canvas and tin shack with a dirt floor and no running water any house could appear desirable. The housing cooperative meetings were emotional and tearful. The DAA officer advised that a list should be drawn up and some criteria of need formulated, an obvious response to the situation from one used to allocating resources on impersonal rational criteria. But this was a difficult task when such an exercise in impersonal conceptualisation was foreign to those involved. Where needs had always been personal and pressing, it was now necessary to weigh the needs of one family against another. Any formal list would be reacted to personally by a group of people bound together by kinship and generations of mutual experience. A listing of criteria of need for houses represented a very significant break with tradition, especially for people who had never had enough resources to think of 'allocating'. However rationality triumphed and such a list was drawn up with those who had been in the cooperative longest at the top. A certain number of houses were to be allocated to reserve dwellers, and the number of children of a family was to be taken into account.

Despite formal recognition of the importance of suiting houses to Aboriginal needs, financial constraints plus perhaps lack of imagination meant that this did not happen. As many people as possible were housed at minimum cost. Not only were the houses small and poky, but they were made of the cheaper flimsy materials. Thus a family of 12 might be allocated a small three-bedroomed house, having had no experience of housing other than a humpy on the reserve. Most of the houses were seriously inadequate, although the fact that cooking and eating outside was favoured by many Aborigines relieved the pressure somewhat. Often no one knew how to use an electric or gas stove or any of the other appliances and a dearth of sources for wood meant that some fences and verandahs were converted to fuel. However those given a house by the government were not expected to voice dissatisfaction or disillusion, and the fact that some of these houses were treated with less than good care, and a few were visibly damaged, gave rise to tales of outrage among the good white citizens of Brindleton. A hole in the outer wall, dismantled verandahs, or broken windows and fly screens led to tales of 'brand new houses utterly wrecked'.

The continuing domination by the DAA due to the need to keep to the guidelines and to account for the use of funds, combined with the policy of Aboriginal self-management, meant that the DAA officer worked in close cooperation with the manager of the housing cooperative. After three years in the position, the manager evinced a complete acceptance of DAA policy concerning the reserve. If the families living there begin to build with tins, I was told, we will move the tins. Others closely involved with the housing cooperative belonged to the same family as the manager, which may be nepotistic, but is neither surprising nor sinister. Kin-based groupings are a fundamental part of Aboriginal society. But in the new context of the allocation of large government funds, problems arose. The manager's family were seen by many Aborigines as running the housing cooperative, and few others felt any duty or cause to go to the meetings. This attitude often involved resentment, and it conflicted with the official DAA view of the cooperative as an even-handed community-based organisation.

A final and continuing problem with the housing situation is the conflicting meaning of housing for blacks and whites. As mentioned above, the paying of rent is not taken for granted by those who have always lived on riverbanks and reserves. It seems not to have occurred to the officials involved to warn future recipients of government housing that they would become tenants, making rent as well as electricity bills and sometime other expenses an ongoing responsibility. The 'pride in the home' that a public servant would take for granted was not necessarily present. After one house had been badly damaged, a middle-aged Aboriginal man told one of his old white workmates, to the latter's astonishment, 'They don't last very long you know these houses'.

In the opinion of the DAA officer, the knowledge that more houses were coming should have reduced the rivalry and tensions surrounding the allocation of houses. But the blacks had little faith in the future, and if some were getting houses was it surprising that others were disappointed and resentful? Few understood the process of funding; why were the houses not all allocated at the same time? How did white people, like the school teachers and police, come to have houses automatically? The new DAA officers who came to provide for Aboriginal needs were themselves housed immediately, with subsidised rent, and in far better houses than the housing cooperative built. The school teachers complained about the inadequacy of their housing at length; Aborigines who heard these complaints were puzzled.

In the late 70s the cooperative decided to buy houses in town, as it was easier and faster, and there were a number for sale. Apparently wider choices thus became available to those waiting to be housed, although, as the waiting list remained substantial, it was a case of taking what one was offered or waiting an indefinite period. Some individuals did not want to live 'up town' and refused offers of such houses. While DAA policy allowed the housing cooperative to choose between building or buying houses, there was a strict embargo on building houses or providing facilities on the reserve. That is, the DAA state chief officer prohibited houses being built on the place which had greatest significance to most Aborigines in the town.

The state branch of DAA called an annual area meeting to decide on the allocation of the money received from the Commonwealth government. The housing cooperatives and other companies sent representatives from each town to argue out the needs of one town against another. Clearly those towns which, by some chance, had representatives with experience and understanding of these processes were at an advantage. Many recognised that Aboriginal needs were being weighed against each other, and the DAA officer was there to explain the basis and the limits of the funding, and perhaps how unity was not strength in such a situation. The meeting would in the end reach some kind of consensus, with each place making demands on the basis of need and previous funding. After each meeting the Aboriginal chairman would regularly send a telegram to the Minister to say there was not enough money and they would not take part in such meetings in the future. Being forced to scrap over inadequate funds was not a pleasant experience, and was recognised as something the government was forcing on the people. The DAA officers who seemed to support such protests were reprimanded by head office.

After the money was allocated, the local budget was worked out in detail, a task conducted by the local DAA officer and accountant with the housing cooperative. Quarterly returns had to be lodged accounting for the spending. No Aborigines in the housing cooperative took part in these proceedures.

In the early 70s housing loans were allocated to two Aboriginal families at an extremely low interest rate. Also under a scheme for funding individual businesses a small shop at the Aboriginal end of Brindleton was opened by two people who are efficient managers and hard workers. As their clientele is not affluent, and often is in need of credit, the business has never been very lucrative.

The new patrons

The enlightenment era saw bureaucrats from outside the town taking up a role as patrons of Aborigines in rural areas. Not only the DAA and later the ADC (Aboriginal Development Commission), but the Aboriginal representative organisations and independent pressure groups increasingly had links with Aboriginal communities in country towns. Local branch committees pursuing educational, health and other objectives were formed. It seemed possible that such a network of outside supporters for Aboriginal communities could break the previous domination of the local establishment. In fact a break from the past is occurring, but slowly and in unexpected ways.

Many different kinds of Aboriginal organisations have come into being since the new government initiatives were developed. The housing cooperatives, medical and legal services, land councils and education committees each have different features. Smaller towns may have only one or two of these groups. Each organisation has sets of patrons. The housing cooperatives are clearly under the wing of the government bureaucracies, the DAA and ADC. By contrast the medical service organisation is part of a nation-wide Aboriginal body with a radical political approach to issues. The state and national education organisation is narrower in its focus, and takes a pragmatic and opportunistic line. The local education organisations are also offered patronage by various school teachers.

The NSW Aboriginal Lands Council has a more complex background. The disillusionment about the NSW Land Rights Act (1983) led to conflict about tactical responses, which caused splits between different areas. The other important Aboriginal organisation in the state, the Aboriginal Legal Service, has also been active on a number of political fronts.

In the western towns the local branch of these organisations is seen to be controlled by a set of relatives. There is a degree of rivalry between them, and some cynical comment from others in the community about the personal interests of those who run them. Nonetheless there is an acceptance by Aborigines that that is the way things work. Specialisation is seen as natural. Of course there is nothing surprising about this, but because the issues are so crucial for the community and because the bureaucracy expects perfect representativeness, the situation often gives rise to criticism.

The embargo on building houses on the reserve applied widely but not everywhere in NSW. This policy was a rational response to a certain set of ideas about Aboriginal disadvantage. In this view, the reserve epitomised Aboriginal problems and would always represent previous conditions of deprivation. There was little objection to the policy by influential whites. The shire council said that the Brindleton reserve was too difficult to 'upgrade' as it was subject to flooding and, unlike the golf course and cemetery, too expensive to put a flood bank around. But also, fear was expressed that the building of permanent and functional houses on the reserve would serve to split the population of the town into racial groups and would increase racial tension. There were of course those in the town who would not have minded such a split, but disapproved of money being spent on Aboriginal housing. Aboriginal views on the subject were not widely heard. While some shared the view that town housing was preferable to reserve housing, many wanted and still want to live there. Some find it a peaceful refuge from the whites and from drinking and fights that are associated with the pubs and the town.

The tradition of Aborigines in Brindleton is closely tied to the reserve. For many years there was no alternative to reserve living, but this is the very reason the reserves in NSW towns represent the tradition and unity of the Aboriginal communities. When Shirley Smith says anyone who was down there with me on the Cowra mission is an Aboriginal (Read, 1984), she is referring to a common definitive experience which is one basis of Aboriginal identity. The notion that reserves represent the worst aspect of Aboriginal life and deprivation is based on the very naive idea that material comfort or discomfort is the essential criterion of deprivation and that all suffering associated with poverty is debilitating. From the foregoing it appears that the relationship with the rest of the population is the source of deprivation. It is the painful inequality with the majority of whites, whose control of the status criteria and the purse strings is an unquestioned fact of life, which comprises the disadvantage experienced by Aborigines.

Finally these government policies are directed to a group defined by race. This clearly has the effect of confirming the dichotomous character of the population. For one thing those blacks who are taking advantage of the offers of help with education and housing are doing so as Aborigines, denying by implication that they are a part of any other group such as other working people, unemployed people, or exploited or deprived groups. Were they to follow any other strategy the funding would be very likely to dry up, and working-class unity or companionship with the white poor could hardly provide equivalent rewards. So Aboriginal disadvantage is in relation to white society rather than to the influential employers and rulers of the town. The conflict is understood in terms of racial deprivation.

But housing, and many of the other benefits, are largely welfare provisions not likely to create independence. Only a few Aborigines will gain those secure and respectable jobs, such as liaison officers, which have been created largely to service other Aborigines. Those who do are the more 'assimilated'. Thus the whole uplifting exercise of the enlightenment is destined to regroup the black population dramatically and increasingly. There are many signs of the way this is occurring and of some resistance to the process. Before turning to that issue we need to take a closer look at the nature of the town.

Chapter 4

The dominant culture

INTRODUCTION

The barriers to the government policy of Aboriginal 'self-management' in towns such as Brindleton have not been analysed even superficially. For instance no one has asked how management by the local shire council could be avoided. Management by the police has not been seen as a barrier to self-management. How could the hegemony of whites at this local level be countered? It seems that the rhetoric of self-management does not mean anything more than funding of local organisations to provide some basic economic and material resources, specifically government funding for houses, health services and education. Besides the barriers to self-management which were discussed above, there are ways in which the local council can exert a degree of control over the deployment of such resources. Further the whole institutional structure of the town militates against any radical change in either the racial structuring or other forms of hierarchy.

The aspects of the dominant culture to be discussed here are those relevant to the racial divide. That is, rather than a description of the white population's various lifestyles and institutions, I will attempt to show the way the lives of people in Brindleton are contained within strict limits. Some of these processes are direct and violent, and we will begin with the way the council and the police function and especially the way they control Aborigines. There are conflicts between these two bodies, with the council demanding stronger measures to police the town and the police asserting that their actions are subject to the legal system.[1] But the actions of these two bodies are complementary as will become evident in the following account.

---

[1] The police are engaged in a struggle with the present government over the curbing of what were regarded as excessive police powers of arrest. The Summary Offences Act was introduced by the previous government to curb the demonstrators and unionists of the 1960s and 70s. It allowed the police to arrest someone in the street for behaviour which they considered a nuisance, such as being drunk or swearing. The repeal of the Act in 1979 led to a protest by police which appealed to public fears concerning threats to law and order.

RULING BRINDLETON

The shire council[2]

The activities of this elected body are governed by a quite specific tradition, the major theme of which is the domination by country councillors. A system of ridings has ensured that from its inception in 1956 until 1983 there were six country councillors and six from the town. Although the vast majority of voters live in the town, country councillors say that this level of representation is quite justified by the huge area for which the council is responsible. The country representatives are all graziers although some usually live in town. One has been on the council for nearly 30 years and others have held their places for several terms. Of the others, the majority are shopkeepers with one or two working-class councillors representing conservative Labor Party views. The shopkeepers recognise that their interests are in many ways the same as those of the graziers. There is a certain deference offered to graziers by both shopkeepers, or business men as they prefer to be called, and other local people.

While the abolition of ridings may preface changes in the council's functioning, the recent election of one or two candidates who represent other political views has made little difference to the operation of the council. It is dominated by the same forces, and run in the same way as in the past. The president of the council and the shire clerk work together and keep the council meetings running quickly and smoothly. It is seldom that any discussion of issues or priorities is allowed to intrude on the lengthly business of deciding which roads need attention next and how to get more money, mainly for the roads, out of the state or federal governments. The meeting procedures show some indiosyncratic characteristics, but as the president and shire clerk are more knowlegeable than others about such things they are never challenged. Certain issues are discussed and not others, and certain decisions are speeded up rather than discussion being allowed.

This is not to imply that there would be frequent dissension were discussion encouraged. Those who apparently understand and can deal with state and federal governments, for instance by sending telegrams to ministers or participating in a graziers' delegation to

---

[2]The events recorded took place between December 1981 and May 1984 inclusive. Seven meetings were attended in one town, and councils in two other towns were visited.

Canberra, are regarded as powerful and effective by other councillors several of whom have little experience of such activities. Those councillors who would question certain decisions or information are treated with impatience and often are unsure of the way to go about such disruptive activities.

The abolition of the ridings in 1983 was recognised as a potential threat to this cosy system of decision-making by consensus. Councillors spoke with some alarm and disgust about the possibility of 'vocal minorities' being able to elect members to council. The new system might mean that 'political argument will dominate the council'. There is no doubt that 'political argument' is seen as bad and time wasting. It seems that the councillors recognise that there are agreed principles and priorities which dominate the council proceedings and that these would be challenged by the 'vocal minorities'. As Wild found in Bradstow there is an 'overwhelming dread of dissension' among the councillors (Wild, 1974:132).

An example of consensus was the council's blocking of the state government's attempt to establish a 'proclaimed place', an alternative to police cells as a place of temporary refuge for drunks. Even though one councillor supported the idea, there was no discussion of the issues involved such as what the proclaimed place would achieve or whether the council had any responsibility towards alcoholics. Rather the proclaimed place was viewed as another attempt by outsiders to foist the Aborigines' problems onto the townspeople. At a meeting with a representative of the Department of Youth and Community Services, one councillor said, 'Should not this be called an Aboriginal welfare centre? Brindleton is already plagued by nuisances at that end of town. It appears it is on the route home. One resident had five windows broken, his wife repeatedly abused and children bashed.' None of the councillors took seriously the assurances that the service was for all residents.

The council simply refused permission for a series of suggested properties to be so used, until finally the state government told them they would be overruled if they did not allow the development. When the president and shire clerk presented this ultimatum to council they had already arranged for an ex-council employee, who was on the point of leaving town, to sell his house to the relevant government department for the proclaimed place. Council members agreed to give this property the relevant clearance when it was explained to them that they must be seen to be cooperating with the welfare and social service provisions or the future funding of various schemes could be jeopardised. With a little grumbling, but in the belief that they had made their point and were even being clever in siting the proclaimed place near the police station, the council thus succumbed, still insisting that they had never actually refused to accept a proclaimed place. They had only, they asserted, been obeying their electors' instructions concerning the unsuitability of the suggested locations.

The status of the skilled employees of the council, such as the engineers and the health inspector, are a subject of conflict. The Brindleton council is convinced that they are employees and not required to make decisions. But the expertise of the engineers and their control over council's road equipment means that the country councillors in particular are not able to control them very closely. The council's grader is a constant bone of contention, as the country councillors all see it as for their own use.

Another example of the appreciation of traditional roles by the councillors and council employees is evident in the extreme subservience shown by the women, known as 'the girls', who work in the office. The younger ones never speak or look at councillors but provide them with tea and other refreshments. The older office assistant does a great deal of the council's work without acknowledgement. She complains bitterly in private. Nevertheless 'the girls' all dress in their best for the council meetings and accept their inferior status by deferring with alacrity to the wishes of the clerk and councillors. Their dealings with those who come to the council chambers tends to reflect this heirarchical view of the world. The adjacent council library also welcomes only those who are clean and confident of their right to be there. Aborigines are seldom seen in the vicinity.

Not all local councils in the west still adhere to these somewhat feudal notions of their role and, with the abolition of ridings, there will be more representation from 'vocal minorities' including blowins, Labor Party loyalists and Aborigines. Eventually this will lead to a less nepotistic and more rationalistic approach to local government.

While most of the blow-ins voted at the local election in 1984, many blacks did not vote. Like many of the poor whites they do not consider that the council has much to do with them. But through the Aboriginal organisations there were seven Aborigines who stood on an Aboriginal ticket and one who stood as a Labor Party candidate. The number should not have been a disadvantage because of the system of preferential voting. One was elected, though had all eligible Aborigines voted for the Aboriginal candidates at least three could have become councillors. Several sympathetic whites indicated that it was a pity that someone had not helped the Aborigines at the election to make sure their best candidate or even two candidates got elected. However not all Aborigines think that Aborigines are the best candidates. For instance one of the country councillors, who always takes sweets and icecream to the reserve before council elections, has retained the votes of some of the old rural workers.

With the election of an Aboriginal councillor in the November 1983 elections, the gossip and denigrating asides about Aborigines in the council chambers have been muted. The man elected has experience of working with whites in the town and his mateness and good humour may smooth the social interaction to a degree. But he is unlikely to make a significant impact on council as, like some other councillors, he has little knowledge of the way government funding operates or of the formal rules for meetings. Furthermore, without a careful reading of the minutes and the agenda, it is easy to be outmanoeuvred in council meetings especially if one does not go to lunch with the other councillors. However, from the start, the presence of an Aboriginal councillor created a new slant on the usual spate of complaints. As the representative of the Aboriginal community he became the target of accusations. 'What are you doing about your lot down there', he is asked and 'Your people were playing up in the pub again.' His first reaction to these challenges was to join in the complaints while denying that they were his responsibility.

Common phrases used by the councillors indicate their attitude to the people they govern.

'Whatever you do for them it's not enough';
'There's a right way and a wrong way of doing things';
'They want us to do everything for them';
'We need to approach him verbally'; and
'If you leave it in the hands of the shire clerk and myself'.

There are frequent references to 'a certain element' in the town who are responsible for the council's problems. In fact there are two 'certain elements' one a 'vocal minority' and the other the recalcitrant Aborigines.

The method of making council appointments, the suspicion of union demands and the attempt to keep a close surveillance of the council workers are all indications of the strong conviction that care must be taken to keep up the old standards. The harsh nature of the regime was apparent when a request came in the form of a letter to council from two of the council workers about overtime. Their foreman was an Aboriginal who had been with the council many years and had inherited the right to do the overtime when his predecessor retired. The council acceded promptly to the request of the others that the overtime be shared by the three of them. There was virtually no discussion of the reasons for changing the precedent.

Perhaps the height of obstructionism was reached when a candidate for election to council, who was a wage earner, asked whether the council meetings could be held at night. He was told it was not possible because, were the meetings to continue late into the night, councillors would have to miss a day at their place of business the following day!

The shire council puts out news items in the local paper, as do other organisations in the town. There is no reporter on the paper so the vast majority of news items are reports sent in by clubs or associations. Occasional articles appear highlighting some concern of the shopkeepers or councillors, but few other views are aired. As the newspaper depends on advertising from the town's business people, and on being sold in their shops, the editor feels he cannot afford to cross them. One of the issues which has been aired several times in articles written presumably by councillors or members of the Chamber of Commerce, is the level of vandalism, break-and-enter and other petty crime in the town. After years of lobbying the Minister for Police, the council succeeded in having the police station manned for 24 hours a day. Since then there have been further attempts to have public complaints of alleged lawlessness in the town dealt with by more severe penalties.

Another campaign referred to above, which used the newspaper to promulgate its views, involved disapproval of the transient traders. The Chamber of Commerce wrote in no uncertain terms to the Country Women's Association, whose building had been used to sell the cheap clothes, explaining that the group could have taken $20,000 out of the town. Further, 'A dollar . . . has been calculated to turn over three or four times before leaving, so in actual fact this could have meant a cash flow loss to your town of $60,000. This amount of money could have kept someone in employment for a full year'. The knock-down argument behind this original economic theory led the council to refuse permits to trade to those who were in competition with business houses already operating in the town. It is clear that the poorest section of the population were of a different mind from the council. Their dollars are turned over only once.

The council objects to some others having their views printed in the paper. When one long letter to the editor criticising the council in some detail appeared, it was suggested at a council meeting that the editor be told that he should not have printed it. It was pointed out that there is, after all, a right way and a wrong way of doing things.

The shire council spends over three million dollars a year. Of this only about 27 per cent is from rates. Over two-thirds of the total expenditure is on the country roads. The council's allocations of funds is not based on a clear policy. For instance road maintenance money gets used on whichever road one of the country councillors makes the most effective complaint about. Decisions are essentially ad hoc. A dissident councillor said with some bitterness, 'It doesn't suit greedy people to have a policy. They call it flexibility.' Queries about the conditions and spending of particular grants are discouraged. On one occasion a councillor's enquiry about the spending of a grant was discouraged because, it was claimed with a wink and a nod, the grant was the result of a special private deal between the shire clerk and 'Neville' (Wran), the then NSW State Premier. Enquiries from the relevant funding body in Sydney showed that the capital grant had come in the normal way from the Premier's department. Such secretiveness and misinformation encourages the suspicion which is widespread among the older residents that the council fiddles the books. Such accusations concerning local government councils are not uncommon, but no doubt are quite without foundation.

The white man's burden

A major activity of local councils is applying for funding from state and federal governments for a wide range of activities. While the Brindleton council is assimilationist to its boot straps it has been forced to accept that governments have, in recent years, been funding resources for Aborigines. There is absolute and extreme disapproval of this policy, expressed openly by the majority of councillors. The reason given in public is that spending money specifically for Aboriginal projects is divisive. Money should not be spent on one section of the population. The view expressed in private is that the government is throwing money away on those who neither deserve nor appreciate it while the roads are, as always, in desperate need of upgrading.

However there is also a recognition that the council can make gains by emphasising that the Aboriginal population is assisted by the

council, or that the Aboriginal population makes more expenses for
the council. The fact that these two claims involve somewhat different presentations of the council's evaluation of the Aboriginal population makes for some difficulties. The disparaging tone of
complaints that the Aborigines' habits create an extra burden for the
garbage collection service (as an argument for extra funds) sits ill with
the claim that Aborigines will be welcomed to the community centre,
which should therefore be funded from DAA resources. In one submission it was stated that the large Aboriginal population means
that the council needs to spend more money on health services
because 'they cannot be trained'. Following this appeal, the DAA
supplied $10,000 for a clean up of the Aboriginal end of town.
Another submission was made to the DAA asking them to pay
one-third of the cost of the sewerage scheme for the town. The
submission asking the DAA for money to help complete the community recreation centre was accompanied by the information,
elicited from one or two Aborigines, that Aborigines were going to
make use of the centre. These requests are sometimes successful.
Even when they are unsuccessful, the council makes gains because
replies will cite other moneys supplied directly to Aboriginal organisations for similar purposes. Such information is of great interest and
use to the council.

But while taking credit for acting on behalf of Aborigines the
council also tries to educate the Aboriginal Housing Cooperative by
reminding them of untidiness, of unsightliness, and of their duty in
various capacities. Once the council asked the housing cooperative
officially whether they had discovered the culprit in a case of vandalism at one of the cooperatives' own houses. Councillors do not
disguise their predominant view of Aborigines as troublesome and
needing to be controlled, but they are aware that they must present a
somewhat different view to the state and federal governments on
whom they rely for funding.

The council also has had quite direct control over some aspects of
resident's lives. Many of the council's proceedings have an air of
noblesse oblige. They may decide to do some work free for sports
clubs or allow some organisations exemption from paying rates.
Decisions about what services should be supplied to the Aboriginal
reserve has, until recently, rested with the council. Now that the
housing cooperative owns the land the services have to be paid for
but the council still has some discretion about supplying them.

The response to requests from the Aboriginal community, usually the housing cooperative, is marked by a distinct attitude which is often punitive. At its most benign this is exemplified by the comment of one of the councillors (a well-heeled man who tries to be fair), after a meeting with the Aboriginal Housing Cooperative; 'Did you notice how they want everything done for them?' He was referring to the request that the council mow the grass beside the road at the Aboriginal end of town. The council mows the grass in other parts of the town regularly. The response of the council's health inspector to the request was more direct. He said he would certainly not let the council's equipment be used to mow *that* grass as it was full of broken glass and must be cleaned up first.

Through various committees the council has a say in most events in the town. There is a council representative on the board of most organisations. The Community Development Committee was formed to solve the problem of unruly youth. The council, through this committee, employs two government-funded youth workers, one white and one black, whose job it is to develop activities for the youth to keep them out of trouble. However the people appointed have no training for this job and are closely monitored by the councillors who seem to disapprove of most things that anyone else suggests. At one meeting concerning the possible activities of the youth workers, particularly among Aboriginal youth, one of the policemen from the town made a series of suggestions which were all rejected on the grounds that the youth workers should simply be facilitating those activities that parents arranged. We don't want to 'do everything for them'.

The way they manage to do nothing for them is exemplified in the efforts of one Aboriginal parent, Bill. The youth workers had complained that they had arranged various sporting events and no one turned up. 'Aboriginal parents will not cooperate' they asserted. When Bill heard this he said 'I will get them to a meeting anytime' and a few days later he sent a handwritten note to the youth workers with a rather peremptory request that they attend the hall for a meeting the next day. It should be understood that this is the usual way such arrangements are made in the Aboriginal community. The youth workers took the note to their patron, one of the councillors, who wrote a formal letter to Bill asking that he inform the committee, as employers of the youth workers, if he wanted to make any arrangements with them and that he give sufficient notice for proper arrangements to be made. There was no meeting with parents after that.

There are two community halls in Brindleton, both built in recent years. As mentioned above the Aboriginal Housing Cooperative began a community hall at the Aboriginal end of town, followed for years by the painful business of writing submissions for funding to complete it. After that hall had been started the council submitted a plan for a Brindleton Community Centre which was intended, it was claimed, to serve the whole community, unlike *some* halls which would divide the community by serving the interests of only one section of the population.

This community centre was begun two years after the hall, and the council also had trouble getting sufficient funds for its completion although the local Lions and Rotary Clubs helped raise some money. During a state government election campaign in the late 1970s a large grant was handed to the council by the state Labor government to complete the community centre and this was outbid by double the amount from the Federal Liberal Minister of Aboriginal Affairs. Local DAA officers and Aborigines believed that Aboriginal money was being spent on the community centre, while the Aborigines' hall was still unfinished. This caused fury to the extent that a direct protest was made in the form of a punch directed at one of the prominant MPs campaigning at an election rally in the town. Subsequently, perhaps as the result of this blow, the Aboriginal hall was given sufficient funds for its completion and opening in 1983. It is a far less elaborate and less expensive structure, and events there are more noisy and less formal than at the community centre which is mainly used for the playing of sport and is predominantly attended by whites. The 'Aboriginal' hall is used for discos, bingo and meetings and is dominated by blacks.

At the invitation of the Aboriginal Housing Cooperative the shire president officiated at the opening of the Aboriginal hall, and he took the opportunity, among other encouraging remarks, to deplore the divisiveness which this hall *could* represent. Only a very small group of somewhat unenthusiastic Aborigines were there to heed this weighty advice, although five councillors dutifully attended. The real opening occurred that evening when a ball was held, attended by most of the Aborigines in the town and by selected whites from a number of organisations, including the DAA and the school. There was a buffet meal, a local band and dancing, in which whole families joined with much evident enjoyment. There was even a fight towards the end of the evening, by which time the bouncer was having trouble forbidding the consumption of alcohol inside the hall.

The admonition is made frequently by the council that it is divisive to speak in terms of colour or of Aborigines as if they were a separate community. Thus the request that the council fly the Aboriginal flag on National Aboriginal Day has been regularly refused. In 1982 the council's Australian flag was stolen on National Aboriginal Day, an action that councillors could interpret as expressing Aborigines' determination to be divisive.

Inspecting health

Not only does the council determine how the town's resources are spent, it polices building and health regulations. This results in surveillance of the living conditions especially of the less-affluent section of the population. The council has the power to inspect properties to see that they conform to building and health regulations. They issue licences for buildings, collect rating information and condemn buildings or manners of living that are, in their view, a health hazard or are offensive to the eye. It is clear that a great deal of discretion is used. For instance despite many complaints and a petition about the unsightly condition of his premises, the council showed patience for many months towards one of the older business men in town. The condition of his health was considered too serious for the final notice to be served.

Far less sympathy was shown to two newcomers who fell out with the council after being refused permission to use their premises as a boarding house. On the grounds that the building was not kept in good condition council sent the health inspector to inform the residents that they could face prosecution by council if they did not clean it up.

The housing and health inspector is the person responsible for carrying out these tasks. He can enter private premises 'at any reasonable time' to make an inspection. The health inspector in Brindleton is indefatigable in his work. If a caravan is parked in a vacant lot it will not be long before a letter is received demanding rate payment. He knows every building in the town, and has very strong and simple views on what constitutes a health hazard. Council must approve a clean up or a demolition, but the only reason to demur is if they imagine that the resident is a ratepayer who might complain. Thus the section of the population most subject to such surveillance is the poorest section, which includes virtually all of the Aboriginal population. There is some protection in law from having one's home suddenly demolished, such as the requirement that notice of closure be given in advance. But the law is only available to those knowledgeable and confident enough to take advantage of it. The council might also shoot your dog. The dog population is a source of many complaints and an ordinance inspector was appointed to shoot 'stray' dogs many of which are, in fact, owned by Aborigines. He is not universally popular as is clear from his request for protection.

The effect of these controls on the lives of citizens can be widespread. Thus in March 1983 it was reported to council that 27 stray dogs had been destroyed, 64 notices had been served on unsightly allotments and the health inspector was authorised to effect legal proceedings if his orders were not complied with. Letters of intention were to be sent concerning inspections of eight further properties and notices were expected to be served requiring demolition or repair within two months. Other months show a lesser but steady steam of inspections and orders, some to the Aboriginal Housing Cooperative. The reserve gets its share of attentions from the health inspector. He complained at one council meeting that a temporary influx of people to the reserve was going to create a problem for sullage collection; penalty rates would have to be paid to council workers if a weekend collection was necessary.

The punitive attitude of the shopkeepers on council is evident in their request to the Minister of Police for permission to impound bicycles left lying on the footpath. The Minister politely replied that he did not think it was really appropriate to amend the law in this way. It has been decided since that council will supply bicycle racks in the main street. Also somewhat obstructive was the response to one councillor's suggestion that council mow the grass and redirect stagnant water at the house where the 'Indian Nuns' run a child-care centre. The health inspector rejected this idea, saying it is up to the parents to keep their children out of the water. Another councillor asked where the money was to come from.

Another form of monitoring by the council was the attempt to obtain from the school information on truancy, particularly the names of absent students, to help catch thieves. They also had discussions with the truant officer at YACs but reported; 'Unfortunately when parents are confronted the story is almost invariably "sickness" "no shoes" etc etc'. The councillors are outraged that the parents refuse to assist the truant officer and the council to control the children.

The council sees the police as insufficiently effective in the control of vandalism and crime but are told repeatedly that it is the law itself and the court system which ties the hands of the police. A solution was suggested to council in February 1983. The shire president had discussed 'anomalies' with the police relating to what he called 'Police offences in public places', for instance, breaking bottles. He continued:

> The police Act is sometimes difficult to prove and incurs only a hundred dollar fine. The local government act is relatively easy to enforce and incurs a $300 fine and the Police wish to proceed under this section. Section 640 indicates that police are quite able to act under the Local Government Act as they are deemed to be acting for the council. The police in this case retain the penalties.

It was resolved by the shire council that the police be authorised to act on council's behalf in matters related to offences in public places under the Local Government Act. Whether the court was able to increase the penalty for breaking bottles to $300 is not known, but the example illustrates the council's indefatigable search for ways to achieve 'law and order'.

What then is the power of the shire council? They determine the terms of the public debate by informal control of the newspaper, through their influence in organisations and informal social life, and through the deference shown to them by others who run the town's institutions. They try to manipulate public opinion by their air of authority and control over communication with government ministers. The overt conflict that erupted over radio programmes (see below) shows that when their bluff is called they have little independent power, but can call on a range of patrons in higher places, often in the name of peace and public opinion.

POLICING BRINDLETON

Law and order

A common emphasis on property as the basis of health and happiness is reflected in the fury expressed about alleged Aboriginal carelessness with their own and others' property. Gubbs (whites) show extreme irritation with do-gooders from the cities who show sympathy towards Aborigines and make accusations about racism.

This is due to the conviction that the local reaction to threats to property and to bad behaviour generally is the same as anyone would have. Criticisms of too generous government handouts to people who will drink or otherwise squander the money is felt to be normal and certainly not a racist response. Outrage at the destruction of houses or of public property is felt to be fully justified. The Brindleton citizens are convinced that these city people do not know how bad the behaviour of the Aborigines is. The commonly expressed views about Aborigines are seen as just plain common sense (cf. Lawrence, 1982).

Despite the forlorn and frantic air about the councillors' complaints, the crime against property in Brindleton is virtually all petty crime. Theft of cars for joy-riding; house break-ins with little taken besides money; frequent shop break-ins for cigarettes, clothes or alcohol; school, club and church break-ins are all regular events. Occasionally more serious destructiveness occurs. There are a number of commonly accepted 'facts'. The main one is that there is an extemely high level of theft and vandalism nearly all committed by young blacks. A second is that their parents don't care and the police can't do anything. A third is that the situation is getting worse and people are buying guns to protect their property or planning to leave town. Offensive behaviour and vandalism are said to be increasing. The main street is 'a sea of broken glass' on 'pension' night after the social security cheques arrive and tales of drunken men lying in the gutter swearing are told with horror. The police and courts are said to be powerless due either to the repeal of the Summary Offenses Act, to legal aid 'getting them off', or to the law not providing proper penalties.

In fact most people know little of the processes of the law but do know that *everyone* knows who broke into the club last weekend and that the police can't or won't arrest them. Many believe that the police have too few powers and would like draconian measures taken. Some believe that the government no longer allows Aborigines to be put in goal or even prosecuted. Many say there is no respect for the law because such light penalties are awarded. On one occasion a young offender allegedly arrived back in town on a bond after a conviction in a higher court. The policeman who had prosecuted him was still on his way home. Such anecdotes are recounted to demonstrate how weak and ineffectual the courts are. Another popular belief is that the homes to which the young offenders are sent provide an enjoyable holiday and they are sent home to vandalise the town during the holidays.

The national press is seen as deliberately blind to these problems and unwilling to tell the truth because 'everything is for the Aborigines now'. By contrast, the local newspaper can reflect the local orthodoxy. One headline announced that one town was 'The Break and Enter Capital of Australia'. The article which followed fulminated against vandalism and break-ins and asked the townspeople to write to the council with information about their experiences. Armed with the peoples' complaints, the council could ask for more police or for more power to be given to them.

The police

The following table shows that the number of police officers in country towns varies, not only in relation to the total population, but in relation to the population's characteristics.

Table 4.1: *Level of policing in four NSW towns*

Town	Shire population	General duty police	Ratio
A	4,300	25	172:1
B	7,400	15	493:1
C	11,000	13	847:1
D	6,000	5	1,200:1

A 24-hour station and district HQ; 30 to 35% Aboriginal population
B 22% Aboriginal population
C Very small proportion of Aborigines
D No Aboriginal community
Source: NSW Police Department and Census 1981.

The number of police stationed in Brindleton is high per head of population mainly as a consequence of continuous lobbying by the Chamber of Commerce and the shire council over many years. The increase was supposed to reduce the level of break-ins and vandalism, but all these policemen have not been able to catch the thieves. The tactics of the young offenders, like that of a guerilla army, are sufficiently flexible to allow for changes in changed circumstances.

The police duties in Brindleton are not onerous, at least in terms of time. The high level of court appearances on relatively trivial charges such as failing to indicate the intention to turn a corner in a motor vehicle, may be a consequence of the police not having enough to do. The major police duties are patrolling the pubs, clubs and football games, answering calls to attend fights and domestic disputes, policing traffic, sometimes attending to disputes or complaints in the outlying villages (which might take one or two days), managing the police lock-up and attending court. The patrols around the town by car are not time consuming as the town has few streets. The police organised a series of 'Blue light discos' for some months as part of a state wide attempt to prevent youngsters getting into trouble; these created some extra work.

It is apparently difficult to recruit police to Brindleton, but some are simply sent there. Like the school teachers, they complain about the isolation and lack of entertainment in the town. Most stay the required time of three to four years and then go elsewhere. Thus, like the schools and other government instrumentalities, the police station is manned mainly by people unfamiliar with the town and with no long-term interest in it. They feel themselves to be in a foreign place. A few of the more senior police stay for longer periods. Occasionally marriage to a local leads to permanent residence. But most police are isolated from the rest of the town and they are a large enough group to achieve a degree of social self-sufficiency.

One reason for the social isolation of the police is that both black and white populations complain about them. While it may be common for police to feel embattled, two aspects of Brindleton make the problems more severe. In a small town they are unable to avoid contact with some of those who will voice complaints. Also the complaints are totally contradictory. The vocal whites complain of a lack of police protection from theft, vandalism and drunken abuse. It is openly stated, or at least implied, that it is the Aborigines who cause this kind of annoyance and they should be policed more harshly.[3] The council and the Chamber of Commerce make frequent personal and written representations to the local Superintendent of Police and to the Minister of Police, demanding protection from such crime. By contrast the black population complains of victimisation, brutality, unjustified surveillance and discriminatory practices.

In recent years a police/Aboriginal liaison unit has been set up in NSW and, as a result of its activities, meetings have been arranged between police in many NSW towns and any local Aborigines who wish to come. Such a meeting in Brindleton was held in the hall at the

---

[3] In late 1985 a law and order campaign was instituted in many NSW country towns orchestrated through the shire councils (Cuneen, 1986).

Aboriginal end of town, with about 30 people present and five police officers one of whom was the officer in charge. The meeting lasted three hours, during which time a large number of specific and general complaints were made by the Aborigines. There were no allegations of brutality in police cells, although some have been made privately. Rather complaints centred on alleged discriminatory practices.

For instance it was asked why police looked for suspects among certain families, sometimes waking them in the middle of the night. Why was surveillance of domestic gatherings by police in their cars, and spotlightling of back or front yards, carried out only at the Aboriginal end of town? Why were the police cells dirty, the food poor and sometimes no water provided? Why are there so many police in towns where there are a lot of Kooris? There were also complaints about being called black bastards. An older and more intricate story of injustice which concerned the price of a chicken, aroused considerable amusement because the complainant showed a degree of confusion. Perhaps the most potentially explosive moment was when a woman shouted 'That constable said my sister gave him VD' but, amid gales of laughter from the Aborigines, the policeman, relatively calm if a trifle pink in the face, denied he had ever had the disease.

The response of the police was twofold. First they said that particular complaints should be made formally to the sergeant at the station and would be investigated. Second that most complaints did not denote any form of discrimination, but rather were normal police practice. For instance spotlighting would occur if there were suspected prowlers. 'You are not being picked on, I can tell you that', the sergeant said with authority. Concerning the police cells it was asserted that someone was paid to clean them daily, and the police suggested drily that people should try to avoid being put in them. The sergeant noted that there had been no appreciative comments about the way police take victims of brawls to the hospital. 'All we hear is the swearing', he said. He also said he hoped that the police would get cooperation from the community and that the kids would be kept off the streets and away from the business houses 'because that is where they come to our notice'.

The assessment of the meeting a little later indicated that some of the criticisms of the police had smarted, and the frustration felt by some Aborigines had not abated. While a few thought the meeting was a success, one policeman complained that it was just a gripe session; Aborigines had not realised that their problems were self-made. One policeman said 'The boss tried to be too diplomatic at the meeting. The reason we look at this end of town for the culprits is that by past experience it is 95% juvenile Aborigines who break and enter.' Aborigines complained that the police did not admit that they were doing anything wrong. They had thought the meeting was to allow them to explain their complaints.

Given the old and notorious hostility between police and Aborigines (see Chapter 2), the fact that such meetings occur is a somewhat surprising achievement; police, like other people, would usually avoid sitting still to be criticised. While local conflict may be alleviated to some degree, there is unlikely to be any change in the underlying reasons that Aborigines are policed in a way that they find intrusive and unjust.

As the police personnel are virtually all outsiders, their interpretation of their role, especially as regards the black population, takes a somewhat different form from that of the older residents including the councillors. However, unlike the school teachers, the duties of the police towards the black population are recognised as different from those towards the white population. Of course the police are resocialized into the realities of Brindleton by their colleagues who explain who should be watched, who should be shown leniency and the unofficial basis for keeping the peace. As one policeman explained, 'You can't have the new constables arresting the leading businessmen for DUI (driving under the influence).' They are told to be tactful because the police would find the town uninhabitable if the influential citizens or their friends were alienated.

This same flexiblility allows for some individuals to be victimised. Some black families are 'known' to be troublesome. One member of such a family, known more for political anger than crime, believed he was being subjected to so much police harassment (such as being stopped and indicted for minor infringements of traffic regulations or vehicle fault), that he walked to work across town for weeks. Conversely a young white man told me he had failed to give way to a police patrol car one night when he was extemely drunk and stoned. One of the policemen he had almost collided with was a fellow footballer. He was told to drive straight home and the police escorted him. He complied, showing them due deference, and heard no more about it. This personal rather than impersonal application of the law is considered by both the police and those who benefit from the treatment to be tactful and sensible policing in a small town where 'We all have to live together'.

Most of the Aboriginal population has personal knowledge of the police from a quite different point of view. Those of twenty of more will still have memories of the earlier regime where the police would regularly visit the reserve, enter the humpies and shacks, and arrest people for being drunk, often having to awaken them first. When one policeman arrived in Brindleton 15 years ago, it was illegal for Aborigines to be drunk on the reserve. 'So we would go down there at night, drag people out of their beds and take them down to the lock-up. The children were left without mother and father. We didn't worry about them' (cf. Beckett, 1964). This policeman thinks things are getting better as such treatment has ceased. 'But', he says,'hostility to police is bred into them. The little kids chuck rocks at police cars.'

There is no need to appeal to a breeding process. Even those who have never been in trouble are fully aware from friends or kin, or from being present, that police and blacks are mutually hostile. The police do patrol the Aboriginal end of town frequently. Police are believed to initiate trouble and they have weapons, their superior officers and the courts to back them up. It is also fairly clear to the Aborigines that the police dislike or mistrust them, and some do not hide the fact, openly denigrating Aborigines individually and collectively. Abusive swearing and violence are a usual part of the interaction between police and Aborigines, but the police can arrest and fine Aborigines while their own abuse goes unpunished (cf. Wilson, 1978). The police are reputed to be afraid of attending fights at the Aboriginal end of town and on occasion they have suffered violent attacks after answering a call. Police argue that they should not attend until they are called or they might exacerbate the conflict. However it seems more common that their arrival leads to anger being deflected onto them.

Another arena where the activities of police are familiar to the Aborigines is at the Sunday football matches. There is often conflict among Aboriginal spectators towards the end of the afternoon, and the police patrol will be called upon to stop it in the early stages. This is no easy task for young police who have little familiarity with the kind of abuse and anger regularly evinced in what are often old feuds in a close knit and complex community. The crowd often becomes excited. When one young and very white policeman was called by a furiously angry Aboriginal woman to deal with a man who had abused her, with a large excited crowd standing about, his face showed paralysing fear. If a violent fight begins it is no easy matter for two police to deal with a large crowd who have been drinking for most of the afternoon. A particular conflict can often become the occasion for the expression of other antagonisms and many people may become involved. Police can become the target of attack. Once when a fight involving over a hundred people erupted in the street outside the football ground, the police are said to have used tear gas to disperse the crowd. A good deal of effort was put into keeping that event from the attention of the urban media. Several Aborigines told me that the police were right to stop the fight that way.

Thus the policemen in Brindleton feel that their lot is not a happy one. They have developed certain convictions about their role which serve to distance them from the complaints which come from two sides. Their defence against the council and their ilk consists of a superior knowledge of the law and blaming the law's weakness (especially the repeal of the Summary Offenses Act) for their inability to stop the 'crime'. They also feel themselves to understand the situation better than the locals because of their knowledge of much more serious crime elsewhere, and with many police now given some instruction on social deprivation, they can feel themselves to be more enlightened concerning Aboriginal problems than the councillors.

Their defence against the accusations from Aborigines also consists of a superior knowledge of the law, as well as an understanding of their own discretionary powers. They accept that there is an 'Aboriginal problem' and, because Aborigines deny that this definition of the situation is accurate, the police are not seriously challenged by their criticisms.

Answers to complaints about the police lock-up indicate the kind of personal judgements which underlie some of the policemen's attitudes to Aborigines. The food is said by police to be good, and the trouble is that the Aborigines are 'used to junk food and cannot eat a decent stew'. The cells are cleaned daily; it is the inmates who dirty them very quickly. This situation was carefully demonstrated to a reporter who came to the town to follow up one such story. He was shown a clean cell, and then taken to lunch during which time an Aboriginal prisoner was put in the cell. When the reporter was shown the cell a couple of hours later it was dirty. This story was told to me with much satisfaction, but I have not heard the reporter's or the prisoner's view. Thus, while all agree that the police are less brutal and despotic than in the past, the black population still feels victimised and harassed. One longer-serving officer blames the young police who, because they have been brought up in bad stations such as Kings Cross, are prejudiced and have a ghetto mentality.

There are other ways that the Aboriginal community is affected by the law. Police are called upon by Aborigines to control much dissension within and between kin groups. Some such occasions are defined as domestic violence and others as brawls. In all cases the police operate according to their understanding of the law rather than according to the wishes of the Aborigines. While there is nothing surprising about this, it needs stating because the need that Aborigines have for police to control internal dissension creates a number of conflicts. In the literature which quantifies and analyses the problems Aborigines have with the law this aspect of their relations with the police is seldom discussed (Eggleston, 1976; ADB Report, 1982; Hanks & Keon-Cohen, 1984; but see Beckett, 1964). I would argue that, while individual Aborigines rely on the police in some circumstances to protect them from other Aborigines, this reliance has grown up in a situation where interpersonal violence is common. This violence is in turn a response to the violence which has been endemic in the controlling of Aborigines since the first settlement. It began with killings, and continued with the violence of the Aboriginal Protection Board, reserve management and police intrusion. The fact that police must now be called frequently to stop blacks hurting each other is a final ironic tragedy (cf. Wilson, 1982).

The courts

The court house in many country towns is a tourist attraction, not of course for its function as the venue for the punishment of crimes but for its architecture. The magistrate's court in Brindleton usually sits about two days each fortnight and the district court sits occasionally. I attended one two-day sitting in its entirety in 1983. The following is a summary of the charges.

Table 4.2: *Cases involving Aborigines*

Assault or resist or incite to resist police	27	(12 individuals)
Serious alarm & affront	6	
Assault (not police)	7	
Total	40	

From limited observation at several other court sessions this balance of cases, while not typical, seemed similar to others in that more Aborigines are charged and most of their charges involved conflict

Table 4.3: *Cases involving whites*

Break enter & steal	4	(2 individuals)
DUI plus associated charges	6	(2 individuals)
Higher PCA* & dangerous driving	2	
Total	12	

* Proscribed concentration of alcohol

Table 4.4: *Cases heard at the Court of Petty Sessions (for the year 1982)*

Offence group	No. of cases	Convicted Fine	Prison	Other	Not Convicted
Against persons					
Against person	44	14	3	6	21
Offensive behaviour	30	28	—	—	2
Resist arrest	13	12	1	—	—
Total	87	54	4	6	23
Against Property					
Break, enter, steal	11	10	—	1	—
Larceny	10	7	1	2	—
Unlawful posession	6	3	—	1	2
Damage	10	7	—	1	2
Total	37	27	1	5	4
Driving & Drink driving	66	56	4	3	3
Firearms	9	7	—	—	2
Other*	13	9	—	—	4
Total**	212				

* The category 'other' contains 8 different offences mostly minor.
** There are fewer cases for the year than might be expected from Table 4.3 because many of those cases were for mention only or were held over from previous session.
Source: Bureau of Crime Statistics.

with the police. Many of the Aborigines before the courts face multiple charges.

It is clear from Table 4.4 that the largest category of behaviour which results in court appearances is to do with attacking or offending people, and that most of those attacked or offended are the police. That is, 43 of the 87 cases are offensive behaviour (charges brought by police), or resisting arrest (by police). An unspecified number of the other cases involved attacks on the police. The second largest offence is to do with driving. The third largest is offences against property.

The court procedures themselves show what is acceptable and respected behaviour in a number of informal ways. The dress and deportment of many of the Aborigines is strikingly different from that of the police, lawyers and magistrates, though the Aboriginal legal aid lawyers dress informally to try to bridge that gap to a degree. Those more neatly attired and confident seem to elicit more respect from the court. But the deference to the magistrate and court procedures shown by lawyers, police and the more respectable accused cannot be matched by many Aborigines who often evince a sullen or frightened manner. The language used in the court is at odds with that used outside it, even by the same people. Perhaps the most bizarre example is the producing of evidence in cases of offensive language. Words that are heard frequently in the street and pubs are produced with intense solemnity by policeman as used against themselves. 'He said, fuck off, fucking cunt cop, your honour.' A string of repetitions of the same terms follows the policeman's reporting of his restrained response. The task of the magistrate is made difficult by the need to disapprove constantly of such behaviour that must, over time, become extremely familiar. Perhaps he is in danger of suffering from cognitive dissonance! There is clearly a large degree of arbitrariness in the decisions about the context and import of such language (Wilson, 1978).

While Aborigines regard the court as a place to be avoided, the court staff attract dependency. The clerk acts on behalf of the court as a go-between for many of those who appear before the court, or who are seeking the assistance of the court. Particularly as regards the payment of fines and domestic disputes he has a good deal of discretion. Further, some women, mostly Aborigines, approach him asking for a court order or restraining order to keep control of a violent husband. His advice is all prefaced on his notions of probable outcomes. He assured me the problems are mostly due to unjustified jealousy and lack of communication. He often calls in a husband to try to smooth troubled waters. So, for diverse reasons, it is difficult for many Aborigines to avoid involvement with the legal system.

The two lawyers for the Western Aboriginal Legal Service (WALS) are stationed in Dubbo, and travel to the courts in the west as required. Most stay with the service for some years and get to know the local population well, often staying in the town for some days and perhaps attending a disco or the pub and visiting Aboriginal friends and clients. Unlike the police and teachers these lawyers show a commitment to the populations they are serving. The police and many whites in the town regard them as 'weirdos', but also, more seriously, as the enemy of law and order. When a policeman was complaining about the legal service giving their clients bad advice, that is, to plead not guilty, I asked why he thought they did that. He said 'Have you *seen* them?', as if their informal dress and longish hair was sufficient explanation of such a legal aberration. In fact the justification for defending a client rather than habitually pleading guilty is clear. One role of the ALS is to reverse the situation whereby the law becomes another tool in the wider oppression of Aborigines. 'ALS's have tried to expose and grapple with the underlying attitudes that give rise to discriminatory police behaviour' (Lyons, 1984:147).

Thus the ALS lawyers' role is seen as in opposition to the white citizens, and their lack of social interaction with the white population seems to confirm this. The loyalty of others such as the magistrate, the police prosecutor and the lawyers in the town who drink and lunch together and with members of council and other important citizens is clear. It has not escaped the notice of Aboriginal clients of the court who commonly assume these people all represent the prosecution. Such an assumption, in terms of wider social processes, may be fundamentally accurate.

The magistrate is reputed to give higher sentences to those who have pleaded not guilty if they are convicted. He allegedly believes they should not waste the court's time. This is the basis of the argument that the legal service is disadvantaging the clients by advising them to plead not guilty. Also the WALS is seen as discriminatory. Legal aid is available to whites, but they must submit an application and show that they earn under a certain amount. Any Aborigine gets free legal aid when they arrive at the court. While the policy of the Aboriginal Legal Service is to represent all Aborigines (Lyons, 1984:144), the service provided by WALS is limited as they have many clients and often have to interview them briefly just before the court sits.

According to the court officials the magistrate deals in the same way with white and black juveniles. Juveniles are only sent away when they have been before the court three or four times and have been on probation. If the third offence is serious, and certainly at the fourth offense, the youth is sent away. But I was told 'regardless of how long he is sent for he will be back within 3 months or sooner'. This is the leniency complained of bitterly by the shire council, the Chamber of Commerce and numerous other residents.

There is a powerful orthodoxy of views surrounding the town crime. Though the majority of robberies are minor and often by way of unlocked doors, righteous anger is aroused by the reports even among those who do not suffer from burglary. Expressing anything other than outrage, or even considering possible causes of the problem, is likely to meet with anger and suspicion of disloyalty. Orthodox ideas concerning the situation are nurtured, especially by the council and by the Chamber of Commerce. The latter body complained at one meeting about how the ALS was 'hindering justice' and sent letters concerning law and order to the newspaper. Such public statements reassert the legitimacy of the complaints and the illegitimacy of any interest in or sympathy for the 'vandals' or the 'certain element'. When the brand new ambulance was stolen and crashed the week after it was delivered, the whole town knew about it. They also knew that the culprit was back in town three weeks later and stole another car. In the face of such apparently senseless destruction, it is more than one's social life is worth to attempt to discuss causes and solutions to the problems of 'the certain element'. But this element is, for many, simply the Aborigines.

Criticisms of Aborigines in the town are repeatedly justified with stories which demonstrate an alleged lack of responsibility — mainly towards property, money and work. The stories usually feature an individual whose behaviour seems inexplicable to the speaker except in terms of some inherent depravity. The solutions are in terms of forcing them to account for money, forcing them to work for the dole, goaling them at length for any destruction of property, taking the children away from them when young to teach them proper values and other such punitive measures. It is the shopkeepers and other business people who usually talk in these terms because they are the ones that have been most often subject to such attacks. But other institutions in Brindleton contribute to the racial divide and are subject to less direct attack. We shall examine how education, health and welfare services become embroiled in these processes.

EDUCATING BRINDLETON

The schools

The functions of schools are, of course, far broader than indicated in the curricula. Schools are a part of the wider society and operate as part of a local community also. In Brindleton, it is at the schools that most interaction between sections of the population, which are otherwise separate, takes place. Thus for interpersonal relations between black and white, the school has crucial significance. The schools do not challenge the dominant racist ideology of the town. One reason is that the enlightenment philosophy which dominates the thinking about Aborigines within the education department, and which most teachers espouse on their arrival, does not prepare teachers for the situation they find themselves in.

This philosophy emphasises the fact that Aborgines have been and are oppressed by white racists. It is supposed that an anti-racist attitude is sufficient armour against joining the oppressors. But in the face of unexpected difficulties it is not perhaps surprising that the local 'realism' is usually adopted. Were there a clearer understanding of the basis of the conflicts then, under courageous leadership, the school could act to counter, to a degree, the prevailing processes in the town. Instead it takes part in recreating the racial divide by not challenging it. There are from time to time efforts to help Aborigines, but that is a different thing.

The first educational institution which Brindleton children enter is the pre-school which since 1960 has aimed at giving children from disadvantaged backgrounds a 'head-start', particularly in language development, using the 'direct action' method. This involves repetition of patterned grammatical forms, rewards and self-esteem exercises all of which are intended to counter the effect that a deprived home environment has on the child. The pre-schools in different towns show more variation in their methods than the other schools, but they all face similar conflicts.

The method of recruitment to the pre-school is aimed at reaching all the children in the town who have a need of such a head start.

Using the birth records from the hospital all four-year-olds are invited to enrol, and if there are too many then the 'brightest' are excluded. There is a nominal fee of $2 a week and a bus collects the children and delivers them home after each half-day session. Some white parents do not send their children because the pre-school is seen to cater for blacks or backward children. Some Aboriginal parents do not send their children, or stop sending them for a number of reasons to do with the alienation from such an environment felt by child and parent alike. There are Aboriginal staff who conduct regular home visits, but a few children who would be considered most in need often do not remain long at the pre-school despite their efforts.

The pre-school has been a project of educational psychologists at the UNSW and Wollongong University for many years. It is well funded and well staffed (see Table 4.6). Parents are encouraged to take part in running the place, but few black parents come unless cajoled for a particular reason. Then it is likely that the most 'assimilated' will turn up. Others will evince timidity and discomfort. Thus the pre-school, with the best intentions and considerable resources, cannot remove the barriers between the black and white populations. One reason is the lack of awareness of the nature of the racial division.

There is no overt recognition by those who determine the programme that there is a racial problem. It is believed that certain children are denied opportunities, so if 'opportunities' are offered with the smile of friendship, all will be well. The attempts to monitor the longer-term effects of the programme have been conducted by experts, usually psychology students, who, during brief visits to the town, administer tests to a sample of ex-pre-school children at various stages of their later schooling. These assessments show some average differences from some other students (Moffitt *et al.*,1973: 141–4). Those who fund the programme are convinced by this research of the programme's long-term success. While I would not wish to deny this claim, or to detract from the value of the pre-school, it is clear that after 25 years the Aboriginal population still suffers severe educational disadvantage. For instance in 1984 there were 28 primary school children in the remedial reading programme of whom 60 per cent were Aboriginal. The lower streams at the high school are almost entirely Aboriginal and no Aborigines who stay in the town complete high school.

On leaving the pre-school a child may go to the state or the Catholic primary schools. After that there is high school in Brindleton or some can choose to go away to boarding school elsewhere. Since the late 1960s school attendance by Aboriginal children has been more closely monitored than previously, and all now attend primary school at least. But, as with some of the white rural workers, the illiteracy of the parents remains a handicap for the children. For those who have left school the local technical college provides a range of courses from basic literacy to computing skills and including cake decoration. The courses offered depend on the availability of local teachers.

Table 4.5: *Student population of Brindleton (1983)*

School	No. of students			% Aboriginal
	Aboriginal	Non-Aboriginal	Total	
High school	95*	180	275	3
Primary	48	154	202	24
Infant	52	90	142	36
Catholic	58	87	145	40
Correspondence	0	38	38	—
Total	253	549	802	31.5

* Aboriginal students in high school are defined as those on the Aboriginal secondary grant. The principal asserted that 8 of these, though on the grant are 'not identifiably Aboriginal' and do not identify with Aborigines (see Chapter 5).

The preference Aborigines show for the Catholic school could be due either to its being nearer to the bulk of the Aboriginal community, to a large percentage of Aborigines being at least nominally Catholic, or to the positive policy of this school towards Aboriginal education. Despite such a policy, the same kinds of tensions exist as in the other schools. The attempts by the teaching Sisters to gain cooperation from Aboriginal parents in assisting their children to gain an education does not always meet with the enthusiasm they would wish. Virtually no Aboriginal parents pay the fees. At one stage the Bingo game organisers were asked to pay $30 to $40 each week to help the school but instead it was paid into the funeral fund.

For a large percentage of teachers Brindleton is their first appointment, and the majority leave after the required two or three years (Table 4.6). Especially for the senior staff, such a school is seen as a stepping stone to better things. Since 1969 the principal and deputy

Table 4.6: *School staffing figures for Brindleton (1983)*

School	Total	First Appt.	1	2	3	4	>5	ATAs	Other	Teacher/ student ratio

Headers: Certificated Teachers (spanning Total, First Appt., Years in B: 1, 2, 3, 4, >5); Support staff (ATAs, Other); Teacher/student ratio

School	Total	First Appt.	1	2	3	4	>5	ATAs	Other	Teacher/student ratio
High school	31	18	8	9	8	4	2	1	5	1:8.6
Primary	12	7	0	5	2	0	5	2	1	1:17
Infant*	10	5	2	4	0	1	3	1	1	1:18*
Catholic	9	4	2	3	1	1	2	2	2	1:16
Pre-school	6									1:4.5

* This figure includes the correspondence school which has 3 teachers and 38 pupils.

have arrived together for their three years, and departed together, so that a new regime begins at regular intervals. It is notoriously difficult to get staff to go to western NSW. The primary and infant schools have a few married women who remain for longer periods. The high turnover of staff does not mean that the teachers all dislike the town. Many enjoy their two or three years in the west because of the sunny, mild winter climate, access to sporting facilities, and other features of small town life. But most would not consider staying; isolation, the lack of privacy and difficulties with Aboriginal students are the usual reasons given. I was told repeatedly of problems associated with Aboriginal students. They are said to be cheeky or sullen, emotionally unstable and unable to concentrate. Teachers say 'If you have a rowdy Aboriginal class next door it is hard for everyone.' Also teachers find contact with Aboriginal parents difficult as many such parents have had little schooling themselves, and the teachers lack experience of the Aboriginal social world.

A teacher explained to me that the school is a forum where the white and black communities get at each other and the teachers are caught up in the middle. There is some truth in this assertion in that the expectations of these sections of the population are different. On the one hand the Aboriginal Education Committee feels the school is one accessible white organisation which they may be able to influence. Their children complain about school and about their treatment there. The white parents, on the other hand, perceive the school to be favouring the Aborigines. In a competitive school system they worry about their children being held back by the blacks who are apparently non-competitive and non-achieving or, some would assert, badly behaved and stupid. A number do not have uniforms and do not care about tidiness. On the occasion of a school display in the town for which parents had spent a lot of time making sure their children were spic and span, a few of the Aboriginal children spoilt the show with their untidiness and uncooperative attitude. It is natural, I was told, for white parents to feel resentful in this situation.

There is a general view among the staff of the high school that any discrimination shown by teachers is in favour of the Aboriginal students. That is, some teachers are conscious of trying very hard not to upset black kids, trying to encourage them and treating them more leniently than the white kids. Other teachers complain about the black kids, and are sympathetic with white parents' feeling about the injustice of the Aboriginal Secondary Grant (ASG). Such teachers are not averse to some minor redirection of funds towards other needy students.

There is a stigma attached to receiving the ASG, known as 'the grant'. Teachers are well aware that several students who are on the grant do not particularly wish to be known as Aborigines. There is embarrassment or defiance shown by those who are handed their portion of the grant money at the school and the teachers at the school always know which students are and which are not on the grant. Some of the parents have it paid directly to the school, and others have nominated an agent to receive it. Of course the school is in favour of the funding of Aboriginal education: it provides the school with additional financial resources.

Besides the ASG, there are two areas where specific attempts have been made to improve Aborigines' access to education. One is the appointment of Aboriginal Teacher's Aids (ATAs), and the other is the introduction of Aboriginal studies courses. The ATAs are seen by the teachers as useful helpers and, especially in the high school, as liaison people to assist with truancy problems and difficult parents. There has been no attempt by the school to use them to make any fundamental change in the relationship the school has with Aborigines in general or with Aboriginal students.

The ATAs for their part show a high level of deference to the teachers, although through the Aboriginal Education Organisation (AEO) there have been demands made that the high school alter some of its practices. However the teaching staff find it comparatively easy to have their views prevail in any conflict with the ATAs. Through appeal to common sense notions about common eduational interests, the ATAs are encouraged to see the need to get the Aboriginal students and parents to behave better rather than complain about the teachers who are, after all, doing their best in difficult circumstances. When one of the ATAs was asked to write a reference for a senior staff member who had to face a partly Aboriginal selection board, the combination of being flattered and encouraged to do so by her white patron (for the patron's own reasons), led her to write him a favourable reference. An ATA who left the school was similarly flattered by the send off she was given. 'They must have valued me a lot; I never realised', she said, indicating a lack of awareness of the duplicity so evident on such occasions. Thus are the ATAs compromised and tamed by the schools that employ them.

Efforts to include in the school curricula information about Aboriginal culture are also vitiated by the need to pander to the sensibilities of the establishment. The past one hundred years are not a major part of the subject matter of Aboriginal studies courses. The material that is thought of as Aboriginal tends to be about exotic cultural practices which are no longer in evidence or about artefacts. If these have any meaning to the young people in Brindleton, it is a negative one. Such traditions or language from the past that are still familiar to a few old people have never before been regarded with anything but contempt or disdain, and some of that negative evaluation has been accepted by many Aborigines.

Thus when an old man, shy, diffident and poorly dressed, is asked to talk of hunting or making spears in the polished and hard-edged atmosphere of the classroom, it seems to confirm rather than reverse the low status of the old Aboriginal traditions. The reliance on retrieving some hand-made objects, whether useful or decorative, from the local community, can result in a rather pathetic display such as that shown at one of the schools for National Aboriginal Day. The children had to file past and stare at the woven basket, several wooden plaques and ashtrays with 'Aboriginal' motifs, and a painting of black girls with large breasts. The back drop was a piece of tapa cloth from Fiji. The history that has made such an indignity possible is not explicated in the school curriculum.

The second limitation on the teaching of an Aboriginal studies course is its position in the course structure. As an elective subject it is not taken by the ambitious students but by the ones in the lower streams who are predominantly black. The teacher who introduced the subject in its first year in Brindleton was dedicated to teaching and thought the subject important, but she was not hopeful of success. As the lower-stream students are negative in their attitude to school in general, she just hopes to keep sufficient interest so that they can pass their time with a modicum of peace and enjoyment.

While many of the teachers remain sympathetic to Aborigines, many are irritated and dismissive of the claims about racism made by their Aboriginal students. Very few recognise that the complaints may be valid in a general sense. In their early adult years, these young blacks are faced with a town where their status and that of their parents and friends is abysmally low. They do not know why this is so, or what they can do about it. They are often angry or hurt about slights and insults to themselves their parents or relations. Even overheard discussion of 'the Aboriginal problem', casual glances of contempt in the shops, or recognition of the disgust with which many whites view Aboriginal drunks, can upset a youthful Aboriginal person who is struggling to establish his or her own identity. These experiences might seem trivial or unreal to the teacher. All the Aboriginal student can blame is white racism, so the 'racist' accusation is made frequently. Outbursts of anger can be deeply hurtful to sympathetic teachers, especially when the attacks come from the very students they have paid special attention to and become fond of. The theory that Aborigines are unable to control their emotions has developed to explain such behaviour. That is, rather than consider the source of the anger, an essential emotional quality is attributed to Aborigines. It is this alleged difference, rather than their different social circumstances in the town, which then absolves the town from responsibility.

There are also more specific cultural discontinuities. The contrast between the acceptant, indulgent and egalitarian values which predominate in the Aboriginal community and the judgemental and moralistic atmosphere at school, is striking. Aboriginal students live it; teachers do not recognise it.

The refusal to talk about or recognise Aborigines' experience of racism leads to the school failing to alleviate quite specific problems of many of its students. For instance teachers are often disappointed that the Aboriginal students will not go on excursions. They appear to have no good reason, and their parents are accused of not valuing the advantages they are being offered. Sometimes it is the fear of being shamed because of not having a nightdress or the correct accoutrements that makes the teenager reluctant to go on overnight trips. When students were to be billeted in Sydney there were probably much more tangible fears about the attitude of white hosts. The subject was not broached, and no Aboriginal students went on the excursion. Thus the teacher's profound ignorance of Aboriginal social patterns and experience vitiates any attempts they make to help their Aboriginal students.

The opportunity for Aboriginal students to go away to boarding school has been available since 1971. For the government, this is the most expensive of the grants for Aboriginal education. Until the late 70s, little advantage was taken of these opportunities in the west. As more families found that boarding school solved certain problems, more students were sent to the schools where there were hostels for Aboriginal students. But since 1981, stricter guidelines have been developed so that an Aboriginal student will only be accepted as eligible for boarding school if the parents are in dire poverty, or the home is massively overcrowded, or some such extreme situation exists.

At the tertiary level the resentment created by the ASG is exacerbated. The majority of technical college students in Brindleton are young women doing the secretarial course. Among the white students in one year there was one girl on the full allowance under the Tertiary Education Assistance Scheme (TEAS), one on the dole, one with no income and one with part TEAS who had a part-time job in the evenings. The Aboriginal students' grant exceeds TEAS, and is not means tested. Thus their money is handed to them regularly, so long as they attend, without their having to fill in forms or prove their eligibility. When the white girls discovered the discrepancy, they wanted to know why they could not have the same support. The Aboriginal girls agreed with them. When the Minister for Education came to the town, three white and three Aboriginal girls went to him as a deputation to ask for the same support to be extended to all those in need. He was most impressed, he said, but not surprisingly, nothing more was heard. This incident illustrates the real inequities, obvious to all, which result from racially specified benefits. It was clear that the Aboriginal students could not have supported themselves without assistance, but it is unarguable that at least two of the white students had equivalent needs. Thus these working-class students, unlike some better-off whites, recognised the need of Aboriginal students for educational assistance.

The document affair

I will interrupt this discussion of the institutions which dominate the life of Brindleton with an account of an incident which deeply disturbed many people in the town. At one time the high school became the focus of attention from the national media because the Aboriginal community withdrew their children from the school, not only in this town, but across the state. They complained of a racist document being circulated in the school. Media attention was at first courted by the Aboriginal organisation, but subsequently was avoided by all. This was because, I would argue, the desire of the journalists to offer support to the Aborigines, without any under-standing of the nature of the dispute, embarrassed everyone in the town and seemed immediately to provide more ammunition for the conservative forces than for those seeking change.

The events which led up to this public attention are understood quite differently by various residents of the town. Not only did groups attribute importance to different events and blame to different people, but there were contradictory versions of events. As a relative stranger, I was the target of a range of accounts and explanations of what had occurred. In all cases there was intense personal feeling involved. I will describe three versions, beginning with that given by one of the Aborigines involved with the Aboriginal Education Organisation.

First version: A blatantly racist document which denigrated and ridi-culed Aborigines was being circulated to the teachers in the school. The AEO got hold of the document, and an angry meeting of a large number of Aboriginal parents in the town decided to withdraw all Aboriginal children from school. They contacted the NSW state organisation and gained state-wide Aboriginal support for the de-mand that the clerical assistant, who had been copying and appar-ently distributing the document, should be sacked. Their resolve was firm. The school refused the demand and called in the Education Department. A meeting with Sydney Education Department officers, including an Aboriginal officer, was held. A decision was made to conduct an enquiry. It was also discovered that the clerical assistant was not the owner of the document.

Before the Education Department enquiry had been held, one of the Aborigines from the AEO, after talking with the Aboriginal representative from the Education Department, called a meeting to form another organisation called Aboriginal Friends of the school. Many of the Aborigines attended, not realising it was subverting the original group's activities. This meeting took the decision to accept the Education Department's assurances and to send the children back to school. It seems that the Aboriginal officer from the Education Department had decided that the fight could not be won outright. Due to these two events the Aboriginal resolve to stay out until all their demands were met collapsed, causing much bitterness against those who were seen as traitors, and much defensiveness by those who were later shown the gratitude of the Education Department for their cooperation. Previously active members in the AEO withdrew, but feel that the whole document affair was a forceful indication that unity and resolve are available in the community. A more tangible gain was the decision of the Education Department to screen teachers for racist attitudes in schools with a high proportion of Aboriginal students and the assurance of Aboriginal representation on the screening committee.[4]

Second version: One of the senior staff of the school in question told the story differently. It was a put up job, he said. A young clerical assistant had been asked by another woman on the support staff to make a copy of a bogus employment application form. It was a humorous thing, though perhaps in bad taste, which actually originated in the United States and had been modified for Australia. This woman had been sent it from Western Australia. The senior staff member claimed that one person on the staff, who was determined to make trouble, asked the clerk if he could have a copy of the document, and rushed to the AEO and told them the document was being distributed to all the staff. This, he asserted, was a lie. But, he went on, another person in the town jumped at the chance, for political reasons, to attack the school and called in the media and threatened the school with exposure of scandals and trouble. This person was in league with the media, which thrives on disruption. The Aborigines in town did not want all the fuss, he said. Without those two stirrers it was just an unfortunate little incident that the media got hold of. One dignified Aboriginal man who looked like an Eastern potentate came to see the principal at the school to apologise for all the trouble, and they formed an organisation to support the school. Most Aborigines give their support to the teachers who are idealistic and dedicated to helping the Aboriginal students. They spend their own time at the homework centre, even when their cars are scratched and they are sworn at. The teacher, who was forcibly transferred because of other evidence, was, in this version of events, really foolish and childish; not racist.

Most of this is similar to the version of the story that many of the whites in the town relate. There is no racism (meaning overt hostility to Aborigines) in the town, they assert, except that stirred up by

---

[4]At the school where the document incident occurred there are insufficient Aboriginal students (below 50%) to qualify for this screening process.

troublemakers. The document was just a joke that would not offend anyone with a sense of humour. The teachers have a hard time with the Aboriginal students, only a minority mind you, but this kind of fuss makes it worse. The city media jumped on the story but do not understand what goes on in the town.

Third version: A third version is that of the alleged stirrers and their few supporters. They say the school, like the town, is replete with conscious and unconscious racism and the appearance of the document was just another example, but a concrete and blatant one that could be made public. While many individual teachers are sympathetic with the plight of some of the Aboriginal children, a punitive and negative attitude prevails, especially among the senior staff. This is evident in the existence in the previous year of a punishment room in the school, called the Black Jail by Aboriginal students. Further evidence of teachers' racist attitudes was brought to the attention of the Education Department enquiry in the form of an audio tape made by a staff member. The existence of this tape was not made public at the time, but the school had been given a copy previously. After the attempts by the school to sidestep the Aboriginal demands and deny responsibility for the document, a 'stirrer' told the school that if they did not let the department know about the tape, then he would.

This tape had been made during an in-service course for teachers on radio and video production. It consisted of a simulated interview between a newcomer to the town and a local male, during which sexual and derogatory comments were made about the 'gins on the reserve' and flagons of wine. The intention may have been to mock the attitude of the townsmen as much as anything else. The existence of this tape was not made public until sometime later, and the Aboriginal community was not told about it, clearly to avoid further protest. But it was the production of the tape which forced the Education Department to agree to an enquiry as a result of which two teachers were given forced transfers, another was reprimanded, and the clerical assistant was exonerated.

This version of the events also stresses, as does the first version, that the solidarity shown by the Aborigines has great significance in itself, but because they were defeated by treachery from those who were virtually bought off, the whole thing can be seen as a step backwards.

One might ask whether the document was in fact funny, in bad taste or racist. Clearly humour can serve different functions in different situations, and there are some Aborigines who could find certain parts of the document amusing just as some women can bear to laugh at mother-in-law jokes. But humour is not merely entertainment. It is constructed within existing power relations. In a situation of structural inequality, where the ego of many young Aborigines is damaged by denigration and shame and where the school in theory tries to create an opportunity for individuals to be free of the stereotyping which many experience, the document represents a nasty reminder of the insensitivity, to put it kindly, of some of the staff. The fact that both the teacher who made the tape and the teacher that took the document to the Aborigines were forcibly transferred, may indicate even-handedness on the part of the Education Department, or simply a convenient solution to an awkward situation for which they have no solution. The schools, with their uniforms and exams, espouse the notion that individuals are equal in the education system, as they are supposed to be before the law. Thus the historical and social inequalities that exist as part of the lives of the students, are mystified within the schools in Brindleton.

INSTITUTIONAL RACISM

Health and welfare services

The conflict between the practices of the health services and those of their clients is obvious in communities where hygiene is poor because of poor access to water, bathrooms and other washing facilities, as well as crowded conditions and a lack of resources of many kinds. The authoritarian and hierarchical organisation of hospitals and health services generally, are characteristics which clearly disadvantage Aborigines both as clients and as prospective employees in these institutions. Some Aboriginal girls and women have been employed as nurse aids at the hospital in Brindleton, but because they are in competition with others who appear to conform more closely to hospital standards, few get these jobs now. Those that take on nurse training have to live in the nurses quarters, for many a daunting and hostile environment.

The characteristics shown by Aboriginal patients, besides the essential one of being ill, are not held in high regard by the hospital. For instance they have too many visitors, especially ill-disciplined children. They look scared rather than grateful. They lack frilly nightdresses and combs. Some are regular patients suffering from such low-status diseases as alcohol abuse. Not being in the habit of taking out private insurance, they have always suffered from being in the charity category. Faced with many practices which are a normal part of the health service the Aborigines appear to be uncooperative. But the fact that they are uncooperative does not mean that they do not want to be healthy.

I have discussed various ways in which the shire council, the police and the schools are involved in re-creating the racial divide and deflecting any structural change. In many of these institutions 'politics' is seen as the enemy of a unified town and the enemy also of rational assistance to the unfortunate poor. This is especially true in the field of public health where the National Aboriginal and Islander Health Organisation (NAIHO) has been trying to extend its control over Aboriginal health. NAIHO has set up branches of the Aboriginal Medical Service (AMS) in cities and some towns. They are run by Aborigines and employ professionals when needed. The AMS is prefaced on the belief that only by developing a health service independent of the Health Department, that is, by making Aboriginal people aware of and responsible for their own community's health, can advances be made in this field. Health problems are seen as part of a more general political deprivation. I will not discuss here this political philosophy and the long drawn out battles that the organisation has fought to create and extend the AMS to more centres. The struggle has had various effects in Brindleton. Some of the local people have been to NAIHO meetings and been strongly influenced by the ideas and rhetoric of the radical leaders of that movement.

But the government has made some resources available for Aborigines within the government health services in recent years, and there are Aboriginal health workers and Aboriginal alcohol counsellors employed in health centres. Their presence has sometimes caused local dissension. A trained nurse at the Community Health Centre complained that her attempts to assist Aborigines were undermined by politics in the form of the young Aborginal health worker who supported the setting up of an AMS. She asserted that the AMS was not interested in health but only in politics. The assistant, she says, threatened her if she would not let him have the centre's car all the time. She was frightened of him. The assistant on his part accused her of racism, and says she had no respect for him and that she wanted to know what he was doing all the time. Such conflicts at the personal level, even among more moderate and thoughtful people than these two, often become bitter and destructive.

This nurse commented with approval on the other Aboriginal assistant who does not want to be an Aboriginal health worker but rather a community worker. 'She says she does not want to work with those dirty Aborigines', I was told by the white nurse with satisfaction. It seems to her to vindicate her own idea that the Aborigines are difficult and need teaching. Any complaints by Aborigines about other Aborigines are thus siezed on as powerful evidence to support the dominant ideas.

Government spending can sometimes have negative effects on previously operating services. The health centre used to be in a rather dilapidated building, easily accessible from the Aboriginal end of town. It was in regular use five years ago. When two smart new buildings, one housing the medical complex for the doctors' rooms and the other the Community Health Centre, opened about half a mile into the white part of town, use by Aborigines dropped off considerably. Volunteers run some activity groups and the centre's cars are used to take people to and from the hospital. But hardly any one comes to the centre besides a few young white mothers with their babies on Wednesdays. This is not only the result of the move, but also to do with the fact that the dedicated senior nurse had left and the staff since have shown little enthusiasm for their work. For the success of government services in a small town, dedicated and skillful personnel are essential. Those health or welfare services which are highly valued, often depend on one person with particular interest and skill.

The story of the clinic on the reserve is told frequently as evidence that Aborigines bring their problems on themselves. There was a small fibro building (known as the clinic) at which clinics were held regularly by the nurse from the Health Commission. In 1980 the clinics were terminated, and it was some time afterwards that the clinic building was broken into because someone needed medication and believed there might be aspirin inside. Subsequently it was broken into again, and the door was broken and then the windows. The towns people simply know that 'they wrecked their clinic'.

The health services are also personally intrusive, though less directly than those of the police described above. Name and age are constantly required on forms. The old people sometimes do not know their age and for women the registering of infants' names sometimes causes embarrassment. Many Aboriginal women retain their original surname and confer it on their children, but it is automatic for the hospital to record the father's surname as the child's surname. A health commission officer, an old-timer in the field of Aboriginal health, explained to me that the recording of personal information, such as the fathers of 'illegitimate' children, was for future reference because of the possibility of incest now that moieties have broken down and there is much travel and men have wives in several towns. In fact this is a fanciful post-hoc rationalisation of an old practice of monitoring Aboriginal habits, and has nothing to do with the moieties which 'broke down' quite some time ago.

Besides the health and medical services, the poorest Aboriginal families have close association with welfare services, that is, the Department of Youth and Community Services (YACS). Here there is marginally less direct conflict between the welfare officers' practices and Aboriginal forms of interaction, but there is more direct control of those in the most dire straights. Cash grants, rent relief, emergency grants and a setting-up grant for a new tenancy (of about $500), are the main forms of financial assistance available. The district officer has a good deal of discretion, within the department's guidelines, as to how much and how often he will grant relief. In Brindleton people are told they should pay the cash grant back when they can; many believe that they should, and some do. They are given $20 to $30 as against the usual $80 in Sydney, because most of their debts are not very large. However electricity bills of over $100 are a common problem. When blankets were issued recipients were told they would not get another for five years, and that *'We* keep our blankets for twenty years'. Of the 700-800 blankets handed out annually by the Brindleton office, until the programme was terminated in 1987, about 150 went to whites.

The philosophy of the district officer of YACS can clearly be of some significance to the lives of the poor in Brindleton. One such officer believed that money given to those who contribute least to society does no good. They should be made to contribute in some way.

> I try to get people to use their own resources. Lots of whites also have a welfare mentality. Our function is to be educational, to help them survive in the long run. For instance, we won't help with social security payment problems any more. They can make reverse charges calls to that department in Dubbo themselves.

YACS instituted an Aboriginalisation policy in 1983 which consisted of reclassifying the Aboriginal community workers, usually untrained local people recruited intitially for liaison work, into Assistant District Officers. This means that they will now have to make decisions about issuing money and will have authority and obligations under the Child Welfare Act. That is, they will be forced to police truants from school and make court appearances concerning youthful offenders and neglected children. The change was intended to rectify a situation where Aborigines were structured into low-status positions. It was argued that many were invaluable workers who should be rewarded for work which was, after all, at least as useful as that done by those who were more highly qualified in formal terms. Even though the increased repsonsibility is accompanied by increased pay, some do not welcome the change. But the promotion can only be refused at the cost of the job because the position of Aboriginal liaison officer will no longer exist.

For those who live in their own home towns, the more responsible position carries potentially explosive conflicts. The department recognises this problem, and such people may choose to be employed elsewhere. If there is a suitable vacancy, a newly promoted Assistant District Officer may be transferred to another town, presumably where there are other Aborigines. Thus the expertise which was originally valued, of personal familiarity with the town and informal liaison to benefit the Aboriginal community, will be lost. Apparently it is believed that any Aboriginal person can perform similar functions in any Aboriginal community.

There are other institutions which are important to the functioning of the town, but I will finish this account with the comments of an officer of one of them who has remained in Brindleton for longer than usual because she likes the place. Her view is that the lack of initiative in the town is due to the lack of commercial television. She adds:

> The Aboriginal people like to live as they do; slow and easy. Many drop out of the youth employment training schemes. There is no direct racial conflict; everyone knows everyone. If you know them there is no fear. Sometimes they swear at you if they are drunk but mostly they know me and say hello. The stories of violence in other towns is exaggerated for news.

Of a recent news items of an attack by white youths on blacks in another town she says, 'How did they know it was whites fighting blacks? You don't have to be black to be Aboriginal now you know.' Thus this white public servant shows ignorance, stereotyping and insensitivity, under the guise of the reasonable considerations of a kindly human being.

Breaches

The permanent residents of the town are not all represented by the 'dominant culture' discussed above. While the white working class (those who rely on wage labour for their income) shows little systematic or vocal public dissent from the prevailing ideas about Aborigines, it is among this part of the population that many close relationships between black and white people have been formed. There are two reasons why the barriers to interaction are easily breached in this segment of the population. First, familiarity develops through working together, and while the work place may foster notions of racial difference, and rivalry may encourage antagonism, there are also many occasions where common interests prevail. Second, the sense of honour among working-class whites does not depend on the display of propriety evident in the manners, dress and material comfort which is characteristic of the middle class.

For some working-class people, the blacks are fellow sufferers from the snobbery and contempt of those that rule the town. Contrary to the popular notion that the working class displays more racism than the enlightened middle class, it is among the wage labourers that the racial divide is most regularly and intimately breached. This is not to say that hostility towards blacks is not openly expressed by some white workers. In a small town such as Brindleton, class positions are not reflected in sharp social divisions so that wage labourers can, if they wish, share the sports fields and pubs with employers, and share their views also.

There are a number of disadvantages faced by poor whites, particularly welfare recipients, which are the same as those of the blacks. For instance, in the early 1970s, white farm hands who lost their jobs on properties came into town with little education and sometimes with large families. Those of 15 years or over did not enrol at school, but applied for unemployment benefits or tried to find labouring jobs. Illiteracy is entrenched in some such families, though the children now regularly attend school. Illiteracy is not uncommon in the town, even among businessmen. The shame attending illiteracy may be greater for whites among their own circle of friends and relations than it is for Aborigines, simply because it is more common among the latter group.

Whites who have to live on unemployment benefits or pensions, or have been forced to ask for cash hand-outs from YACS, sometimes find their penury does disturb their sense of honour and they feel shame. One woman, who was distressed at having to ask YACS for help, continued to struggle to pay the fees at school. The poor whites are more isolated in their suffering than Aborigines, and for this very reason remain subject to the dominant values. White girls at the technical college who have poor education tend to persevere with their studies longer than the black students. Poor white pensioners deny themselves the use of heaters unless it is *very* cold.

One woman who with her husband ekes out a precarious existence doing contract work for landowners, complained in familiar terms about government hand-outs. However it was assistance to the superior 'cockies' that she objected to. She spoke bitterly about their snobbery. 'The cockies get all the subsidies and their places are run down but they have flash cars and their kids go to boarding school.' She also said that the two Aboriginal men she and her husband employ regularly, both notorious for violence and trouble in the town, are the best workers you could wish for. Thus views other than the dominant ones can be found peeping through the social fabric.

Institutional racism

In highlighting these underlying and sometimes overt conflicts, it is easy to imply that people spend all their time cogitating on the problem of race. But most of the time the divisions and practices are taken for granted. For instance a taxi driver answered my opening conversational query 'How's business?' by saying, 'They get the cheques two days a fortnight now.' He assumed I knew who 'they' were. He explained that 80 per cent of his custom was from Aborigines. There is often no hostility in the usual interaction with familiar shop or taxi customers, but there is embedded inequality which remains unquestioned.

A recent writer on Aborigines and the law has said that 'What was once a matter of welfare is now becoming a matter of rights, exercisable by Aborigines on demand' (Hanks & Keon-Cohen, 1984:xv). There are still limits on the exercise of rights though, which lie in informal social practices. The term institutional racism has been used to refer to the informal ways that institutions reflect particular cultural practices and values, and disallow the expression of others. Examples have been alluded to above, and many more are evident in shops, schools, hospitals and offices. The style of language, dress, manners and many assumptions about what is acceptable and unacceptable behaviour, reinforce the system of authority in the schools which are based on European norms. An infant school teacher's comment that in one class only five children were normal, indicates a narrow and clearly culture-bound notion of normal. She believed that abnormal families had led to some children's abnormally difficult behaviour. The fact that many of the children do not conform easily to the very specific behaviours expected in the classroom does not necessarily indicate a neurotic or psychotic condition. Rather it indicates a contrast with the values and practices in the community which the children come from. Even the kind of attention paid to children is strikingly different in the Aboriginal community from that at the school.

The mothers who work at the school canteen unconsciously treat Aboriginal children in a discriminatory way by saying 'speak up', 'haven't you got a hanky'. They would do the same to a snotty-nosed or mumbling white child. They try to bully them gently into conformity. But it is mainly the Aboriginal children who show these characteristics, and this treatment probably confirms the child's fear or dislike of contact with white people. White kids are conscious of different standards. After an Aboriginal boy had paid 25 cents out of $5 for a chocolate bar, a white boy with 20 cents was told he did not have enough. He said to the canteen lady, 'If I was Aboriginal you'd give it to me.'

Language has many forms, though it is usually thought that all in Brindleton speak the same language. One contrast in language use concerns what is known as swearing. This issue is embedded in the racial division, and clearly demonstrates the complexity and the hypocrisy surrounding the issue of respectability and power. As indicated above, the court often hears language that is held to 'alarm and affront' in certain circumstances. Many complain about drunks swearing in the street. One man explained 'I'm immune to it and the police are immune to it. But if a man swears at a policeman he has a right to be seriously alarmed and affronted.' Perhaps he meant that the police have the power to be seriously alarmed and affronted. Those who do the swearing are obviously affronted too, sometimes because police have been called by the publican to interfere with the clients' social interaction.

In the schools the teachers commonly adopt strategies of ignoring casual swearing, but will not allow or rather will punish abusive swearing, especially if directed at the teacher. However this does not solve the problem. Respectable parents are likely to object. Not all are as philosophical as the woman who said, 'I took the view that it's there and you get used to it. I said to my son you don't have to do it just because you hear it. You can swear when you are bigger than I am. .... It is part of their (Aborigines) life and I don't know if we should teach them any better.' Another parent was angry at the double standards. 'My kid got a slap at school for saying "bloody" and the black kid didn't when he said the big F and the big C.' When the parent complained the teacher said 'I would have thought that you would want your son brought up differently from that kid.' The parent considered this ludicrous. 'Children should not be taught differently because of what they are used to; they should all learn to the same standard. If a thing is wrong it is wrong. Either you leave it all to the parents or you enforce the rules.'

But the high moral ground concerning language is not monopolised by whites. Aborigines are outraged by the use of the swear word 'bleeding' especially when applied to men, as in 'you bleeding prick'. The association with menstruation is seen as unutterably shocking, although in some circles bleeding is a euphemism for bloody. By comparison with 'bleeding', 'the big F and the big C' are commonplace for most Aborigines.

Many people told me, some with approval, that while ten years ago Aboriginal students were shy and hung their heads, many now hold their heads high in defiance and give cheek or hostile comments to whites. Teachers are called 'white cunts' by a minority of Aboriginal students, and many who thought they were there to help the poor disadvantaged Aborgines find it very difficult to retain a professionally sympathetic outlook when subjected to personal abuse.

White views of black family life

It is popularly believed that the family is the institution in our society which forms the foundation of social life. This view is certainly dominant in Brindleton, and many of those who discuss the problem created by Aborigines for whites consider it is family life which is responsible for the supposed depravity of Aboriginal youth. These opinions are based on little information, but are usually offered with an air of authority and confidence and even concern. These 'authorities' on the intimate life of Aboriginal families have often gained their knowledge by seeing them in the street or discussing them in the pub.

It is difficult to convey the chilling effect of everyday comments about 'them' which are constructed in the common sense language of unobjectionable values. For instance the view that 'they have too many kids' leads to the relating, approvingly, the story of one doctor who was reputed to give the women pills or hysterectomies when they were in hospital. I was told 'They like the little kids but when

they are 4 or 5 they ignore them.' Stories embodying family tragedies
are told with a knowing air. One man explained to me 'Violence is a
way of life with them. If father is shouting at his kids all day, and then
he gets really angry he has to do something worse. That's why the
kids get bashed.'

An incident of violent rape was described to me with the same
explanatory aim. 'They said to me "well what would you do if your
woman was going with another man". They don't seem to think of
talking about it or separating.' It is not only that destructive or other
negatively valued behaviour is often seen as peculiarily Aboriginal,
but that the white population see it as their task to explain and proffer
solutions for what they define as Aboriginal problems.

Old and drastic solutions are sometimes recommended. A concerned citizen explained:

The problems have to be solved by taking the children away.
Only 20 per cent of the kids are a problem, but it is their parents
who are responsible. Some are alcoholic or unemployed or
abused, and then there is the high probability, though not a
certainty, that their children will be delinquent. For instance if
you go up to the pictures on Friday night you will see kids of only
7 or 8 bringing their younger brothers and sisters to the pictures
in prams. The parents are probably at parties or in the boozer.
And when the film finishes, sometimes at 12.30 a.m., the kid
wheels the baby off home. Now I ask you what chance has that
kid got? That's the way the kid is going to grow up.

Some popular notions about Aborigines are positive. One policeman
gave the blackfellow credit for letting you know and attacking directly
if he was angry. 'A white guy will tamper with your brakes and kill you
sneakily.' But the fact that whites will defer more readily to police
means they get let off more. 'The blackfellow will challenge you and
act smart when pulled up. Naturally the cop will react badly. Anyway',
he added, 'wogs and ethnics in the cities are just as bad with knives
and guns and there are tribal problems among the Vietnamese.'

A thoughtful citizen with a responsible job in Brindleton told me,
'Those who threaten to shoot people, I don't agree with, because you
don't know who did it, even if you know the families.' He implies that
the anger and punitive action is justified were one to be quite sure of
shooting the right person. We need now to explore further how it is
that such apparently well-socialised and upstanding citizens can hold
such fierce and primitive views.

Chapter 5

Beneath the surface

INTRODUCTION

The previous two chapters have been concerned with mapping out the surface contours of the town. They have been largely descriptive, although throughout attention has been directed to the contradictions and deceptions involved in the popular understanding of what is going on. It should be emphasised that no sense can be made of the racial division if it is seen as static, or as independent of the will of those who make up the town. That is, the people cannot be allocated to neat or discrete groups even according to the categories they use themselves. For instance a number of individual Aborigines are regarded as honorary whites, but only in certain circumstances and by certain whites. Those who say there is no racism in the town have no difficulty in pointing to one or two Aborigines who are accepted members of white organisations, to intermarriages and to particular friendly efforts on the part of whites. And further, some of the most politically active blacks are regarded as 'coconuts' in certain circumstances as we shall see below.

Despite these confusions, there is an intense struggle in progress. The struggle is only articulated by those who see the town as oppressive for Aborgines and who therefore oppose both the incumbents of powerful positions and the ideas they espouse. Some of those who oppose are white and some are black, but there is little unity within or between these groups about the diagnosis of the ills or about the tactics to overcome them. There are temporary groupings formed which take up an issue or form an organisation. At times there emerges some agreement and some clarity about where differences lie. It is the political activity surrounding the more overt forms of struggle which shows the difficulties inherent in fighting such an amorphous entity as a racism which is denied existence not only by those who practice it but also by many of its victims. In this, I would argue, racism is not different from other forms of legitimised structural inequality. That is, I am not using the term racism to refer to prejudice or discrimination shown by individuals. Rather the actual division of the town into two essentially unequal groupings is itself racism. That is, all the processes which perpetuate this inequality, and continue to explain and legitimate the inferior position of one group on the basis of some essential racial difference, can be said to be part of the racist processes.

This chapter will therefore be devoted to examining first what some white people are striving for and what others are resisting concerning the position of Aborigines. Then the blacks' struggle will be discussed. Not everyone is striving to change their society, or to defend the status quo. Various groupings of people are involved in furthering one set of ideas or organisations, and in countering other actions and ideas. Many such activities relate only indirectly to the racial division.

The groupings which cluster around sets of ideas are not tidy and easily identifiable categories of people. There are those who represent extreme and uncompromising positions at the end of the continuum on which I am focussing. There are many others who, while not actively involved in any of these activities, and avoiding comment on them, would, when forced to act or comment, be characterised as belonging to one or another of the groups. Of course the ideological bases of these groupings have been extracted from a mass of ideas which are at once more complex and inconsistent than at first appears to be the case.

I characterise the two sets of ideas as hard-line and soft-line. The hard-line is identified centrally as anti-welfare, while the soft-line recommends better welfare provisions to overcome disadvantage. As well I will discuss do-gooders and stirrers. The latter two terms are popular ones, and as such they are neither very specific nor used quite consistently. However it is quite clear that the terms are powerful and precise in their political implications, and it is the politics of the situation that I am interested in here. Aborigines are included in these groupings, although many would occupy a somewhat distinct ideological position at the heart of what I will call an 'oppositional culture'. While there are other organisations which people devote energy to, such as the tourist promotion group and the historical society, none arouse the emotional intensity that surrounds the efforts related to Aborigines.

Before the description of these groupings is undertaken, it is necessary to discuss some economic misunderstandings which are widely held in Brindleton. Some of these have been mentioned already. Here I shall focus first on one of the most popular and recurrent aspects of complaint about the blacks, welfare spending. After showing that welfare spending is rather more general than is recognised, the rationale and activities of those who support welfare solutions to Aborginal problems will be examined. More radical indigenous Brindleton positions on these questions will then be examined.

ECONOMY AND IDEOLOGY

Welfare and subsidies

Because there is a high level of awareness of government money spent to benefit Aborigines, we need to put that spending in the context of government assistance to other sections of the population. The major social security benefits, such as pensions and unemployment benefits, are the same for all sections of the population. Money targeted to Aboriginal housing, health, and education needs to be contrasted with grants, subsidies, or provision of services to other specially designated groups. Clearly in all cases there are sets of ideas either to do with equity, economy or justice which provide a rationale for spending from the public purse. I simply want to show that there are many sections of the population which benefit from spending of public money. Some such provisions arouse resentment and others do not.

The subsidisation and concessions to the pastoral industry, which have been a fact of Australian economic life for many years, have been regarded as a right rather than a problem. All political parties have supported such subsidies to the rural industry (Encel, 1958). Drought relief and flood relief are available, and in 1983 some graziers were eligible for both at the same time; properties are very large. Subsidies are also available for scrub-cutting to supply feed to stock during drought periods. When in financial difficulties it is possible for landholders to borrow money at 4 per cent interest. Some are reputed to borrow that money and reinvest it at a higher rate. I was told 'Some run their places well but the majority let their places run down so that they can live off the subsidies.' While it is no doubt quite wrong to impute such motives to landholders, it is true that many concessions are available for those who face financial problems. Whether this assistance is of benefit to the wider society economically or in some other way, is beyond my charter to decide.

The pastoral industry is the only really productive industry in the region. For the western division the total cash return from the pastoral industry for 1979-80 was $89.5m, the total cash costs were

$53.8m, leaving a 'farm cash operating surplus' of $35.7m (WLC, 1982:151). A detailed study of the economy in one region in the west shows that in 1969 the pastoral sector produced a total output of $7,354,900; the rural processing sector (meatworks) produced $5,539,700; the next most important was the government sector which produced $1,674,600. Transport and communications was the only other industry worth over one million dollars in output. The manufacturing sector of the economy is the least productive (Harvey, 1976:41-2). While there is a good deal of fluctuation, for instance during the wool crisis that Harvey was analysing, the economic *raison d'être* of towns in the western region is clear from these figures.

The prevailing view is that this level of production deserves support and gratitude in the form of government aid, but there are some who believe that pastoralists have the good fortune to be in a potentially lucrative and high-status industry and therefore are well able to pay for their own needs.

Individual pastoralists vary greatly in their financial worth. Average income earned per farm in the western region in 1980 was $91,717, and average costs were $62,192 (WLC, 1982:18, 20), giving an average net income of $29,525. However this covered a range from negative income to a net income of over $100,000. While 12 per cent of lessees had a net income of over $70,000, 13 per cent had negative incomes and a further 21 per cent had incomes of under $10,000 (ibid., 21). If the latter groups were to leave their properties, they might face having to become welfare dependents. The Western Lands Commission enquiry considered that the current welfare needs of these landholders in terms of health and education services should be improved if they are to remain on the land and accept subsistence standards (ibid., 29). The report does not mention the already generous assistance for the educational needs of rural children. Further subsidy could create another welfare dependent minority. In terms of economic rationality perhaps only larger owners should remain. The financial wisdom of rural subsidies may also be questioned in the light of the debt position of many landholders. The western region in 1970-1 showed the average farm debt to be $38,759, while 35 per cent of the sample had debts of over $60,000 (ibid., 33)

Not all subsidies are direct ones. The infrastructure necessary to the pastoral industry, such as roads and railways, has always been provided by the state or federal governments, as have the police and courts that protect the property of those that have it from others that want it. A substantial amount of time is spent by the shire council in allocating money for rural road maintenance. The more direct financial assistance to landholders, such as low interest loans and drought and flood relief, have been mentioned already. As well, prices for fuel and fertilisers are subsidised, and there are tax concessions for a great many consumer durables such as motor vehicles that the primary producers have managed to have defined as necessary to their productivity. If one is far enough outback there is even a tax concession for isolation. Thus, while governments may not understand the outback, they reward those that live there.

The school of the air, whereby isolated children are schooled at the primary level, is provided free of charge together with equipment such as video monitors. Of course such benefits are not only available to graziers but also to the poorer people in rural areas such as road menders, scrub-cutters and fencers. Some isolated families also have the education of their children at private schools heavily subsidised as we shall see below. These people, who are at the top of the socioeconomic ladder, are not under scrutiny and surveillance and do not attract resentment when they appear the least in need of the government welfare assistance which is supposedly for the deserving poor.

Table 5.1: *Numbers receiving benefits and pensions (one postcode area, total population 3,326)*

Date	Unemploy- ment benefit	Sickness & special benefits	Age & invalid pension	Widows & supporting par. pension	Family Allowance fam.	chn.
Jan. 80	169	18	373*	93		
Jan. 81	166	41	371*	117		
Jan. 82	197	47	376**	143	737	1,607
Jan. 83	310	38				

* These figures are for August.
** This figure is for October.
Source: Department of Social Security.

Besides the assistance given to the pastoral industry, the government gives direct support to people who cannot sell their labour, to enable them to live. The level of dependence on social security payments is high in Brindleton.

The January 1983 unemployment benefits and special benefits plus the October and January 1982 pensions gives 867 recipients. Thus 37.5 per cent of those over 15 years old depend on the Department of Social Security for their income either through unemployment or sickness benefits or from aged, invalid, widow or supporting parent's pensions.

The 1981 Census showed 1,330 employed, 159 unemployed and 823 adults not in the labour force. My own research indicates considerable slippage between the latter two categories. My figure of 1,119 employed in 1983-4 (Table 3.3) may indicate a fall of over 200 since 1981 in the number of jobs in the town. The rise of 113 in the number of people receiving unemployment benefits between 1982 and 1983 (Table 5.1), is partly attributable to the increased number of Aborigines who have registered to receive the benefit. It is also relevant that 88 per cent of the women registered want sales or clerical jobs and 75 per cent of the men registered want labouring or farm work.

It is clear from various sources of information that the proportion of families depending on welfare payments for their income is very high among Aborigines. In my experience virtually all on the reserve and the majority at the Aboriginal end of town do not have jobs but rely on the income of those members of the family who receive pensions or unemployment benefits. It is very common for no one in a large household to be in regular paid employment. Many unemployed Aborigines are not

Table 5.2: *Housing in Brindleton*

	No. of households	No. of persons*	Residents per dwelling
Purchaser/ owner	435	1,408	3.2
Housing Commision tenant	125	467	3.7
Other tenant	278	1,006	3.6
Total tenant	403	1,473	
Total	838**	2,881	

* 223 persons not in private dwellings.
** 60 households; no existing information.
Source: 1981 Census.

registered with the Commonwealth Employment Service.

Along with the high level of dependence on social security, comes dependence on public housing. Fifty-two per cent of households are owner purchasers, 15 per cent rent from the housing commission and another 33 per cent rent from others. The latter figure includes the Aboriginal Housing Cooperative, other government departments and private firms. The 48 per cent of people in rented accommodation show a higher residency rate, though this is a disparate category consisting of accommodation owned by government departments or by private firms for their employees, as well as a substantial number of dwellings which are rented from the housing cooperative, from the housing commission, the Land Council or privately.

There is a high level of government spending in Brindleton. On the one hand industry is subsidised, and on the other hand a minimal income is provided for those who have no paid work. Other spending on health and education is supposedly for the benefit of allcomers. However there are significant inequities to be found in the sphere of education spending. The most striking is the public perception of the subsidies which are available to markedly different socioeconomic groups.

ASG and AIC

The Aboriginal Secondary Grant (ASG) was discussed above in the context of the school, but it is also a well known and particular source

Table 5.3: *Aboriginal Secondary Grants (1983 figures)*

	Book & clothing allowance	Living allowance	Student allowance
Fortnight (during term)			
Junior		$ 17.00	$ 3.00
Senior		$ 24.41	$ 6.00
Annual			
Junior	$ 330.00	$374.00	$ 66.00
Senior	$ 400.00	$537.00	$132.00
Total annual allowance			
Junior	$ 770.00		
Senior	$1069.00		

Source: Commonwealth Education Dept.

of comment in the town. 'They get paid to go to school you know' is a frequently repeated piece of information. The ASG is the only direct government allowance to which Aborigines are entitled and others are not. This is a cash grant available since 1970 to all Aboriginal secondary school students without means testing (Watts, 1982:19). These students are not required to pay school fees, fees for excursions or for equipment. There is no assistance provided for primary-school children on the basis of their being Aboriginal.

Another kind of educational grant which benefits students in the district is the Assistance for Isolated Children (AIC) provided on the basis of distance from the nearest school or transport to school.

Table 5.4: *AIC annual allowances (1983 figures)*

	Basic allowance*	Max. additional allowance*
Primary	$866	$1066
Junior Secondary	$866	$1266
Senior Secondary	$866	$1537

* Basic allowance is not means tested: additional allowance is, and is awarded proportional to income.

There is free travel by rail (unlimited) or coach (3 return trips a year), provided by the state government to any student at boarding school. Both Aboriginal and isolated children are eligible for this free travel.

According to figures from the Commonwealth Education Department, the total number of students in all of NSW receiving the ASG in 1983 was 6,558 of whom under 200 were at boarding school. The total number of students receiving the basic AIC boarding allowance in 1983 in NSW was 4,355. There were 1,408 receiving additional allowances. There were 1,138 at special schools, and so not eligible for further assistance. That is, 44 per cent of those eligible in all of NSW get an additional allowance. Given the number of low farm incomes in the western division, we can presume that the proportion is considerably higher in the west. Fifty-four per cent or 2,838 of AIC beneficiaries are primary producers. Again, the proportion would be considerably higher in the west.

The Isolated Children's Parents' Association (ICPA), which secured these benefits, was founded the year after the Aboriginal Secondary Grants were instituted. It is one of the most vocal and public pressure groups in the far west, and also must surely be one of the most effective. The members lobby the local member and ministers by letter, phone and deputation with facts, figures and pleas that country children should not suffer because of the rural recession, drought or flood. They have mounted elaborate annual conferences in Perth, Alice Springs, Darwin and other centres since their inauguration in 1971, and have gained support in every state. Their activities are widely reported on in the country press, and they produce a glossy journal called *Pedals* detailing their successes. These include the gaining of extensive government subsidy of private boarding-school fees, as well as a second home allowance and correspondence allowance. The ICPAs activities parallel and compliment those of the Livestock and Grain Producers Association (LGPA). A grazier explained to me that the ICPA had been very good for the wives. They had enjoyed the involvement and had learned new organisational skills and gained confidence. It was a western NSW branch of the LGPA which spawned the ICPA when there was a threat that a country high school hostel would be closed at the end of 1970.

The minimum amount of money involved per isolated child of any age is between the junior and senior Aboriginal secondary student's maximum allowance. The basic AIC allowance of $866 is not means tested. Many graziers seem to regularly achieve a low taxable income so would receive additional assistance. Some of those who get additional assistance pay more in educational fees than they declare as disposable income for purposes of taxation!

A rough calculation in one area in western NSW shows that 95 Aboriginal children in the town receive about $85,500 in educational assistance, whereas 62 isolated children who are boarding away receive about $90,000. There are in addition about 25 Aboriginal students at boarding school who receive similar support at the highest level of isolated children's funding. Including those, we give the figures for one district in Table 5.5.

The fact that most of the Aborigines' money stays in the town should be an important consideration in the way these subsidies are viewed locally, considering the sensitivities of the shopkeepers and the number of times a dollar is said to turn over in the town. However this appears not to be taken into account. Since 1983 it has been made

Table 5.5: *Estimate of education allowance paid in one district in 1983**

	Isolated children	Aboriginal children
Number	62	120
Total subsidies	$89,900.00	$104,490.00
Per child	$ 1,450.00	$ 870.70

*The calculation cannot be exact as no breakdown was available giving the number of isolated children in each category or the extent of their additional allowances. A conservative average estimate of $584 has been used.

more difficult to gain a boarding allowance for Aboriginal students, and in 1985 fewer were away at boarding school. Without full support there is no possibility of such students going away and this means that many receive little secondary schooling. Thus the spending on Aboriginal education is being reduced whereas the most recent Commonwealth budget (1986) has considerably extended the isolated children's allowance.

In the late 1960s, the Commonwealth Education Department built a hostel in Brindleton so that isolated children could board there and attend the local high school. The LGPA had lobbied for its inception. It was argued that the cost to the Education Department would be set-off against considerable savings on the boarding subsidy and travel expenses. Country students could go home more often. Potentially the standard of the local high school would improve through the demands and ambitions of grazier parents, although this was not part of the grazier's argument for establishing the hostel. None of these advantages seem to have been sufficiently weighty to ensure the hostel's survival. A few students boarded there during its first year of operation, fewer the second and it is now closed. The parents claim that the supervision at the hostel left a lot to be desired. But it is also true that the costs to parents are really not very different from expensive city schools given the fact that the government subsidises the latter. Finally there is the conviction that the local state school cannot possibly provide as good an education as the high-status private boarding school. In terms of what many of these parents expect from the 'hidden curriculum', this is no doubt true.

It should also be mentioned that all students in the more remote schools receive some educational subsidies to counter the effects of isolation. Sixty per cent of school pupil's excursion fees are paid for them; a radio station is provided which is partly for educational purposes; a remedial reading centre is funded in the same way.

The Aboriginal Secondary Grant does create some problems for the teachers in schools. Besides some white parents refusing to pay fees because Aborigines do not have to, there are the conflicts among the students. Sometimes white children have trouble getting money for excursions or equipment, while Aboriginal children do not want to go on an excursion or make use of the equipment. Some teachers find this situation intolerable and many talk of this as part of the Aboriginal problem. Aboriginal kids, it is asserted, become irresponsible, ordering the most expensive material for their woodwork class and losing the books which are supplied to them. Furthermore they are aware of their privileged position, and some take advantage of it by demanding as much as they can. The irresponsibility which the policy is alleged to encourage is supposedly illustrated in the story of a secondary-school white boy in the industrial arts class, who had saved over a considerable period $35 for drawing implements. When he came to the teacher to get them an Aboriginal boy said 'Sir I want those too.' The teacher claimed he was obliged to provide this boy with the same equipment because of this sudden whim. Teachers can buy the most expensive fabrics for the Aboriginal girl's sewing while the others must be thrifty with their parent's money. Further, given that Aboriginal students get a book and clothing grant, should the teachers demand that they are provided with these things and punish them if they do not have them?

There is another problem created by the grants to Aboriginal students and that is the decision about who is eligible. Each year in most NSW towns there have been a number of applicants whose eligibility has been disputed either by someone in the Aboriginal community or by the education officer or assistant. When this occurs applicants are asked to provide evidence that they are Aboriginal by producing a statement from an Aboriginal organisation that they are accepted as a member of the community. They must also make a declaration that they consider themselves to be Aboriginal. I do not know how the descent criterion is policed. (see pp.108–11 above)

It is the first criterion which is often difficult to fulfil because the individual concerned may have been fostered, or adopted or have obediently assimilated in an earlier era. Often the local Department of Education officers deal with the disputed cases which come to their notice because of complaints from Aborigines in the town. These days the final arbiter of who is eligible is an Aboriginal bureaucrat.

'Everyone has the right to an education.' Such rhetoric is common to the ICPA and the Aboriginal Education Consultative Group (AECG). Their political styles in achieving educational assistance are very different, but the fact that they are in some sense in competition is recogised by the ICPA. However local knowledge of and reaction to 'welfare' provisions for Aborigines contrasts markedly with the lack of concern about the 'subsidies' for isolated children. The stigma attached to welfare dependence is markedly absent from government assistance to those who have the most authoritative voices in the rural community.

Hard-line resentment

One of the negative effects of the enlightenment policies which is very apparent in Brindleton is the resentment aroused among whites. Welfare dependence is a more apparent and accepted part of Aboriginal life than for any group within the white population. But for the white population welfare policies are a major source of complaint. There are many exaggerated stories of government handouts to Aborigines. It is widely believed that Aborigines get more than others and have money available for anything they want.

Few of course know the details of government schemes, and this ignorance allows hard-line views to thrive. An Aboriginal family moving into a new house, a new car with a black driver, a woman from the reserve buying new clothes for her family or black youths spending money at a disco are all commented on as indications of 'our taxes' being wasted. It is asserted that if they are handed it on a platter they won't appreciate it. Some of the comment is hostile and vicious, made in ignorance of the source of the house or car. Some houses are from the usual housing commission source, and the car may be associated with health commission business. Of course were the sources of funds known, many whites would still not approve. But ignorance allows the situation to be seen as due to crazy government misapprehension of the Aboriginal problem. The better informed also disapprove of much of the government spending on the grounds that if people are provided for without having to work they will become irresponsible. There are many stories which seem to support such views.

Perhaps the best known and the saddest is to do with the destruction of houses. A stranger in many country towns will be regaled with stories of 'brand new' houses that have been given to Aborigines and within months have been wrecked. The older stories of the floorboards being taken up and burned are being replaced with tales of broken fibro walls, smashed windows and torn fly screens. These events are related as if they represented a common occurrence and as if the destruction was due to some intrinsic characteristic of Aborigines. It is true that some houses provided for Aborigines have been damaged irretrievably, and others superficially, but the reasons are at once more complex and more understandable.

The reason why some wood from houses was used as firewood is that there appeared no other way to provide for heating and cooking. For many Aborigines, moving into a house was a sudden and unprepared change from a lifetime in a dirt-floored shack with no electricity, gas, or even running water, and where cooking had always been done outside on an open fire. The knowledge of how to use a gas stove, let alone what to do when a fuse blew or the toilet blocked, was quite absent. A story I was told twice with quite different emphases illustrates this. One story teller said 'Listen you wouldn't credit how stupid they are. They try to heat the bath water by putting the electric heater in it.' The other said 'Do you realise that people are put into houses with no information provided on how to use the appliances. One woman nearly electrocuted herself trying to heat the bath water with the electric heater.'

This lack of experience with what are called 'normal' houses has other implications. Children have to be trained to treat cheap furniture, fibro walls and flimsy sliding windows with some care, not to put things down the toilet bowl and to be wary of the dangers of gas and electricity. Indulgent child-rearing practices make such training difficult to achieve quickly. The sudden change of lifestyle from the free and communal environment of the reserve where much of the time was spent outdoors, to the neat, restricted, overcrowded and nuclear-family-centred house has been traumatic for many. There are reasons other than lack of knowledge which have occasionally led to damage, such as when a woman was hospitalised the day her large family moved into a house. But much of what whites consider damage, such as torn fly screens, discoloured walls or loose guttering, is not considered damage by the residents.

Many whites are convinced that Aborgines are not economically deprived. One public servant described to me a man he said was in clover with a weekly income of $140 from social services. He paid a low rental and needed no car or other such expensive possessions. Being Aboriginal he was said not to want the usual consumer goods.

In fact he had a wife and three children. The public servant pretended to envy this man who, he said, was free of economic worries.

The level of consumption is considered an index of wealth, and Aborigines are sometimes conspicuous consumers, albeit only of alcohol, taxi rides or school tuck-shop fare. Stories about the amount of cash that Aboriginal children have at school are repeated with much moral outrage. The white child with her thrifty 50 cents is contrasted with the profligacy of the black child's $5 note spent in the school canteen. 'They all got $100 each this week' I was told, when black youths were seen spending money at a disco. This cash spending is taken to mean that they are not poor for if they were they would not 'waste' their money. Such convictions are central to the beliefs of whites in Brindleton.

Were the edicts of those who rail against the provision of something-for-nothing followed, the bulk of the Aboriginal population would still be living on the reserve without running water and without jobs to earn the money which supposedly enables others to rent or buy a house. The implication of hard-line views may thus appear the antithesis of the DAA policy of providing houses for Aborigines. But the most important difference between the hard-line and the DAAs soft-line, is that the latter has the resources and power to implement its views. The insistance by DAA that no houses were to be constructed on the reserve has, I would argue, been a new form of destructiveness. Had the reserve community been supported, Aboriginal identity would not be so threatened in Brindleton.

THE PLIGHT OF THOSE WHO HELP

Hard-line and soft-line

I have discussed the objection expressed often in Brindleton concerning assistance to Aborigines, and have described the hard-line views which involve hostility towards Aborigines in general. There is another set of ideas which I will call the soft-line, held mainly by those in the so-called helping professions, usually blow-ins, many of whom are involved directly with Aborigines. Some of the town's older residents also take a soft-line on Aboriginal issues, but their views are seldom heard. The soft-line begins from a different set of ideas about society, one of which is a belief in the essential equality of human kind which leads to the acceptance of the validity and necessity of welfare provisions for the poor. However the soft-line of thought shares certain characteristics with the hard-line and the common elements will be disussed first.

Ideas about Aborigines expressed by both are in the form of complaints. The hard-line violently opposes any special provisions for Aborigines unless they be harsher ones. People speak with anger and resentment at vast cash hand-outs to those good-for-nothings who spend it on booze. Those who follow the soft-line would like to see humane solutions to the Aborigines' problems which they define as largely to do with material deprivation. They say the government would be wiser to provide work than to create a welfare-dependent minority. Thus while the hard-line sees Aborigines as problems, the soft-line sees them as having problems. Both blame the victim and would focus change on the Aborigines themselves. That is, while the hard-line recommends bludgeoning them into changing their habits, the soft-line would help them to do so.

Both sets of ideas share a range of explanations for Aborigines' behaviour. One that is common appeals to tribal or geographical rivalries as the cause of hostility. Thus fights are said to occur because the people from elsewhere are in town. Alternatively it is said to be old tribal enmities that are at the basis of conflicts among Aborigines. The trouble with such explanations is that they are myths. That is, they are repeated and called upon in many circumstances and in the absence of any first-hand evidence to support them. Some fights may indeed be the results of old enmities or conflicts born of different geographical loyalties. But neither tribal differences nor living in different places can actually explain destructive hostility. Such 'explanations' are repeated, not because of their accuracy, but because they give the impression that there is an explanation known to those who are *au fait* with Aborigines in the town. For many people who take little interest in the town's problems unless they are directly affected, such popular notions are convenient.

Another article of faith common to both hard- and soft-line views is that there is no racism in town. The soft-line taken by a woman who has lived in Brindleton for about 15 years, and has a responsible job which entails regular contact with some Aborigines, shows the kind of reasoning entailed in denying that racism exists.

In Brindleton there are distinctions but when something is wrong in town they all pull together. You don't get that in the cities. OK, there are some people who won't go into the pub where there are too many black people, but that is freedom of choice. I don't look on it as a distinction. There are a lot of people I would not invite into my home, black or white. I have had, and will have, black people in here. But there are a lot I don't associate with because of a class distinction. I don't know them and I never come across them. It's not a racial distinction. There is hostility . . . yes, but it is more of a traditional thing, among the older residents who have brought up their children that way. If they knew a lot of them (Aborigines) I don't think it would be as bad. The itinerants seem to get on alright. They accept what is there, except that they get very very hostile over the vandalism and I don't blame them. The drink and the vandalism causes most problems because you can't go away and leave your home. It is not directed towards a particular person. I think it just boils down to lack of parental control among the younger Aboriginal children . . .

If you want to know what it's like living down the other end of town and be confronted with the Aborigines drinking and throwing fire bombs and everything, you need to talk to a resident down there. Apart from a wild party or two we don't know what it is like. You can't blame them for being bitter. I don't like the concept that you go down to the supermarket and they are sitting outside drunk. They never say anything to me but you don't know that they wouldn't. The same thing might happen if a white was sitting there drinking too. In Sydney you see whites drunk in public. But if you face the facts it is the Aboriginals that cause most of the problems.

The Aboriginal organisations seem to be educating some of them but is it to what they want or what we want? The housing is alienating some Aborigines from others by living up town.

Such reasonableness and the desire to see a solution is a characteric of many soft-line views. There is no recognition of the past and present structured inequality, or of historical and cultural differences. Everybody is equal now, but the behaviour of some is still not right. Racism, rather than being a dimension of the towns existence, is reduced to a few individual's traditional attitudes. There is no appreciation of the way power and wealth have accumulated in the hands of whites only, and that it is those whites whose values are supposed to be adhered to by all. There is no recognition that perhaps the blacks adhere to another system of values, and recognise an ongoing injustice which creates bitterness and anger.

Soft-line complaints are about the same behaviour as that of the hard-line. Repetition of stories of Aborigines' supposed depravity is a rich and never-ending source of social comment in a town which, until very recently, depended largely on self-generated entertainment. Videos are now common.

It is difficult for those who take a soft-line not to be drawn into the discussion of the vandalism or drunkenness of Aborigines. They cannot deny that the latest break-in occurred. They cannot but be aware of drunks and the few cheeky children. It becomes a problem therefore to defend all Aborigines from the hard-line attack. Many opt for remaining silent or joining in the complaints, because to defend or even try to explain the behaviour complained of puts one under suspicion of condoning it.

But the soft-line is characterised by the support of moves to improve the lot of the Aborigines, and some are involved in achieving this. Some teachers cooperate in providing a homework centre for the high-school children because one reason they do not do homework is that there is nowhere at home to work. The youth workers' aim is to provide activities for the young people to reduce boredom by giving them something to do. There is a sewing circle where a kindly white woman uses the classic schoolroom style to teach a group of Aboriginal woman to sew. The churches in various ways also try to provide some entertainment and to help Aborigines to overcome those habits which annoy the white population so much. As discussed above, several government departments are engaged in the same kind of helping role.

Despite the good intentions behind this activity, there is little change observed. The homework centre is poorly attended. The same few women come to the sewing class to use the machines and for the company. They are already 'assimilated'. The churches find that the services they provide are accepted without creating any groundswell of change. A doctor in western NSW who saw himself as a 'change agent', and worked very hard at helping Aboriginal organisations for their own betterment, had some success but also considerable frustration, and in the end went on his way without fundamentally altering the situation of racial inequality (Kamien, 1978).

The history of the homework centre provides an example of the dilemma facing those who help. The fact that many Aboriginal students do not do their homework was raised at a meeting between teachers and the Aboriginal Education Consultative Group. The crowded home conditions, often lacking a table or a quiet place, and disturbances from others, were cited as causes for the lack of attention to homework. The homework centre was set up. Funding was available to pay teachers as tutors for those on the grant and to provide some equipment. In Brindleton in 1983, five teachers and the Aboriginal Teachers Aids volunteered to be part of the scheme and attended regularly.

At first the centre was held at the Aboriginal end of town in the hall. However it was found that other children came without work to do and disrupted the group. Students began to turn up late without work and, as time went by, few attended. It was decided to hold the centre in a newly opened community house which was a long way from the Aboriginal end of town and necessitated a bus being provided. After the novelty of the bus ride wore off, attendance dropped to two or three regulars, and the teachers felt that their efforts were in vain. Neither the teachers nor the ATAs could really explain the lack of interest the students showed in their own educational advancement. It was an embarrassment to the ATAs, and they were left bemoaning the laziness or the ingratitude of both the students and their parents.

There are a number of reasons for the lack of success of such enterprises. In the case of the homework centre, any parent knows that coercion is often necessary if homework is to be completed. While the lack of good conditions explains why virtually no Aboriginal students do their homework, it is naive to suggest that they will leap at the opportunity to do it if given the right conditions. Educational disadvantage could be expected to include a widespread dislike of educational institutions, and even of teachers. A scheme by which TAFE provided teachers for older Aborigines who needed literacy skill foundered partly for the same reasons; the young men and women felt uncomfortable with the teachers they had complained about for so many years.

But those who would do good have a more general problem. The very definition of Aborigines' problems, no matter how sympathetic, are not based on a close and continuing knowledge of Aboriginal aspirations and desires. The lack of personal interaction makes this inevitable. Despite the familiar sight of Aborigines around the town, most whites have virtually no personal, domestic or social familiarity with blacks. Thus those few whites who support the Aborigines find themselves providing patronage or charity rather than comradeship and support. They teach the more ambitious blacks how to deal with the bureaucracies rather than offer their services to independent black initiatives. A consequence of this personal separation of blacks and whites is that the common sense notions promulgated by whites are not challenged by black common sense notions born of their experiences of the racial divide. One essential component of black common sense is suspicion of whites' motives for helping and sometimes outright hostility to patronage.

Those Aborigines who are employed as ATAs and in other jobs as go-betweens, are often least representative of the main Aboriginal community. They are confident enough, and perhaps personally ambitious enough, to work in an alien environment. They would already be less inclined to avoid whites than many other blacks. In trying to do their jobs well they are likely to face conflicts with other Aborigines. They have to be tactful. It would be hard for an ATA to explain to a white teacher that many blacks heartily dislike all teachers and even laugh at them. The ATAs increasingly lose sympathy with the students who are nervous of white teachers or who disrupt the homework centre. Thus they are put at odds with those they are employed to represent.

Of course these are not the reasons alluded to by most of those who help Aborigines. More common is the tendency to blame Aborigines for not taking advantage of the opportunities being offered. One young professional blow-in assured me that what was wrong with the Aboriginal organisations is the people in charge of them. In his view the more ambitious or noisy rather than the selfless dedicated people run such organisations. He asserted that Aborigines have power now, in that they can veto school appointments in schools with large Aboriginal numbers (cf.p.185 fn.). In this view Aborigines are not really as badly off as we might think, and anyway their problems are their own fault for not choosing the best leaders, or for some other lack of good sense.

Do-gooders and doing good

It is ironic that do-gooding is so different from doing good. It should be understood that the term 'do-gooder' is commonly used to refer in a derogatory fashion to those who are trying to do good. While the term implies that they are not succeeding, it is significant that the very notion of trying to do good for Aborigines is considered laughable from a hard-line point of view, and regarded with sorrowful regret by those who take a soft-line and believe they know better. The young helpful builders described above (p.141) are the classic referents for the definition of the do-gooder. One function of the term is to indicate the silliness of certain views of Aborigines. It also indicates a breach in white solidarity. That is, it has gained currency as a warning against simple-minded kindness towards what the experienced and practical people see as an intractable problem.

The health inspector of Brindleton greeted my entrance to his office by saying, 'More do-gooding buggers. They don't get anywhere; nothing changes. Aborigines keep their own yards clean by throwing the garbage over the fence into the neighbours.' I had not expressed an interest in Aborigines but, as he considered himself an expert, I enquired as to his view of the situation. 'Close the reserve and build them decent houses in town and tell them to look after them and keep them clean or leave. Conform or get out. Should say the same to migrants.' I had been told this man was a character, a bit of an extremist but no fool. Those who wish to assist Aborigines must constantly run the gauntlet of similar hard-line sentiments in Brindleton.

I want to depict the plight of people who would like to do good. The term do-gooder is used here not only as a convenient short-hand, but because the irony of the term is a useful clue to the irony of the situation. The do-gooder is characterised by the conviction that he or she can help the Aborigines either by speaking or acting for them. Doctors, health workers, school teachers or officers in the government departments such as Youth and Community Services, may be do-gooders. Not everyone in these jobs is included. Many do not publicly identify themselves as especially interested in Aborigines, and remain quite separate from the Aboriginal organisations. Such people may be cynical or sympathetic but evince an impersonal and apparently objective attitude.

One aspect of the do-gooder's plight is that they confront mockery, and feel compelled to defend the Aborigines against denigrating comments. The most common defence consists of explaining the reasons for behaviour which others complain of. Defending the Aboriginal Secondary Grant is another common task. Thus do-gooders will explain at somewhat tedious length that the bad behaviour is caused by certain bad experiences; that drinking and petty crime are the result of boredom and depression; that the Aborigines should be helped to overcome feelings of inadequacy and low self-esteem and that the grant (the ASG) is one element in the solution. It is a matter of environment which interventions by the state and other organisations can remedy. The agency for change is always aligned with the dominant society.

It may be that some do-gooders do not consider the ASG the best form of aid to educationally deprived Aborigines. But to say so would put one in the company of those for whom 'the grant' is the epitome of what is wrong both with Aborigines and with the government. Thus because the battle lines are crudely drawn, those with sympathy for Aborigines feel forced to defend and support government initiatives also. Faced with a particular issue people will appear either pro- or anti-Aborigines. Issues which arise may not be important in themselves, but many feel forced to take sides in a battle which is being fought on grounds already laid down. The outsiders cannot call a truce. They are drawn into making tactical judgements and considering the effect of their actions in all their complexity. Mostly they are from urban environments, and thus more accustomed to discussing social conflicts than facing the consequences of real disagreements over political or social priorities. Some become so aware of the hostility generated among whites by positive action by or on behalf of Aborigines, that they come to believe it better not to act at all. Others are more conscious of the discord and mistrust among the black community, and for this reason lose faith in the possibility of doing good.

The resentment described above cannot be reversed with arguments pointing out long-term objectives, or explaining the difference between social forces and the individuals affected by them, or by describing the historical basis of cultural difference. Some do-gooders dismiss the townspeople as racists. But older residents who take a hard-line, harken back to the old days when there were none of these problems about the Aborigines, that is, the days before governments were providing services for Aborigines. There was employment available then, and exploitation. To many of these people welfare benefits have created the current problems. Their knowledge of the town's history cannot be countered by a school teacher or a social worker telling them of the injustices Aborigines experienced in the past.

A telling example of the do-gooder's plight is provided by staff of the Community Youth Support Scheme in Brindleton. CYSS consists of a small house which is, through commonwealth government funding, staffed with a project officer and a secretary. Such centres were set up when the extent of youth unemployment began to alarm government welfare bodies. They were intended to provide some training for young people. In most towns, the CYSS is attended by a group of unemployed young people who become identified with the centre. In Brindleton this group is almost entirely composed of young Aborigines. The social workers who come to town to work in the CYSS spend most of their time with their young Aboriginal clients. At a social event, or even at the pub or the shops, they will often be made aware of the townspeople's attitudes to their job. Such people usually begin to isolate themselves from white townspeople.

The difficulties such people face from being caught up in situations fraught with ambiguity and contradictions lead to intense relationships developing between those engaged in the same kind of endeavour. Those who take seriously the possibility of assisting Aborigines, or redressing the hostility of the majority, are thrown together. The same people will be involved in various committees and will know the same Aborigines who are involved in such groups as the housing cooperative, the education group or in equivalent organisations in the health or welfare field. For the three years of their residence in the town, a number of blow-ins live constantly in an embattled situation, and spend their time expressing outrage at the racist whites and encouraging the active blacks. Many are concerned about the day to day injustice and expressions of hostility towards Aborigines. But they are also aware that solutions are not easy to envisage.

The lack of close personal relations between the black and white populations leads to these do-gooders relying on a few Aboriginal comrades as their source of Aboriginal opinion. But these people's views have usually been nurtured in the context of the particular enterprise that is being developed, and often their first naive and radical aspirations come to be expressed in terms that are understood and seen as reasonable by their patrons and intermediaries. The art of the possible is introduced very early, and these active Aborigines begin to explain to their fellows what has been explained to them by their white patrons. This process reflects the real limitations of the enlightenment policies, and tends to alienate anyone trying to implement them from the black community. But if the Aborigines in this situation refuse to follow the advice of their patrons, it is likely that little will be achieved in the short term although, as was the case in the document affair, this depends on what is considered an achievement.

An associated occupational hazard for the do-gooder is martyrdom. Working for Aborigines does not necessarily earn gratitude. Such activity can attract the epithet 'blackfella lover' from the very blacks they are reputed to love. One such person would often spend several hours before a meeting carefully informing, encouraging and transporting people 'for their own good' to discuss something 'of great importance to their own and their children's future.' He would explain in detail to them beforehand what was going to happen. Often he would have to explain again afterwards why things did not go as planned. In conversation with me this man often told me who were the good people, meaning those who would work hard to attain the objectives about which it was assumed all were agreed. I do not wish to imply that he was insensitive to Aboriginal wishes. He listened to what people had to say, and understood the reluctance of some to cooperate, the lack of confidence of others, and the rivalries and frustrations which made many Aborigines less than enthusiastic. However he never doubted that education — leading to good jobs and higher status — was the key to any improvement for Aborigines. As we shall see below these priorities entail a number of problems. They may not accord with either Aboriginal aspirations or future job prospects. This man also never doubted that the town whites were the enemy, and that the organisations and intitiatives he worked so hard to develop were the right ones.

His weakness though was the need for some kind of recognition of his efforts. Among Aborigines he was careful not to create personal dependence, and deliberately underplayed his own role, though to me he once claimed to have 'created' one of the Aborigines who was active on committees. While many Aborigines did value his efforts greatly, one young woman liked to point out that he was well paid, and after all that was why he did the job. He was vulnerable to slights and wanted those other involved whites to see him as the expert, the one who knew what was really going on. The intense personal involvement of this individual in what is essentially a struggle for others, highlights the inherent tension in the situation of an outsider implementing a policy intended to benefit a community.

The hardening process

As mentioned above, many of the blow-ins who take a soft-line on welfare questions do not become do-gooders. Instead they distance themselves from the issues by adopting the objectified and homogenised view of the Aboriginal population which is general in the town. This process can be observed in the resocialisation that occurs when new residents arrive. A young school teacher will arrive for a first teaching job feeling enlightened sympathy for the Aborigines, who are seen as victims of the ignorant racism of country people. The teacher is disgusted with the one or two older hard-bitten colleagues who have become cynical and make snide jokes about some of their 'coloured friends'. Such people seem to be the cause of the Aborigine's problems. She is friendly towards the Aboriginal kids, and shows understanding of their problems. But while some of the children respond, others remain shy to the point of apathy, and one may show harsh defiance. She begins to dread having to take the lowest stream, the 'D' level class, which is mostly composed of Aborigines and which is renowned as difficult to control. The senior staff are reassuring. 'Just keep them reasonably quiet' they say. 'It's not your fault.' The implication that it is the kids' fault is one the young teacher prefers to feeling inadequate. Then she is regaled in the staff room with stories of the depravity of an Aboriginal parent. She has seen drunk Aborigines in the town. A redefinition of the problem is occurring.

The *coup de grâce* is achieved when the new teacher's car is scratched, the flat is broken into when she is away or she is called a white cunt by a boy she has been trying to help. The focus of the problem comes to be not racism, but the Aboriginal problem. In common with others, she begins to believe that problems are created for her by an intractable black population. In this way adherence to orthodox views is achieved.

The dominant ideology of the town is effectively enforced in the main by informal pressures to align with the orthodox opinions. But the consensus is always under threat from outsiders. It is well known that the city people believe that the town is a racist one so, when Aborigines publicly deny that racism exists, much is made of the event. A story told with great relish concerns a young traveller who came into the bowling club. He said to the one black woman who was playing the poker machines, 'What have these white bastards been doing to your people lately.' She said 'It's them whites that haven't got rights. We get everything now.' The story is repeated often in an attempt to show that even some who profit from the situation can see the injustice of blacks being favoured. The naivety and inexperience of outsiders who 'haven't lived with them' is also being illustrated. Perhaps this is a sufficient explanation of why some blacks are accepted for club membership.

Contradictions are recognised even by children. One of the more dedicated anti-racists, a blow-in, spent time trying to explain to her primary-school daughter about the family difficulties the Aboriginal children faced. One day the girl revealed that an Aboriginal child had been tormenting her physically for some time. The mother said 'Why didn't you tell the teacher?' The little girl replied with a touch of self-satisfaction, 'But you told me they do things like that because their parents are poor and they don't get enough to eat. I didn't want to get him into trouble.' The white man's burden is learned early in Brindleton!

I have tried to show that, contrary to some of the more naive but very widespread notions in our society about Aboriginal disadvantage, it is not simply prejudice which creates problems for Aborigines. Many with goodwill are inveigled into joining the ranks of those who bemoan the behaviour of the blacks. This is partly because they have no other way of understanding the conflicts which confront them. Resisting the dominant view would invite enmity and anger, and involve fighting entrenched interests and accepted priorities. The purveyors of the new enlightenment theories are struggling in the pool of their own middle-class mores. The modern notions of equality of opportunity, individuality of aspiration and even a limited cultural relativism, are asserted against those, both black and white, for whom such notions are foreign or socialist.

How can the point of view of a young welfare worker prevail when he says that there are more important things than the shopkeeper's window which has had a stone through it for the sixth time this month? How can his feelings of sorrow at the suffering of the families of Aboriginal alcoholics be conveyed to the publican who fulminates against the vandals? How can the self-righteous vilification by the shire councillors be countered? In the next section we shall see how the stirrers answer these questions.

STIRRERS

Who is the stirrer?

The stirrer is an important character in the drama of Brindleton. She/he is feared, hated and despised by almost everyone. Visitors will be assumed to be stirrers if they are Aboriginal. Whites will also be suspected if they take an interest in Aborigines, but it may be they will be found to be only do-gooders. The mark of the stirrer is that he or she talks about the racial division in the town. Anyone voicing complaints about the Aborigines' situation is thought to be stirring. Anyone identifying racism as a problem is also considered a stirrer.

Aboriginal leaders in Canberra or Sydney are all stirrers, and are referred to with intense venom by the hard-liners and with righteous anger or sorrow by some soft-liners. The occasional blow-in who takes up an issue and fights on behalf of the Aborigines, is shunned by the whites and by many Aborigines also. Those few Aborigines who voice anger and complaints publically are denigrated and vilified almost universally by the whites. Many of the Aborigines and their white supporters feel that the hostility and anger aroused by stirring is to be avoided at all costs because the repercussions are worse than any gains could warrant.

One way the stirrer is defined is as someone who comes into the town, stirs up the blacks by telling them their rights, and then leaves them feeling disgruntled and with no way of righting their wrongs. Unlike the do-gooders who are considered naive and ineffectual, the stirrers have 'political motives'. This accusation is an obscure reference to hidden motives related to wider political radicalism, to personal ambition or to the gaining of notoriety. The document story, referred to above, could only be explained as a consequence of the activities of stirrers. Any other explanation of the concerted and effective action of the Aborigines would imply that they had a real grievance, and also that they were capable of organising such a protest.

The alarm about stirring is related to the town's knowledge of its reputation for racism. There have been newspaper stories and television programmes in the national media related to racial tension in many western NSW towns. Events such as the police being called by the school, and a school student incarcerated for attacking a teacher, claims of racism in high schools, and Aborigines being excluded from pubs or clubs, have been bruited abroad in a way that has caused a good deal of resentment and distress. The reports were often neither accurate nor fair, but it was the very discussion of such issues by outsiders which enraged some and upset others in the town. In some cases the reporters believed themselves to be dealing with a simple situation of direct victimisation of a passive and virtuous black population by nasty and irrational whites. The conservative whites in town believe that the city media, and especially the ABC, is in league with the radical stirrers. An ABC reporter who telephoned the Brindleton Shire Council for a comment on an Aboriginal meeting was told 'Thank you, we don't want to talk to you.'

The stirrer is fired with a sense of righteous anger, is impatient, and does not mind becoming intensely unpopular. He or she begins from the premise that there is something wrong in the town, whereas those who would counter that view say the town is harmonious except for the stirrers. If forced to consider why there is conflict at all, many will begin discussing the characteristics of the black population. The do-gooders will also mention the racists in the town, but this is in terms of what they say to or about Aborigines. No one discusses 'race relations' in wider terms, because that would be stressing racial differences. The thought of trying to improve interaction does not spring readily to the minds of those who would really prefer not to interact at all.

But the stirrer will not accept the relatively comfortable categories and concepts of orthodox views, whether soft- or hard-line. He or she is confronted every day by events which offend because they are unjust, and yet are ignored or supported by the rest of the population. The generalisations made about blacks in conversation, the patronising response to an Aboriginal leader's demands, the casual humiliation of an untidy Aboriginal customer and the pervasive signs of Aboriginal poverty and depression, all are a source of indignation for the stirrer. Unwillingness to remain silent about these events means she/he is constantly at odds with others. When a policeman told one stirrer with provocative satisfaction, 'We have two six foot cops coming to Brindleton; then those blacks will have to behave', the man asked, 'Who has threatened you that you need all that muscle to protect you?' The policeman replied defensively, complaining of having to deal with drunks. 'I had to pick up one old man with maggots in his hair. I had to wash my hands.' This 'stirrer', closely involved with Aborigines, was deeply distressed that the old man's human tragedy could be related in these terms. This kind of aggression and inhumanity in the face of the depressed Aboriginal communities fills him with bitter fury.

There are a number of responses to the stirrer. While many who are do-gooders might initially have sympathy for an uncompromising attitude, the demand for action rather than agreement in principle will eventually alienate those who do not want to condemn others or challenge popular views. Some will be embarrassed at being expected to chat to Aborigines in the street. The conflict created by the stirrer is deplored, because it shows no understanding of the reasons for white hostility towards the blacks. The hard-line response is to try to run the stirrers out of town. Such people recognise the enemy, and try to turn the tables by accusing the stirrers of being racists because they talk of race.

The powerful witch-like status of the stirrer derives from this challenge posed to the accepted ways of thinking and talking about the racial divide. A most significant attribute of a stirrer is that he or she acts and speaks in ways that cannot be ignored. Yet the spectre of the stirrer is a force for conformity. The fear of being seen as a stirrer is an effective check not only on words but even on thoughts.

It is not hard for Brindleton people to dismiss the stirrer as disturbed or even deranged. To put one's social relations in jeopardy by daily confrontation with the rest of the town can seem a pointless excercise. For many it is the mark of madness. It also serves to warn the younger and more vulnerable souls of the folly of trying to change things. The tension-filled social relations that result from stirring are a warning against remarking on expressions of prejudice towards blacks. One is protected from ostracism by ignoring insults or slights directed at Aborigines, and by joining in deploring the destructiveness of Aboriginal youths and the waste of government money on this undeserving poor. Too much concern and sympathy may lead to one being classed with the stirrer. Thus the spectre of the stirrer helps to keep the hearts and minds of the majority of the population from considering too carefully what lies at the base of the inequality in the town.

Dedicated whites are caught between a desire for radical change and the fear of creating more conflicts. One way of avoiding the label of stirrer and remaining politically active is by not specifying issues in terms of race. If the health or youth initiative is not said to be specifically for Aborigines, and if the campaigning is not accompanied by accounts of Aboriginal disadvantage, then the orthodox ideas about Aborigines can remain undisturbed. Thus, while the boundaries of the categories of do-gooder and stirrer are not clear, the contrasting strategies make the political implications of each quite different.

One youth worker was under suspicion of being a stirrer because of his very suspect tendency to spend a lot of time with Aborigines. He was often to be seen in a black crowd outside the pub, or among the young Aborigines at the milk-bar. He was told that he would lose the authority needed in his job if he mixed with them. He was accused of taking advantage of young Aboriginal women. He was said to be an outsider, a misfit who could not get on with his own kind. His superiors presented a clear warning that his activities should change.

An event which shows how stirrers are made concerns a young welfare worker who asked a visiting 'expert' to explain to the Aborigines their rights concerning getting out of the police cells when arrested. There had been complaints that people were kept in longer than they should, without being charged. But the 'expert' asserted that the moment was inopportune for such an explanation. The police would see such advice as provocative and their cooperation was needed when the new proclaimed place opened in the near future. If upset by criticism they could undermine its functioning by sending the disorderly drunks to it in large numbers. Such political pragmatism outraged the young welfare worker. He refused to accept the advice and went to the police station himself and asked the sergeant to explain the rules. In the event there were no dire repercussions.

A teacher who took a quiet stand against pervasive racism in the school by suggesting positive steps that could be taken, and by offering assistance and advice to the ATAs, was warned that she was going in the way of a previous notorious stirrer. It was suggested by the senior staff that she might not get recommended for promotion. Another teacher had spent time at the pub with Aboriginal friends who were involved with the legal service, and had driven them home. As he drove back through the town he was followed. Eventually he was pulled up near his home by the police wagon, breathalysed, and the car checked. He had not been drinking, but the car was given a defect notice. Thus the risks taken by those who breach the racial rules are not just of ostracism, but can be to career or even liberty.

White stirrers and black activists

If the stirrers are seen as so intensely threatening one might well wonder as to their effectiveness. Do white stirrers just create conflicts to no purpose, or can they incite revolt or disruptive demands? It may appear from the document story above that they trigger effective resistance, and many see such events as entirely due to the stirrers and entirely reprehensible. But while the stirrers who were involved played a crucial part in providing information, the actual demands made on the school and the organisation to support them came from the Aborigines. There are few occasions when stirrers can effectively work with blacks and there are a number of related reasons for this.

First, the stirrers are no more generally popular among Aborigines than among whites but for slightly different reasons. Many blacks simply do not want trouble, and see the activities of stirrers increasing rather than alleviating their problems. These are the people who are aware that whites will be tolerant and even friendly if they are not annoyed by drunks, vandals or rudeness. The more active or angry

Aborigines do not trust the stirrers, partly because their motives are not understood, and also because their politics show a different style. For most Aboriginal activists independence of black organisations from white helpers is of crucial importance. Further there are few blacks who can understand the sense of outrage on their behalf which energises the stirrer. They are aware that such people become isolated and shunned, and of the reasons for such treatment. While they may applaud their activities it is from a safe distance, for such tactless and insensitive people may not make the best of allies.

A second reason for the separation of white and black activists is that few white supporters of Aborigines are aware of the internal dynamics of the Aboriginal community. For instance a blow-in was grooming a man who appeared to have a lot to say for a leadership position but, 'When a vote was taken by secret ballot to elect a leader or leaders, this man received only one vote, presumably his own. Almost unanimous was the vote to select another man who eschewed the limelight, was semi-literate but articulate and highly regarded by most residents of the township' (Roy, 1984:2).

For the leadership of a blow-in and a stirrer to be accepted by Aborigines would require a familiarity and close identification that is rare for whites to achieve. It is difficult for newcomers to realise that the town has nurtured its conflicts and habits for many years, and what appears inequitable and irrational to the blow-in may seem to be a part of nature itself to many older residents, black and white alike. People are used to avoiding highly contentious issues, or to joking about the hypocrisy and deviousness that often protects white sensibilities. While black activists and white stirrers may sometimes seem to be speaking the same language, the meaning of the stirring phrases is different for each. Thus the stirrers are often as alien to the blacks they support as to the whites they challenge.

While the stirrer's rhetoric might be appealing to black activists, it is based on convictions that blatant injustice related to racial differences should not be tolerated. For those Aborigines who have tolerated it for as long as they can remember, such an attitude seems somewhat quixotic. Blacks are not so sure about the possibility of achieving justice and equal opportunity by challenging the whites who rule their town.

If stirrers are not effective in their attempts to change the town, why are they so hated and feared? I believe it is because they challenge the view of the world which justifies and takes for granted the lesser social worth of Aborigines. They refuse to accept the circular logic which says that Aborigines are lesser human beings because, look at them, they live in poor houses and make trouble for the rest of us, so let's keep them out there where inferior people belong. The real threat is to the sense of honour of the majority of whites who, in refusing to accept that they are racist or unjust, must then blame the Aborigines both for their own position and for the anger that some display in the face of it.

I have said that the politics of active Aborigines is different from that of the white stirrers. One difference is in their knowledge of the entrenched attitudes of the dominant whites. It is such attitudes which excite the stirrers constantly. But hard-line whites, whether in powerful positions or youthful bar-flys full of bombast, are reluctant to expose their opinions in front of Aborigines. The soft-liners are careful to be polite and even kind towards Aborigines they come across. Thus few Aborigines have much idea of the extent to which they are discussed and denigrated, or of the patronising way their affairs are referred to.

Politically active Aborigines in Brindleton adopt at least some of the vocabulary of the black power movement. The rigid racial categories, and the implacable verbal hostility to whites, are difficult for whites to either agree with or discuss. For many moderate but active Aborigines also, they are alarming and misconceived. Those who are active in Aboriginal organisations do not approve of the propensity to upset white people which is evident among the radicals. For many, Aboriginal advances are still dependent on cooperation with the whites. Alienating their patrons would seem pointless.

The tactics of the stirrer usually involves instigating or supporting grassroots organisations and, besides attempts to confront injustice in the town, they make demands on institutions couched in rational terms. These demands are generally for those things which will create opportunities for individuals to gain a better education or a better job. Thus we are back to the position of the do-gooder. Indeed the aims of both kinds of whites are similar. Their tactics differ. But all share a view of black disadvantage that is derived from what are commonly called middle-class mores. The emphasis is on the discrimination suffered by blacks and on the physical poverty of their living conditions. There are misunderstandings embedded in these views which we will now try to dispel.

What colour is poverty?

There is a fundamental error of interpretation which mars much writing about Aborigines' problems, and it is constantly looming on the edge of this work. It has been mentioned before but it is time to confront it in relation to the structural position of Aborigines in Brindleton. Are we discussing a race or a class problem? Are we considering Aboriginal poverty, or poverty suffered by Aborigines? Is deprivation of a different kind when associated with racial discrimination? Many works which give statistics showing Aboriginal disadvantage imply that such disadvantage is created by racial difference.

My argument is that poverty and deprivation are created by specific processes which can affect any people. That is, poverty, like wealth, is created in Australia as part of a capitalist economic system. Private ownership, wage labour and unemployment are necessary aspects of this social system. However this is not to say that the process of social demarcation is the same everywhere. The way a particular group is affected by these processes, and the local understandings of such demarcations, are historically specific.

Further both those who are advantaged and those disadvantaged by this particular form of differentiation will use their imaginations to retain control of their resources, extend their freedoms and, according to their lights, improve things. For many whites in Brindleton this would mean making Aboriginal families smaller and tidier; for many blacks it would mean removing the stigma attached to large families.

The enlightenment policies designed for Aborigines were made without a close examination of the situation which was to be righted. The emphasis on remote Northern Territory communities, as discussed above, was evident in policies, but in NSW the more relevant assumptions concerned the nature of deprivation. Material deprivation was seen as the central problem, and crucially to do with the lack of proper housing. All blacks were thought to want, above all, better housing and to need, above all, better education. In this their aspirations were assumed to be like those of whites.

The faith in education shown by an overwhelming number of people involved in Aboriginal issues is related to two things. First, education is seen as a route to employment opportunities. There is little recognition that the kind of work that most rural Aborigines want is unskilled labouring. There are no policy discussions on how to bridge the gap between such humble aspirations and those that are seen to stem from educational qualifications. The second point stems from this. Education itself is seen as creating the knowledge of other avenues for success in the most general sense, that is, as assisting an assimilation process. One could learn to save money and to keep house better. Such ideas have a lot in common with the theory about the culture of poverty developed by Oscar Lewis.

Oscar Lewis' (1966) theory concerning a cultural pattern related to conditions of poverty in urban environments has been harshly criticised. The criticisms relate less to his description of the supposed culture (but see Valentine, 1969) than to the implication of his views that it is this culture that is at least partly responsible for the perpetuation of poverty. Despite the dismissal of his views by many serious sociologists, the term 'culture of poverty' has been seized on with such tenacity that it is necessary to examine it further. The term is used, largely, I would argue, among those who are in some way concerned with the problems of the poor but are not themselves poor. For such people the term 'culture of poverty' seems to epitomise, and even explain, what they observe. It summarises the fact that certain material conditions produce a certain pattern of responses some of which are common to groups in many different cities and even countries.

In fact these common elements are fairly unremarkable and relate closely to the material conditions of life. For instance the preference for immediate rewards, which Lewis says is characteristic of the poor, rather than the delayed rewards which are the result of saving one's surplus resources, would appear to me universal. It is the practice of foregoing immediate rewards that would, at first sight, seem to be more in need of explanation. Lewis' argument depends on the fact that delayed rewards, in simple terms of buying things, can be greater than immediate rewards. But this is only true when one has a large enough income. Such advantage could only be translated to the poor if they were willing to forego the immediate reward of, for instance, eating, for the delayed reward of eating better. One could hardly begin to save for a house when lacking enough to keep warm and pay the rent. In other words, given pressing needs which exceed the ability to pay for them, the notion of delayed rewards makes little sense.

Lewis seemed to imply further that this inability to delay satisfaction was generalised to other than material desires, but his evidence for that is shaky to say the least. Other aspects of Lewis' depiction of the culture of poverty seem accurate enough at the most general level of behaviour, but not so embedded in the psyche as he would have it. But it is really the function of this culture which is at issue. Lewis (and many of those who deliver welfare services to Aborigines in western NSW), believe that it is their culture, adapted as it is to a particular environment, which traps the poor. For Lewis, this is so because the values preclude their taking long-term economically rational strategies. For welfare personnel in NSW, it is because the culture consists of values and practices that preclude acceptance by the bulk of the white community. Instead of seeing this as a white pathology of intolerance which requires therapy, the whites suggest changes in the black community to make acceptance easier.

An example of such 'blaming the victim' (cf. Ryan, 1972) is evident in the interpretation and activities of a welfare officer who assisted in running a water polo club which included a majority of black youths. He did so because 'Their greatest need appeared to be acceptance by the white community to allow them to develop skills to compete in the wider society'(Roy, 1984:2). The rejection by whites and the competitive nature of society are both taken for granted. 'The swimming pool committee became nervous seeing the parents in such large numbers arriving from the Aboriginal reserve' (ibid., 5). This nervousness is not considered surprising or shocking, yet the timidity of Aborigines in the face of such reactions to their very presence is the focus of treatment by those who would cure the social pathology of racial hostility. That is, it is the reactions of the blacks, their culture, the way of life, that are seen as the basis of disadvantage. Roy says:

> Middle class values such as punctuality, accountability, formality and impersonality in organisations are alien to these people. It was impossible for instance to deny a child a barbecue because he did not have his 50 cents; all his relatives who attended with him would be insulted and get up and leave. Similarly, one could not insist on regulation swimming shorts or demand that games begin on time (ibid., 6).

I take no exception to the author's description of the values which these Aboriginal people do not share with the white middle class. However it should be pointed out that the games did begin, people did pay, and the children did not go naked into the pool. What the author is recording is that middle-class propriety was constantly threatened by the lack of emphasis on those formal rules. He is, in my view, correct in implying that such lack of emphasis on disciplinary rules often shocks and frightens whites who are in positions of authority in such places as public swimming pools. But his description does not indicate how peculiar and anti-social these middle-class mores appear to the blacks.

Rather than their culture being a barrier to acceptance, my view is that their culture today is a response to non-acceptance, and the only bastion of defence against rejection and all the other forces that weigh on them. That is, it is an arena where a sense of honour is based on different criteria from those among the dominant white groups. Aborigines are aware of the judgements made by whites. While some try to conform to those judgements and most simply avoid coming into contact with them, there is a core of opposition to the judgements which can be called 'oppositional culture' (Willis & Corrigan, 1983:97).

I hasten to say that I do not argue that this culture takes a particular form, but rather that the ideas and practices of Aborigines are all part of a creative response which has developed in particular conditions and which will change as circumstances change. It is the fact that the 'culture of poverty' is judged to be a culture of inferiority that is one aspect of the problem of the poor. But this is not because of the characteristics of the culture, but rather because the culture has been created in a situation of economic, political and ideological powerlessness. It is an assertion of identity from a position of inferior strength, and it affirms values which are in conflict with those which dominate society. The next section will explore this oppositional culture.

A final example of political conflict will illustrate the fact that the borderline between accepting oppression, challenging it or making a tactical retreat, can be thin. The local radio station was training some young Aborigines in making and broadcasting audio material. They made a tape in which they discussed the usefulness of their course, and expressed the opinion that they would be enabled to use this knowledge of the white technology as a weapon against the white system. Such a brave claim from 20-year-olds could hardly be taken as a threat to public order. However, knowing the sensitivity of some powerful citizens of the town, the radio station did not broadcast the material because it was concerned that complaints might be made and the radio licence threatened. One of the whites teaching the trainees was outraged at this censorship. It seemed to her a case of saying to these young men, you can talk so long as you say nice things. Another saw it as sensibly cautious.

This incident followed another consisting of a very firm complaint from the shire council. An item was printed in the local paper accusing the station of seminating (*sic*) racially inflamatory material during National Aboriginal Week, and a letter was sent to the station by the shire council threatening them with loss of licence. It was not clear what exactly was being complained of, and the council responded to enquiries from the radio station by saying 'you know what we mean'. Letters of complaint from supposedly offended residents were produced, which also failed to specify what was being complained of. A meeting between council members and the radio station board was held, with much mysterious tut-tutting. In the end it became clear that they were referring to the songs of the Aboriginal group 'Us Mob' and the talk of Fred Hollows, an opthalmologist who spoke in fairly strong terms, as he has often in other places, about the injustices suffered by Aborigines. Though it was clear that the shire council had no direct power over the station's licence they did know members of the funding bodies and, compared with the blow-ins who ran the station, had a good deal of influence over what is known as public opinion. It was clear that council members firmly believe their own opinions to be identical with those of the public.

Political action to change the power structure of the town is thus intermittent, individual and inneffective. But there is a more general challenge to the hegemony of the powerful whites which often goes unnoticed, but which underlies any effective protest and which fuels continuing rebelliousness. It is not a serious political threat but rather an arena where other values are legitimated. I call this arena an oppositional culture.

OPPOSITIONAL CULTURE

Culture or opposition?

If it is true that 'Dignity is as compelling a human need as food and sex', (Sennett & Cobb, 1973:191) then one strategy for powerless groups is to create their own arena of dignity. The necessary conditions for a dignified bearing can be redefined. Dignity need not for instance depend on wearing shoes in the street or on 'neat attire'. Being apprehended by the police does not preclude a sense of dignity when one's father and aunty have had the same experience. Sitting on the ground playing Bingo is not undignified for Aborigines in Brindleton. The judgements of the wider society can be rejected to a degree if one's self-image does not depend on the good opinion of those who dominate the economic and political arena. Members of a group can gain their sense of honour from the group's integrity. From this viewpoint, rather than the culture of Aborigines being a barrier to acceptance, it is their defiant reaction to rejection, and their haven from the indignities meted out to them. I use the term 'oppositional culture' to specify the active creation and protection of this arena of social meaning in an embattled situation (Willis & Corrigan, 1983). I do not argue that all or even most Aborigines take an active part in this creation. Many are passive and some oppose the opposition.

It has been made clear already that Aborigines are a varied group in lifestyles, aspirations and loyalties. In discussing the oppositional culture I refer essentially to that large grouping which mostly resides at the Aboriginal end of town or on the reserve which is closely interwoven with ties of kinship and marriage and most members of which have little interaction with, and little knowledge of, whites.[1] Some people try to limit their involvement with this group and remain on the periphery. Some 'leaders' and 'spokespersons' who are well known to some whites from their involvement in organisations are nonetheless a part of this oppositional culture which whites are seldom aware of. For most people of course it is not a self-conscious identification with a particular cultural group, but simply an acceptance of the identity conferred on them by growing up in the Aboriginal community. Thus this 'community' which represents an 'oppositional culture' is as complex and contradictory as any community. It is, for instance, bound together by its meaningful conflicts as much as by a notion of common purpose.

In popular usages, the term culture refers either to the exotic practices of other societies, or to the artistic pursuits of our own. The Aborigines in Brindleton have nothing that the whites will call culture in either sense of the word. This issue has been mentioned already in relation to the teaching of Aboriginal studies in the schools and the bringing out of the artefacts on National Aborigines Day. It is difficult for Aborigines to counter the grazier's comment 'The old blacks were admirable; they had traditions; the young ones are no good . . . they have no traditions left. This cultural revival is a load of crap.' There seems to be no immediate evidence to show that they are wrong. However it cannot be denied that Aborigines have an identifiable pattern of life and one that is, perforce, in opposition to that which dominates the wider society.

To describe Aboriginal social life in Brindleton as oppositional culture is to accept that certain of its features are an immediate trigger

---

[1] My knowledge is more limited in this area than others and comes from personal familiarity with a few individuals, with one family and from observation at public events. It would have required at least a doubling of the length of my fieldwork to become a participant observer with this oppositional culture, to overcome the discomfort of being initially treated as a welfare officer, and to get past the politically active people whose views are not representative.

to white hostility. Rather than being accorded dignity, many Aboriginal practices in Brindleton are disliked, disdained or pitied. Were Aborigines passive and silent in the face of such judgements there would be little need for the vilification to continue. There would be no point in continuing to actively dominate a population that had accepted subordination. Rather than showing shame, oppositional culture acts as both a challenge to those who would despise Aborigines, as well as a defence against them.

But can the culture of Brindleton Aborigines be considered in this light? Is it the case that Aborigines have created an arena where social value is bestowed using different criteria from that which obtains in the wider society? If so, can Aboriginal culture be seen as admirable, positive and worthy of respect? Many of the whites in Brindleton would find such an idea laughable, and few blacks would describe their values in these terms. Yet, as I will show below, there is a very widespread recognition that blacks adhere to some other set of values from whites. Of course the Aborigines have not been able to achieve independence from the dominant society so that the arena where these contrasting values operate is constantly intruded upon.

Aboriginal evaluations of behaviour in the public sphere are one face of oppositional culture. When confronting a drunken Aboriginal in the street, white reactions vary from disgust or fear to disapproval and embarrassment. The Aboriginal population has a different view of the street scene. Acceptance and understanding are expressed towards the familiar 'bottle men', and relatives will give them money and make sure they get to hospital if necessary. Those who are aggressive or too demanding are dealt with without being humiliated, as is their common experience at white hands. Defiant reactions are understood. If a drunk on the street sees a disgusted glance why would he not swear at the observer? If one is hated why not express one's own hatred? And further, when one is despised for having nothing by the very people who seem to preclude one getting anything and who themselves have too much, why not take from them? The logic of such responses is quite apparent to the black population. It is often those who rail loudest against the blacks whose property is the most threatened.

Most Aborigines of course do not take part in acts of defiance, resistance or public drunkeness but understand very well what they signify. Satisfaction is gained from the story of the Aboriginal woman who threw all her clothes off and shrieked when the police tried to put her in the paddy wagon in the street. A street that is covered with broken glass is jokingly called 'crystal city'. Young blacks gain amusement from the obvious discomfort and disapproval by whites of swearing and drunkenness. Such defiance can have an aggressive edge. Some take pleasure in frightening groups of whites, for instance, by standing about in a silent and menacing group when they leave the club. An Aboriginal girl who was told sharply by the lady of the house to stop whacking the fence with a stick, replied, 'Shut-up you old bitch or I'll get legal aid onto you.' One can imagine the conversations the girl has heard about the power of legal aid to redress wrongs that led to such a bizarre threat.

The attitude of many Aboriginal parents to their children's misdemeanors is in opposition to the powers that be. For many of the Aboriginal parents, truancy expresses legitimate dislike of school, to the despair of the school teachers. Efforts to enlist the respectable blacks in town to assist with keeping students at school and young people from stealing have met with little success. One youth, apprehended for stealing petrol, was pulled out of his car and pushed against the wall with arms and legs spread which is the normal police procedure. In his statement to police he only briefly mentioned the petrol stealing and at greater length complained about the rough treatment by the police. A very annoyed policeman showed the statement to the boy's father, a responsible, respected and unassuming man, expecting him to be shocked at the boy's cheek. The father said nothing, in fact he was not sure why the policeman was annoyed. The policeman said 'If it was my boy I'd smack him in the ear hole and tell him to write down what he had done, not what was done to him. That's neither here nor there.' But the father has heard and seen enough of police practices over the years to be unable or unwilling to take their side.

Independent initiative is not lacking in the Aboriginal community, and when that initiative is at odds with the law it is no less appreciated. One December Friday the social service cheques failed to arrive in the last mail before Christmas, so there was no money for food let alone feasts. Late that night there was a break-in at the cold-store, which was stocked with turkeys and hams for the last pre-Christmas shopping day. A procession of boys was seen in the dim street lights delivering poultry and hams at the Aboriginal end of town. The loss was discovered, and next morning the police wagon followed the same trail as the boys, relieving the overcrowded fridges of their contents. One family had let the dog have a chicken for which they had no space, but most of the rest was retrieved, though it could not be sold. This latter fact seemed to make the police retrieval of the food pointless and punitive to Aborigines, but such attitudes of whites is nothing new. The outrage and fury of the owners of the store, and those who lost their Christmas dinner, was a source of amusement rather than shame in the Aboriginal community.

Perhaps the major contrast with white individualism, competition and material concerns, is Aboriginal family orientation. Assertions of loyalty are confirmed by generalised reciprocity, and status equality is an essential part of kin relations. A whole idiom of speech and a distinct style of behaviour reinforces a cultural identity different from that of the white community. In fact one part of this idiom is the wealth of humorous and ironic comments on white practices. Also a powerful support for the oppositional culture stems from the fact that there are really very few Aborigines who could achieve the material basis for being accorded dignity by the dominant whites. Those who try can easily attract derision from other community members.

The legitimacy of a culture determines whether following its dictates will win honour from others. For instance, while it might be expected that funerals would be generally respected, in Brindleton it does depend on whose they are. A businessman asserts that blacks have the attitude that, 'If Uncle Fred dies in Wilcannia we will all go to the funeral and that is no good to an employer.' It is implied not only that this is part of a careless attitude to work which explains Aborigines being unemployed, but also that there is something wrong with going to one's uncle's funeral. Or perhaps that Aborigines have too many uncles. This judgement about the significance of kinship and funerals is made without consideration of the extent of grief or of what religious or social function mourning practices have. Aborigines faced with such disapproval can only reject the basis on which it is made. If their contrasting values, even when they are as innocuous as going to funerals, are denied any worth then virtually all Aborigines are forced to be in opposition to whites.

But, as noted above, the contrasting values and priorities among the Aborigines are not seen as culture by the whites. On the contrary, the fact that 'they have no culture left' is seen as a part of the social pathology for which various cures are suggested. An experienced health worker in the west, after telling me there was no culture left because no one was circumcised, explained in authoritative terms the way Aboriginal families operate. For instance she asserted that children are neglected but not beaten, that child molestation is unknown, but that, because children do not learn to control their feelings, fighting is common. The 'expert' whites often list some such characteristics as peculiarly Aboriginal. Apart from the inaccuracy and shallowness of such observations, the alleged differences are not accorded the status of cultural practices.

Cultural difference

There is both covert and explicit disagreement in Brindleton over whether, and in what way, Aborigines are to be thought of as different. I have indicated above that a good deal of hard-line effort goes into keeping sympathy and understanding of the blacks from interfering with their vilification. While this process seems to emphasise the differences between blacks and whites, any positive emphasis on this difference is treated with scorn. Since the government policies began to provide services and facilities specifically for Aborigines, it is in Aborigines' interests, in quite obvious material terms, to assert their differences. Aborigines are being asked by outsiders to define themselves separately from whites. But when Aborigines claim to be different, they are said to be threatening the unity of the town. The accusation of racism is made freely of any discriminatory action which favours the blacks or which recognises black grievances.

In these circumstances, what are the options for Aborigines, either as individuals or as a group? It is clear that any unified black action to change their circumstances must necessarily be based on a recognition that Aborigines have common grievances, or at least common interests and needs. Such grievances and needs are emphatically denied by dominant whites, and thus legitimacy is denied to the actions and aspirations of those Aboriginal people who either complain about the institutions that oppress them, or attempt to develop some other organisation to meet their needs. Black organisations face constant attacks and attempts at colonisation. Public figures such as the councillors explain that 'the Aborigines must cooperate with us' and 'they should not be divisive, they should not be racist by setting up separate organisations or speaking of Aborigines as a separate category. We are all Brindleton people.' These calls for togetherness have an appearance of common sense and reason, which makes any independent action appear like rebellion and deliberate disruption of a peaceful community.

However there are clear and recognised differences between Aborigines and whites, many of which have been alluded to already. The different material circumstances are one basis of a distinctive lifestyle which is taken for granted by the Aborigines as much as by the whites. Both see their different circumstances as to some extent natural, a part of the nature of black and white existence. For instance a young Aboriginal woman said of another who claimed to be Aboriginal, 'She's no Koori. She's been to America. Her family is rich.' Whites often remark, 'They like to live like that' referring to overcrowded and dilapidated houses. Money is not necessary for the sense of honour in the Aboriginal community, though sharing is. Those who aquire a car, a washing machine or any other useful thing will expect, though not always happily, that it will be used by a wide network of kin.

It is of course the whites' cultural practices and institutions which dominate the town. Aborigines may feel shame and embarrassment when whites come into their house because of the paucity of furniture and accoutrements which are taken for granted even by poor whites. 'The Welfare' no longer makes inspections as it used to (Kamien, 1978:40). But Aborigines are conscious of white reactions of, at best, confusion and embarrassment when the usual forms of hospitality, such as being offered a chair and a cup of tea, are absent. Aborigines do not visit each other in the way white people do, and many do not know and do not want to know the ritual associated with such visiting. Extended families tend to come and go freely in the houses of close kin, and others interact mostly outside or in the public arena.

Aborigines publically identify themselves in opposition to whites at the Sunday football game when they barrack for the visiting team, indicating that they feel themselves to be outsiders in relation to the predominantly white local team and the town in general. Aboriginal players in the local team also complain that they do not get as many chances to play as do the white players, even if they regularly go to practice. Whether or not this is the case it indicates ongoing conflict.

A play for National Aboriginal Day was performed by school students to a largely Aboriginal audience with noisy children and much movement in the Aborigines' hall. Those teachers and white students from the school who attended were either discomforted or shocked by the apparent chaos, and the younger white children could not believe their eyes that such freedom was tolerated. Aboriginal events are always less formal and usually attended by people of all ages, some with little interest in the proceedings. Drunks are tolerated with humour and only evicted when violent or aggressive.

There are several ways in which Aborigines' values are seen to make them incorrigible. Some households burn the lights all night and run up large electricity bills. 'They don't perceive their situation and live to their income', I was told. The extended families and kin-group responsibility is also seen as a problem in itself though whites are reluctant to say that sharing is bad. The fact that an Aboriginal girl did not want to work full-time was interpreted by her employer as her way of avoiding the extended family preying on her earnings. But her reluctance also reflected the desire not to be richer than her relatives. The employer sees the extended family as the problem rather than the unemployed state of the girl's relatives.

The sharing and support between wide-ranging kinship networks is recognised to be in conflict with individual ownership and the competitive striving for jobs and goods which is a fundamental feature of our society. When a public servant explains to me that 'Money is the tool. If they don't want money you can't do anything to help them', he is clearly aware of the crucial role of oppositional culture.

Social pathology?

Any set of values shows a double-sided quality, confining and liberating. Identification with a tradition provides confidence and comfort, but also circumscribes one's life. A tradition is not *per se* good or bad, although to read many of the emotive statements about 'Aborigine's lost culture' one might assume that it had some absolute value. The opposite might be assumed from comments about many contemporary Aboriginal communities.

But are all cultural traditions equally valuable? Is the apparently high level of violence and drunken destructiveness among Aborigines, the poor health and the high rate of court convictions part of a cultural tradition or is it rather a social pathology to be explained by past suffering? (Wilson, 1982). Surely both are true. The recognition of negative and positive qualities, whatever the status of such value judgements, says nothing about the reality of the tradition.

However the metaphor of social pathology needs closer examination. There is no criteria for diagnosing disease in a whole society, and there are no studies which allow a statistical assesment and definition based on how many alcoholics or how many occasions of violence is to constitute social pathology. While there are Aboriginal families in Brindleton where difficulties are chronic, others show close, caring and responsible relationships. While alcoholism is common and binge-drinking frequent, there are many who do not drink or drink only occasionally. There are many strong and confident people; a high rate of certain symptoms does not indicate that all are infected. It is merely a comparison with some other, presumably more normal, level. Many are aware and active in their attempts to counter destructiveness. For many, drunken kinsmen are simply a part of life which must be dealt with regularly.

There is, at least sometimes, confusion between indulgence of children and neglect, between public and shameless drinking and family distress, between poverty and pathology. The fact that drinking is common may have an insulating effect. The private and shameful suffering of some white families may generate more individual pathology than the public and recognised suffering in some families in the black community. While irregular meals and sleep may cause much distress in some social environments, such conditions are taken for granted by many blacks. If one household becomes chaotic, children and adults can usually find a haven among other kin.

It is impossible to be sure of the level of, for instance, domestic violence among whites in Brindleton, though that causing injury serious enough for hospital treatment is certainly lower than among the Aborigines. Physical violence to women occurs fairly regularly in a few households in the Aboriginal community, and is an accepted form of control in others. A young man who seldom drinks was surprised at my reaction to his wife's bruises. 'She was drinking', he said. 'I can't let her do that. She has to look after the kids.' But casual and supposedly humorous references to 'giving the old girl a tap' are common among the white drinkers. Few white women go to the police in the face of their husband's violence whereas Aboriginal women often do so. As with drinking there is much more public awareness of black violence than of white.

The inspiration and the justification for both drinking and domestic violence came originally from the white men, and have been sustained in conditions of dependency. It should be emphasised that not all of what is assumed to be white culture is to do with punctuality and paying one's way. It may also be relevant to note that no case of direct physical violence between Aborigines and whites has come before the Brindleton court in the last three years. Thus violence in the white and black communities is both different and separate.

Aboriginal views of the situation differ from that of whites. The hypocrisy of white people loudly bemoaning Aboriginal drinking is quite apparent to the Aborigines. It is clear that there are immense personal problems associated with alcohol addiction among most sections of the population of Brindleton. The level of consumption is extremely high (Harris, 1986), and drunken white men are often visible in public, sometimes indeed at their places of work, to make it clear to all that this is not a problem caused by being Aboriginal. The fact that European drinking is mostly done behind closed doors seems to confirm that white people are ashamed of their habits.

Alcohol consumption is as much a part of social interaction among Aborigines as it is in the white community, and it has a positive side which is highly valued. Similarly violence could be considered to have a positive side. Brawls among Aborigines, for instance after the Sunday football matches, could be interpreted as a stouch, a public battle which is cathartic and entertaining and at which little damage occurs. Thus, although many Aborigines recognise that excessive drinking and the associated violence is causing misery and destruction for a minority of people and try in one way or another to control alcohol consumption, there is no overall disapproval of drinking. For most, alcohol and fighting are central to the drama of interpersonal life. When children at school were asked to create a little dramatic scene of their own, the white children acted asking mother if they could go to the disco, and the Aboriginal girls had one of them being bashed on the way home, telling mother, and the two mothers having a brawl. Thus the children take for granted the pattern of experience they grow up with, and the wholesale and absolute disapproval of violence among comfortable whites is certainly not shared by many Aborigines.

Excessive drinking and violence are associated with situations of deprivation and frustration, and there are obvious stresses associated with poverty which regularly create situations of desperation for many Aborigines. While the positive side of kinship networks and reciprocity are often emphasised, the necessity to share can be as weighty a burden as any other pattern of conformity and can, due to financial stringency, lead to severe tensions.

In their depiction of *The Hidden Injuries of Class*, Sennett and Cobb (1973) indicate the way status inferiority affects the identity of those individuals who live out their lives in a situation deemed inferior by themselves and others. Yet it is possible to see also an attempt by such peoples to undermine the power of those judgements and to subvert the notion of inferiority. While the battle may not be winnable, it seems unstoppable. I have argued that there is an Aboriginal culture in Brindleton because there is an Aboriginal tradition. In a hostile environment it is the shameless affirmation of values which are an affront to white propriety that are the positive face of Aboriginality. In many cases I would further claim that it is the acceptance of behaviour which is anathema to white society, such as stealing and violence, which underlies the notion of social pathology. Those blacks who feel no shame are considered sick.

The vicissitudes of opposition

The Aboriginal community does not have a unified view of the matter of cultural differences. There are those who want not to emphasise difference. Those who had recognised that being black did not bring any rewards and obediently had tried to assimilate are now being rewarded if they will identify as Aboriginal. The affirmation of an Aboriginal identity is the price asked for gaining one of the jobs as an Aboriginal liaison or advisory officer. Of course there are not many such jobs, and those individuals perceived as most likely to succeed are usually the least representative of the oppositional culture. This does not mean they do not want to 'help their people'. But that help is often seen in terms of abandoning those values and behaviours that are in opposition to the dominant whites. Thus the affirmation of oneself as Aboriginal is occurring at the same time that many are being enticed with the opportunity to cease being Aboriginal in the ways of the past — to desert the kinship networks as well as depressed circumstances and denigration.

Only a small minority have actually gained these rewards, and only some of them have been seduced into believing that their success depends on rejecting any identification with distinctive Aboriginality. There are also those among the most poor and humble who believe that Aborigines should try to become more acceptable to the whites who rule. One old man, a gentle but regular drunk, told me that if the behaviour of other Aborigines improved there would be an end to discrimination and rejection by whites. He said that white people always spoke to him. He clearly believed that if others were to show deference they could also gain such kindly treatment. This is a rational response, yet one that threatens the unity of Aboriginal opposition.

Some who believe that Aborigines bring trouble on themselves attempt to separate themselves from the disreputable blacks and keep their children from going to *that* end of town and learning *their* bad habits. The price is either some social isolation or joining with that interstitial group which is composed of those who try to identify with both black and white communities. Others deplore the vandalism and drunkenness and say 'They (meaning other blacks) won't take advantage of all that is offered them.'

The ability of blacks' opinion leaders to control the loyalty of followers is severely vitiated by lack of agreement concerning what the wider struggle is about. Thus different tactics are adopted by different people to gain the same ends or, conversely, the same tactics are used when different ends are being sought. White hegemony is maintained with the assistance of police, schools and the welfare institutions, and their power is unarguable. Many blacks do not envisage creating another power base; gaining a place within the reigning order seems the only possibility.

Those who would attempt to make the definition of Aboriginal include aspects of the culture that are in opposition to the dominant world of the whites, and to define these differences in a positive way, are in conflict with those who do not want to be oppositional. Oppositional culture takes pride in flouting the mores of the oppressors. Thus when Aboriginal technical college students have difficulties, not just because of their poor education, but also because of their babies and boyfriends and spending some of the weekend in jail on a drunk and disorderly charge, the more aggressive face of oppositional culture makes a virtue of such events, or at least makes fun of them. In rejecting the humiliation involved in being jailed, the Aborigines are taking an active role in the reproduction of racial separation. They have not conformed and surrendered to white hegemony.

Thus it is in opposition that the ongoing re-creation of a distinct cultural heritage occurs. This culture has its distinctive vocabulary, family form, pattern of interpersonal interaction and even its own economy. I have already mentioned the highly developed humour which reinterprets events which threaten to engulf Aborigine's lives.

There are areas of social life where young people are especially tempted to cease opposition. The attractions of joining the whites in sporting and social events are evident, and the opportunity is there, albeit conditional on conforming in certain ways and affirming certain values. But just as whites try to promote adherence to the orthodox views, so loyalty to the oppositional culture is demanded by blacks. Those who appear to favour the white world in any way may be accused of disloyalty, or derided as coconuts. Culture has thus become a sphere of political struggle. This is not necessarily a self-conscious decision to keep others in line, but a process stemming from intense consciousness of the meaning of behaviour which is threatening to the hegemony of whites. Joking about white habits, such as the delicate sipping of wine at dinner parties, the anxious clinging to money and the anxieties associated with careful avoidance of certain people, is an important part of the way Aboriginal children learn about whites. Such joking is kept very secret from almost all whites. Even one's white friends might be offended if they knew the kind of humour which their habits give rise to. Mimicry is a well-developed source of entertainment among the blacks of Brindleton.

But there are difficulties in presenting a discourse of dissent for a beleagered minority. Some of the older demands such as 'Treat us like human beings' are inappropriate today. Accusations of racial discrimination are difficult to sustain when there is at least some discrimination by governments in favour of Aborigines. The pleas for sympathy for vandals and drunks amount to saying 'If you stop hating us we will (eventually) stop being hateful.' But the oppositional culture does not apologise. Rather it says, 'You hate us for this behaviour; but this is how we are and we will remain so. We do not want to adopt your practices.'

Thus Brindleton is the site of a struggle. It is control of resources and power that enables certain groupings to dominate the town. Graziers and blow-ins could be seen to be in an unholy alliance, in that each in their different way ensures that the black's challenge to white hegemony is contained. This class struggle is thus played out through the idiom of race.

Chapter 6

Race and racism

THE DIVIDING LINE

Racist processes

I have tried to analyse the dynamics of Brindleton in terms of the continuing reproduction of the racial divide. There are other perspectives from which the town could be analysed. For instance the gender division, in sometimes similar but less-contested ways than that about race, determines what women can do in the town. As with sexism, racism is not a conscious and deliberate policy of those who appear to benefit,[1] nor is it simply attitudes of prejudice embedded in individual psyches.

It is, rather, a multi-faceted set of divisions which appear natural or necessary because each reflects the other. At one level it is engendered by the economic inequality of capitalist society. The economy creates unemployment which is suffered disproportionately by those who have come to command little status or power in the society. The state also plays a part in dividing off racial or ethnic groups as targets for its discriminatory practices or, more recently, benign assistance. It is easier to try to provide jobs, health and education for Aborigines than to provide for all who are in need. Institutions which dispense the education, the health and the law perpetuate, by their conservative practices, the hierarchy of status including the racial divisions. There is also the systematic set of ideas and practices which explain and perpetuate the racial division. In Brindleton these ideas comprise a powerful orthodoxy, and in the wider society they are part of a recognition that inequality and disadvantage are deplorable but inevitable. Finally there are the scientists whose part in re-creating or challenging these divisions will be the subject of further discussion below.

Aborigines' position in the capitalist economic order began to be established with the original forced appropriation of the land by the invading population. Where they survived at all Aboriginal groups were reduced to exploited labourers. They became largely fixed into the position that is usually called 'a pool of cheap labour' for rural industry. Considering that these men became skilled stockmen,

---

[1] In fact it could be argued that it is not in the whites interest to live in a town so riven with hostility and tension, yet it is whites who appear to have the upper hand and therefore to perpetuate the situation.

245

bushmen and drovers, they were indeed cheap labour. Subject to laws which dispossesed them and precluded them from ownership of land, and to a system which made other skills and a general education an unattainable prerequisite, they remained the least adaptable section of the labour force. Thus they could not command regular and secure work, could not enforce the payment of proper wages and seldom accumulated any capital or property. The only means of production they could be said to control are the skills of the bush that enable the hunting of porcupine or collecting of emu eggs or fishing. However the land where such production could take place became legally inaccessible. Thus Aborigines were dependent on employment and most vulnerable to unemployment. In the 1970s the lack of mobility and of previously aquired possessions ensured a continuation of widespread material deprivation.[2]

This economic situation, and the particular laws and forces which ensured that most Aborigines remained entrapped in it, confirmed and reproduced other differences. That is, the original differences between indigenous and colonising populations became aligned with contrasting positions in the new social order, which led to a reproduction of cultural difference. Subject to intense surveillance and intrusion during the protection era, Aborigines only source of independence or dignity was in retaining or re-creating a separate domain of meaning and value which I have called an oppositional culture. A necessary ideological element of this culture was the rejection of those standards of behaviour and forms of propriety which ensured that Aborigines would be seen as inferior.

I am not arguing that this was a free and independent choice, nor that such rejection of dominant mores was a conscious or even successful policy. Nor do I want to judge it unsuccessful. The actual effects of such processes is far too complex for such simple judgements. Nor am I arguing that all Aborigines concurred in this oppositional stance. What I do argue is that such oppositional ideas and actions attained a legitimacy within the Aboriginal communities which created the potential for a more aggressive assertion of Aboriginal identity. This was only intermittently realised because of the forces aligned against them. But realised it was, as the rare writer in the area (e.g., Beckett, Reay, Fink) has borne witness to.

---

[2]Stuart Hall, in *Policing the Crisis*, said 'The class relations which inscribe the black fractions of the working class, function as race relations. The two are inseparable' (Hall *et al.*, 1978:394).

Given this oppositional culture's rejection of pride in property (they had none), refusal of respect for the wealthy and powerful (the oppressors), and the repudiation of the judgements made by white society (which held them to be inferior), Aborigines naturally presented a threat to white hegemony. They were a thorn in the side of the local establishments, not sufficiently powerful to rock, let alone topple, the structures of society, and only occasionally embarrassing to state and national governments. The lack of shame and deference to the hegemonical dictates of white society, the sullen or brazen attitude to white disapproval and disdain, seemed to vindicate the hostility of whites. Thus those more powerful in rural areas could usually gain concurrence from their friends in high places for their continuation of oppressive practices.

On the national front, the exposure by active Aboriginal groups in the 1960s of the dire poverty which characterised Aboriginal communities led to widespread attention to the situation which resulted in the new policies of the enlightenment. Because poverty was supposed to be non-existent in Australia, and there had been little national awareness of Aborigines or of racial tensions, the media campaign which resulted when black protests became good copy galvanised the government into action, some results of which I have detailed above.

It now remains to ask whether racism is a useful concept. If race as a system of biologically determined categorisation is not valid, if so-called racial hostility is really about things other than racial differences, and if the whole process of differentiation has much in common with other examples of group closure, perhaps the term racism confuses more than it clarifies? Is it not perpetuating an error by implying that the deprivation and hostility experienced by Aborigines is due in some way to biological or quasi-biological characteristics, or to the erroneous belief in such determinants? Would it not be more useful and accurate to show that racial differentiation is just another form of class differentiation?

I believe that the term racism should be retained, as it has a meaning which accurately identifies one feature of the oppressive process where one group is deemed to be essentially of a different and lesser kind from those who dominate. In other words, it is the convictions about the meaning of inherent differences which gives this differentiation a spurious validity, and this cannot be corrected by rejecting the term. There are genetically given biological differences; age and sex differences as well as height, blood-group and skin colour are things we cannot do very much to change. It is when the process of social differentiation is taken to be equally incontrovertible because of such biological characteristics that we have sexism, racism or even, to use a useful neologism, agism.

Racism is a powerful term which, like the concept race, will not go away because academics deem it inaccurate. It is brief and explosive, with a specific referent of colour and a general referent of conflict and dramatic difference. Images from the colonial era are conjured up. Such associations are increasingly suspect making the implied causal connections easier to challenge. In themselves the terms do not imply anything about the cause of the differentiation, but rather invite a re-examination of the social processes which allow such differentiation to flourish as a set of practices and an ideology. Associated with that task is the need to clarify the contemporary use of the term race and its relationship with notions of culture and miscegenation.

Dividing what? The importance of categories

An earlier generation of anthropologists saw themselves as 'naturalising the bizarre', showing that behaviour which at first seemed inexplicable and irrational did make sense both in terms of the native concepts (the emic or native view) and also often in terms of function, biological, psychological or social. But the anthropologist had to do long fieldwork and careful analysis before the concepts which comprised the understanding of the natives could be grasped. Those other natives, the whites in communities studied in contemporary Australia, are believed to share at least some of the concepts of the researcher. Community studies among white Australians have quite a different emphasis from those among black Australians. Oxley (1973) does not need to explain that it is religion that goes on in the church on Sunday or even what religion consists of, and Wild (1974) can take it for granted that his readers know a good deal about what the shire council is supposed to be doing.

Now there are two problems with this. First, much of the behaviour of the 'primitive' people would be quite explicable in terms understandable to any other human group. That is, people everywhere produce and exchange; mate and reproduce; fight and feast. The particular way such activities are arranged and understood and the more complex rituals do indeed require specialised study before they can be understood. But then so do 'ours', and that is the second problem. Studies of communities with which the researcher has some familiarity face a danger that anthropologists working in other societies do not, and that is, the danger of taking for granted the very concepts and categories that need to be explained.

What goes on in the pub may not be recognised as in need of explanation. Much of the behaviour associated with gender roles was not problematised until feminist scholars pointed out its relationship to male perceptions of the world. And what of concepts that have a wider currency? One everyday concept used by white Australians and uncritically adopted in many analytic and descriptive studies is 'Aboriginal'. It is often assumed that the category is empirically unproblematical and uncontested, even when it is considered to refer to a cultural category. Earlier sections of this work indicated that this is not so.

It became common among social scientists to say that race is a culturally constructed category, but the meaning of that statement is sometimes confused with the assertion that race is a matter of culture. The former refers to the process of categorisation, and the latter to the material from which the category is constructed. The process of categorisation whereby people of a society are allocated to one or another group which is called a race, or to any other category, is a part of the wider process of construction of ideology. The categories created are not an automatic consequence of a certain genetic or cultural heritage, or indeed of any inherent characteristics. Rather the social categories are part of a cultural process of evaluation and bestowal of meaning on certain phenomena such as biological or cultural characteristics. The major characteristics which will influence (but not determine) who will belong to a racial category may indeed be genetically given ones, but the fact that such characteristics are taken to be important is a matter of ideology; a cultural construction.

The assertion that race is really a matter of culture is quite a different issue. It refers to the fact that the criteria for categorising people into groups are cultural characteristics that can become identified as an inherent property of a particular group. This argument states that there are real differences between groups of people such as Aborigines and whites, but that these differences, contrary to popular belief, are not biological, but cultural. Thus the division into racial or cultural groups is a natural consequence of real cultural differences. This view recognises that the criteria for categorisation are varied and flexible. There has been much emphasis placed in recent years on the part so-called ethnic groups play in their own identification. But little attention has been given to the process and practice of categorisation, that is, the way a certain category of people are reproduced as a separate group within a wider society.

The categorisation of people according to country of origin, language background, religion or some loose amalgam of these called 'ethnicity' is common, and the problems associated with that categorisation have given rise to a substantial literature (e.g., Glazer & Moynihan, 1975), as well as a body of work on the wider confusions associated with the concept of ethnicity itself (e.g., de Lepervanche, 1980; Eipper, 1983). The formation of what is sometimes called ethnic identity has also received a good deal of attention in both academic and other literature, indicating that the problem is not only a conceptual one.

In popular language in Australia today ethnicity is used to refer to foreigners and race to refer to black people, usually Aborigines. Thus Aborigines face a somewhat different situation from other groups.[3] One's identity as Aboriginal or non-Aboriginal is very important in a way that it is not important whether one defines oneself as Scottish or Maori, Italian or Indian. When an immigrant ceases to refer to herself as Italian, it is not of great moment outside the circle of her own family and friends. The importance attached to such an immigrant heritage is extremely variable, and sometimes has little meaning to second and third generations of immigrant families. I am not saying that the history of an Indian family in Woolgoolga (de Lepervanche, 1984) or a Greek family in Marrickville (Bottomley, 1979) is less important for the identity of its descendents than that of an Aborigine in Brindleton, but that it is not subject to the same scrutiny and judgements of the surrounding society. Further the emotionality and accusations of betrayal if she should leave her religion or the farm are on personal and family, rather than political, lines.

One cannot, in Brindleton or Katherine, in Townsville or Adelaide, be indifferent as to whether one is going to identify as Aboriginal or not because the surrounding society will not allow such matters to be forgotten.[4] It matters a good deal to everyone in Brindleton that a person's racial identity be known, but it matters to different people

[3]The confusion is exemplified in the statement that for certain purposes of funding Aborigines are not an ethnic minority.

[4]The personal pain caused by these definitions is not confined to country towns. A woman said her adopted daughter 'had something in her' and wanted to know if there was a way of knowing if that something was Aboriginal. It turned out that the girl had been teased as being an 'Abo', and on reaching early puberty she had demanded to know what she *really* was. As the parents did not know her biological father, there was no way she could find out. The parent's view that it was not important was not shared by the girl nor, apparently, by her peers.

for different reasons. To the education authorities it matters whether one is eligible for school grants. The housing officers want to know whether one should go on a certain list. And many people in town want to know whether one is eligible for patronage or denigration. To the Aborigines, it matters whether one is on one side or another. Those who indicate any turning away from kin and community are watched and discussed. Yet there are many whose loyalty is conditional, and who try to separate themselves from the disruption and demands of indigent friends and relatives. Some have achieved virtually complete separation.

Thus my argument is not to do with what being Aboriginal consists of in some abstract sense, but with what it is believed to consist of in different arenas and with the way Aborigines are themselves changing the meaning of the term to include, in most cases, as wide a range of people as possible.[5] Government authorities have changed their definition dramatically several times in the last twenty years, which in itself indicates that the criteria are not a matter of empirical fact or even of common agreement. The question concerning race on the census form in 1981 stated 'Is the person of Aboriginal or Torres Strait Islander origin'. In 1971 and 1976 a tick box was used with categories of European, Aboriginal, Torres Strait Islander and Other provided. Prior to 1971 respondents were required to give their race, and where race was mixed, to specify the proportion of each. Of course no definition of what was meant by race was given.

It is apparent that in western NSW the edifice of racism relies on the notion that there are two races, two different kinds of people, Aboriginal and white. Despite obvious examples of people in between, the dichotomy is held to exist. The confusion is not absent from all kinds of surveys and statistical tables. In many cases 'Aboriginal descent' is specified, a vague term implying an Aboriginal forebear who was a 'real Aborigine' rather than descended from one. That is, it refers to a genetic heritage. This basis of categorisation is not only biologically meaningless, but it also ignores the fact that one must be of 'white' or 'European', or some other descent also. This categorisation recognises and reproduces the social consequences of having an Aboriginal forebear. The definition of who is officially Aboriginal relates to descent, self-identification and acceptance, and, as discussed above (pp. 108-9), creates problems for people who, for any number of historical reasons, do not satisfy all criteria.

---

[5]This issue relates to Aboriginal politics at a national level which needs far more detailed treatment than is possible here.

When whites recognise that the Aboriginal population is not homogeneous with comments such as 'I don't include X. She's different', the supposed compliment is really another attack on the whole category of Aborigines. The fact that not all blacks show the alleged depravity becomes another weapon against those that do. For, if some Aborigines 'behave well', why can't they all? This simple reasoning underlines the binary classification system which is at the heart of the racism in Brindleton. It is the simple logic following from the fact that there is one kind of decent behaviour and two kinds of people which allows the hostility to continue. This categorisation process had the effect of forcing those who by heritage (genealogical or cultural) or from personal experience stand between the black and white populations, to identify with one or another group.

The whites would like to emphasise that it is the *behaviour* of the Aborigines that is the problem, but it is their identification of the behaviour of the *Aborigines* that becomes the Aborigines' problem. The separation, exclusion and vilification is directed at the category Aboriginal. Many whites and Aborigines argue that race should be ignored, and that the town does not have a racial problem but rather a crime problem, an unemployment problem or a problem of bad behaviour by one section of the population. As we have seen, the assertion that the town is divided by race will be identified as stirring. No critical attention is paid to differentiation based on wealth and power.

The answer the schools give as to who is Aboriginal is those who are on the grant. This is not so obvious even to the Aboriginal students. Recall the girl who asked her class-mate why she was not on the grant. The latter girl's white father said she could not get the grant because you had to believe you were Aboriginal. During their teenage years school students begin to discuss such things, and the Aboriginal students try to make a virtue of their position. One dark girl, whose family's strategy is to gain respect in the wider community by their cleanliness, propriety and good manners while remaining firmly committed to the Aboriginal cause, has asserted that certain people should not get the grant. In one case this is for not being sufficiently dark, and in another for not associating with Aborigines.

The students of Aboriginal descent who do not think of themselves as Aboriginal gain approval from most teachers, while those who are on the grant but 'don't appear as Aboriginal' merit disapproval. Perhaps they should pass as white. However both these groups are more acceptable than the reserve people who are on the grant but not apparently making proper use of it. They are not trying to become assimilated. Some of these children are the 'uncontrollable' ones.

Biology is powerful; skin colour can be used in a number of ways to denigrate. Individuals can be included or excluded from the category Aboriginal by different people in different contexts, while the categorisation has an appearance of being involuntary. Someone can be denigrated for claiming inclusion in the category when not sufficiently dark, and for trying to remain outside it when a shade too dark. This flexibility makes for some curious judgements. 'She's as white as I am' is an exclamation implying that the person is somehow fooling everyone by pretending to be Aboriginal. While 'He has a splash' is an explanation for any anti-social tendencies, which are supposedly in the blood.

Among Aborigines the accusations are different. Individuals are said to be 'pretending to be white' or of being 'like a coconut, black on the outside and white on the inside'. Such people are being accused of disloyalty to their own people and also to themselves. A common observation is that 'He has forgotten who he is.' Such statements are often directed to those who have gained a good job, to those who are active in some organisation, or to the younger people who may associate too much with whites. Thus there is a large section of the Aboriginal population who would not be subject to such accusations as they have little to do with the whites. For them also, rejection by the Aboriginal community could not be risked because the wider community is unwelcoming.

However there is a substantial minority which is constantly accused in this way. This is the interstitial group. Most are married to whites and many have jobs associated with government programmes or are active in some public capacity. Some lead private lives, avoiding the pubs, football matches and other public gathering places, but there is a substantial group for whom drinking at the same pub confirms their unity as a social group. However these differ markedly in their political convictions. Nor do they share a sense of loyalty to 'the Aborigines'. Members of this group are most likely to attract accusations of being coconuts, but they are also the ones who make such accusations about others. This is because such accusations do not relate only to relations with whites but to actions and strategies concerning the committees and meetings related to Aboriginal issues in the town. One woman, for instance, denies that her public service job should only be concerned with Aborigines, and refuses to assist those who ask for her help after hours. While she often merits the epithet of coconut, she has a secure place in the social group I have called interstitial.

While these people form a group in terms of a degree of cultural unity and because they have some links to both the black and the white communities, their individual differences concerning issues related to the racial divide do not lead to unity of action. In fact the very reason for the existence of this group, the fact that their family lives are a racial meeting ground, ensures a prevarication about political issues which surround the racial division in Brindleton.

MUNDANE RACISM

Traditions

I had a striking lesson in the meanings of cultural tradition in Brindleton when a local grazier wearing a tartan tie began to talk of his love of tradition. He took great pride in his knowledge and rendering of Australian bush yarns and songs, but also in his Scottish background exemplified in his tartan, his clan and his castle. The drunken Scottish bar attendant who had a broad Scottish accent derided the notion that the grazier, who was born in Australia, had any connection with his home country. Quite an argument developed about the relative claims to authenticity. The grazier claimed, with stories of his forebears taking up land in Australia, and his kin and their property in Scotland, to be as legitimately Australian as he was Scottish. The working-class Scot denied that was possible; he did not accept that the predominantly green tie was a real tartan nor that an Australian could also be a true Scot. The Aboriginal man listening to all this said nothing. His traditions would have added a rather embarrassing dimension to the discussion.

These men were both making claims concerning tradition and culture, but the symbols had different meanings to each. The source of the particular symbols of a culture and its forms of art or ritual is the set of beliefs, values and practices which the whole history of a people has given rise to. When whites assert that Aborigines have no traditions left, they are referring to the particular symbols and forms which were characteristic of the Aboriginal past. But the sentimental clinging to past practices is not necessary to a living tradition. Some practices, such as slavery and corsets, are happily abandoned without the tradition they are associated with being lost. How certain practices or traditions are valued over time depends on a whole range of things; in Brindleton it depends on one's social position. Thus stories of the early grazier families are eagerly sought by the historical society. The history and forebears of the Aboriginal population are not considered of general interest. In fact discussion of the past suffering of local Aborigines is considered to be provocative and unnecessary. Yet, as discussed above, the tradition of Aborigines is a real one, strongly tied in with rural labour, and with the reserve and financial hardship. This tradition needs recognition before the question of difference and culture can be confronted and settled.

The confusion between race and culture, between values and traditions, is evident in this woman's views.

You hear bits about tribal law; that this one is in charge of that one and the family all comes together but I just don't know how much this rings true in this day and age when you have quartercasts who have so little blood. I don't know if it would affect them. The thing that riles the white people is their lack of ownership. If we have worked for something we consider it is ours. They don't. If you are living next door they will help themselves to anything and not consider it stealing. We look on it as thieving, but whether they do or not I don't know. I don't know if it is the tribal influence and whether we expect too much of them, or whether we should expect them to live like we do.

There is here reference to tradition, but it is clearly seen in a different light from that of the disputing Scots or the kind of tradition which is treated with great respect and deference in Brindleton. 'Old Brindleton families' and 'early settlers' are referred to in the newspaper without anyone being confused about their colour.

An Aboriginal man from Brindleton who visited Alice Springs was quite overwhelmed to hear Aboriginal people speaking their own languages. He said 'There's lots of Aboriginal people walking around up there. They look at me as if I wasn't Aboriginal.' His own identification as Aboriginal comes not from genes or any specific consciously practised culture, but from membership of a group that has been so defined, whether it wished to be or not, and yet has been accused of not being authentically Aboriginal.

Mundane racism

Racism should be seen as a process which divides a population into unequal races. Before discussing the theoretical justification for what appears to be a circular definition, I want to highlight the way this dividing is practiced in mundane ways in everyday life. Despite its imaginary quality, the dividing line is kept in place by a whole series of processes which operate to reinforce each other. At the level of conversation, violent threats, disparaging jokes and casual opinion or advice on 'the Aborigines' are an accepted part of everyday life. Among the blow-ins, the discussion of 'their' problems in terms of notions of deprivation and a culture of poverty is commonplace.

Much of the orthodox discussion of 'the problem' makes assumptions about inherent differences using the symbols of breeding and blood. For instance in discussing delinquent behaviour one man said:

The problem goes back to the parents; like breed like. Ronny D. was an assault and rob man and his 14 kids have similar attitudes. Even his daughter who looks white. She gets riled up easy, pig headed, and won't see both sides. She's definitely got a splash in her. The only way I can see to break the cycle is to take the kids away.

The attribution of these characteristics to 'blood' is not as important a characteristic of racism, I would argue, as the casual and confident way such judgements are made by people who know that they will not be contradicted. This mundane racism warrants further examination.

The expression of hatred is common, and remains shocking to an outsider. One man tells openly and casually in lurid terms stories about how the blacks destroyed houses and public amenities, and the danger that 'the blacks will take to you with a bottle'. A guest at a party had a device in his pocket which would signal him if someone tried to break into his car. He displayed it, explaining with relish that if it beeped he would 'go and smash the boong's head in'. After some conflict in the street, a man at the bar says loudly 'If that half coon up the road wants to fight I can fell him with a bit of 4 by 2' (a piece of wood). Several heads nod in approval.

A young man visiting from another small town made his bid for acceptance at the bar by informing his new aquaintances that all the blackfellas should be put out in the outback and they would starve to death. He added, 'The real black ones are OK. The ones who make trouble are part Aboriginal.' Another wise country lad said in reply, 'The old guys made the worst mistake when they took the bounty off for shooting boongs.' Such loud and challenging assertions are a commonplace part of bar conversation. Another who was repeating the old phrases about Aborigines sitting on their big fat bums not wanting jobs, asserted that he could always get a job. He would do so by offering to work harder and for less money than others.

Others make 'jokes'. A government welfare worker who has a cold is asked by someone he rings up from another town if he caught it from a blackfellow. He laughs approvingly. A more savage example is the warning I received from the manager of a club that there might be blackfellows at the disco, but we would be able to smell them a long way off. Such extreme comments are partly a jest, a defiant flaunting of prohibited views in order to shock or outrage listeners for the amusement of the speaker. They also function in terms of the stereotypes and categories which are purveyed in the public sphere.

An everyday strategy of such leading citizens as the councillors is the denial that racism or even races exist. People claim not to look at the colour of a person's skin, that it doesn't matter if a person is black, white or brindle, and that any discussion of race is racist. A reporter from a city newspaper asked one of the council candidates how many Aborigines were standing for election. 'I don't know' he replied complacently, 'I don't look at their skin colour.' Yet one of his friends had commented casually about the Aborigines; 'Ugly looking people; frightening.' These assertions are not seen as contradictory.

The denial of awareness of race is a logical part of the refusal to countenance any measures favouring Aborigines which might solve the problems of structural inequality. For instance favouring an Aboriginal candidate for a job is treated with horror. 'If that isn't racism, what is' they say. 'They complained for years that whites were favoured and that was wrong; now they want to favour blacks.' The idea that having Aborigines in positions of respect and authority in the town might improve the situation in other ways is simply denied.

The only form of racism that anyone will plead guilty to is favouring blacks. Teachers confessed that they practice double standards, accepting behaviour from Aboriginal students that would be punished from others. One teacher said:

> I'd be a racist on two counts. First I don't think much of Aboriginal people in general because they don't take advantage of the opportunities they are given. And second I favour the Aboriginal kids in class; they are praised and encouraged for things you take for granted in the white kids. White kids are resentful of Aboriginal kids getting things free and not being forced to do things.

Another teacher said she did not ask Aboriginal kids to pick up papers because they would refuse to do so and an unavoidable confrontation would result which would undermine her authority. In each case it is an individual's behaviour that is defined as problematic.

The Anti-Discrimination Board reacts to particular events and to certain kinds of views in ways that local people find incomprehensible. One man told the ADB that in 200 years time there would not be an Aboriginal problem because they would be so interbred that they would not be identifiable. The board members expressed shock at what they said was a prejudiced comment from a responsible citizen. This man simply projected the mixing between Aborigines and whites forward to the future and assumed that if there was no physical sign of difference between the two there would be no racial differentiation. As his wife is Aboriginal by descent, but not identification, he lives with evidence of this daily, and naturally considers that all the problems of the Aboriginal people, to which he has given some sympathetic thought, would be solved if all were like his wife and children.

Had he been accused of condoning genocide he would have pointed out that in his opinion it has already occurred. That is, like most of the white citizens of Brindleton and a few of the black, he believes that there is no Aboriginal identity that is worth saving. Poverty and depression and some specific Aboriginal views are recognised, but are regarded in a negative light as problems.

These mundane expressions of racism bear witness to its orthodoxy and legitimacy, although the legitimacy of certain kinds of expression is increasingly being challenged. The powerful local resources which back up the orthodox views are evident in phone calls and letters to ministers demanding better policing. For instance the ADB report on the causes and cures for crime and vandalism was rejected with scorn and in writing. A policeman tried to stop the showing of the Aboriginal film 'The wrong side of the road'. Many other examples were given above. The aggressively propounded common sense of the dominant local whites asserts that the blacks, rather than having the problems, are the problem.

The small group of whites who are dedicated to working for the Aboriginal community in some way constantly deplores the overt expression of racism. The popular way to avoid being deemed a racist is to either like those to whom others show hostility or to help them. In the cities of Australia it is reasonably easy for whites to like ethnics, and one can sometimes have Aboriginal friends. But in the country towns this is difficult. Those who deplore racism have to take the second line and help Aborigines. The reason for the difficulty has been alluded to above. There is little social or domestic familiarity between Aborigines and whites. Few Aborigines own houses or cars and most would not invite someone in for a cup of tea. Thus the anti-racists in Brindleton have a difficult job practising what they preach. They are distanced from Aborigines in ways they have no control over.

Aboriginal responses to racism

The everyday racial hostility discussed above is expressed by whites in the absence of blacks. In quite different circumstances, where Aborigines are dependent on services provided exclusively by whites, mundane racism is apparent to those who are the least able to resist.[6] For instance the social service cheques were formerly distributed through the post office. While many people in Brindleton depend on social service payments, it is those Aborigines who make no secret of their dependence who attract censure as social service dependents. *They* get their cheques on Thursdays. The post office staff show their irritation with the blacks who come at 9 a.m. asking for mail that will not be sorted until 11 a.m. Often it does not come at all because the recipient has moved, has not filled in the required form or some such disaster. Many Aborigines have taken post office boxes to avoid the humiliation of facing impatient staff. The tourist or visitor asking for mail will be served before the humble or dishevelled black. However the significance of the day the cheques come is quite apparent to the businesses in the town.

Those Aborigines who become involved in organisations dominated by whites come up against discrimination expressed in another form. I have already referred to the way the one Aboriginal person on the shire council was called to account for 'his people' who were causing a nuisance to another councillor. At a law and order meeting one businessman voiced the platitude that Aboriginal parents should be made responsible for their children. A young Aboriginal woman pointed out that such a suggestion was rather stupid as the problem was just that. How could those parents who suffered from alcoholism be responsible for their children? They

---

[6]This is a case where the shorthand of racial categories is inaccurate. There may be people who could be defined and define themselves as Aborigines who are employed to provide such services. However the services are dominated by a mode of operation which is foreign to the bulk of Aborigines.

could not even be responsible for themselves. These two people clearly defined the social problem quite differently.

On committees concerned with health or education, Aborigines will often be involved in discussion where the assumptions of the whites who run the meeting are at odds with their perceptions. In such situations it is difficult and even embarrassing to change the basis of discussion. This occurs partly because the norms of everyday Aboriginal family life are not those taken for granted by whites. Aborigines are left feeling frustrated and misunderstood without the power to have their views prevail. For this reason, meetings within the Aboriginal community are more relaxed and seem more productive than those with whites.

Many whites distance themselves from the personal aspects of Aboriginal life out of embarrassment at what it might reveal. A teacher at the infant school advised her junior colleague not to enquire too far into the parentage and relations of the children. The knowledge that two of her pupils who are sisters have different fathers is enough to cause a tactful avoidance of the topic. The mother, of course, may not be at all ashamed. Even whites who may feel no disaproval at the complex and unorthodox family life of some Aboriginal friends will not find it easy to know how to refer to such matters. As kin are so important to Aborigines this virtual taboo on mention of family makes for a real hiatus in communication.

Aborigines are seldom aware of the mundane denigration and are shocked if they do hear it. When an Aboriginal woman heard someone making a long-distance call from the public telephone telling a friend about how bad the blacks in town were, she was outraged. 'That person will believe that story' she said, 'They will never come here to see what we are like.'

While racist attitudes expressed as overt hostility may be the most inflamatory and painful disadvantage which Aborigines face, they are only one element of the ideological dimension which divides the population. The division is, as we have seen, deep-seated and pervasive. It is tied in with other elements of a whole ideology of worth and acceptability. The ideology is replete with contradictions and inconsistencies and is bound up with the material dimension of inequality.

A few situations of overt discrimination have been experienced by individuals[7] and a few whites are known to be hostile to blacks. A

---

[7]When the Aborigines complain of discrimination they often have little evidence that the same behaviour in whites would not receive the same disapproval. So when a white woman complained about the drunk and violent young man at her daughter's

grazier's wife who has been a 'nurse' for the health commission at a small village for years is notorious for bullying those who need her help. A young man in town, well-known for his overt racist aggressiveness, was alleged to scare Aborginal footballers by trying to run them over on the street after some conflict at the football club. Such people cannot be ignored. However such specific cases do not affect most people in their daily lives.

To most Aborigines in the town racism is a feeling of discomfort among whites. But many would not define their discomfort as part of a racist process. One old man said, 'I've got no complaints about the whitefellas or blackfellas. Only blackfellas don't talk to you as much as the whitefellas. The whitefellas say hello, give me a lift. I'm a member of the clubs. Cops will give me a lift if I'm staggering along a bit drunk.' Such deference is complementary to the hard-line, conservative views which are characteristic of some of the old white residents. More generally there is a feeling among blacks of exclusion, of mistrust and of resentment against those who evince an air of superiority about the town.

I have observed earlier that the everyday expressions of racial differentiation are taken for granted and ignored by most people most of the time. The comment of one young Aboriginal man that he had not realised Brindleton was a racist town until he left it is indicative of this fact. But another observation that 'You can feel the racism in town all the time which is why the Aboriginal people stay together', may more accurately reflect the common Aboriginal experience. Such a view is supported by the jokes which satirise the attitudes of whites and the no-win situation that blacks are in. 'They moved from this end of town when we moved in. If we move up town they will have to go to the next village. Then to Queensland.' 'They are afraid the colour will rub off if they get too close.'[8]

A policeman, making conversation with an Aboriginal man outside the courthouse, was bemoaning the drought conditions. His listener replied laconically 'No, this weather's OK.' 'No I mean the drought',

---

classy party it was significant that, instead of the outrage and threats offered by this same woman when drunk Aborigines cause problems, she spoke with sympathy of the lad's teenage confusions.

[8]The Aborigines find they just cannot win. When the manager explained to one of the councillors how responsible the Aboriginal committee would be in controlling the use of the community hall, keeping it locked and checking on any damage, he believed he would gain support for these efforts which were of the kind the council constantly recommended. But the councillor reported to others that use of the hall was going to be restricted and it would be kept locked most of the time. This misinterpretation seemed deliberate.

said the policeman. 'The heat's great.' After a few more such exchanges with the policeman becoming increasingly irritated, the other man said, 'If the drought continues all the sheep will die, and you whitefellas will go away and leave us in peace with our land.'

Ironic comments are made about the fact that a criminal record precludes club membership. 'All they have to do now is convict us all. They've got most of us already.' The council's attempts to counter various nuisances also give rise to some amusement among the Aborigines. Public phones were moved into the street because, it was alleged, the alcove they stood in previously became a place for drunks to lie, children to defaecate and telephone users to complain about. The large plate-glass windows on the main street which have received a number of bricks through them have been replaced with bricks. The breeze block wall base at the corner where the drinking men sit had the holes carefully plugged up because bottles were secreted in the holes when the police appeared. Thus the nuisances are repressed. The town authorities are engaged in a vigil protecting the public face of the town. Such strategies, like the removal of the seats mentioned earlier, is part and parcel of the council adminis-tration of Brindleton.

Aborigines assert that friendships formed at school between black and white students do not last. As they get older barriers arise which are partly conscious policy of parents, but also a response to the separation which permeates the town. One Aboriginal man said 'Some marry black and white but that is when they knew each other at school and were too much in love.' Young people at school are challenged by the racial stereotypes but have little power to over-come them. One young man was wounded by a teacher's comment on the day he left school nine years ago; 'I suppose you will end up like the rest of them at the meatworks, on the grog and in jail.'

There is an awareness of racism in jobs. Labouring jobs will entail joking and teasing on racial lines. Joking is part of the structure of the interpersonal politics of racism in which Aborigines are always the butt of the jokes. In the restrained atmosphere of offices and shops the more subtle forms of discrimination are difficult to specify let alone complain of. They mainly consist of assumptions about friends, family and social life. Few Aborigines work in offices or shops, although there are some who consider either themselves or one of their parents Aboriginal, but are not known as such by their fellow workers. Such people are often very aware of racist sentiments, but fear dismissal or ostracism if they object.

Black racism?

Frequently whites accuse blacks of practising racism. They are referring to Aboriginal expressions of hostility and distancing from whites. If such attitudes and sentiments exist can they be called racism? As discussed previously, racism cannot be defined as a matter of individual attitudes and prejudice. Given that Aborigines are in no position to practise discrimination or even achieve groups closure against whites, this alleged racism, or hostility expressed towards whites, is better understood as a defensive response.

It is clear that in Brindleton the experience of many blacks is of harassment, fear and humiliation at the hands of police, welfare personnel and other organisations. This raises the question of why the war of attrition should continue given an already dispossessed and subject population. One answer could be that it is not a war of attrition but simply immediate conflicts due to young and ignorant police, inexperienced school teachers and conservative councillors on the one hand, and Aboriginal alcoholics and vandals, unemployment, poverty or cultural confusion on the other. Such a view blames the behaviour of individuals. But the history of processes of exclusion, the regularity and systematic nature of white aggression as well as other expressions of a belief in racial separation, precludes this explanation. Racism has been identified with a structure of domination in which the category of race disguises the relationship and holds nature responsible.

An alternative explanation is that the black population is not completely subjugated and powerless. It has not been demoralised and rendered passive. In support of this view is the history of movements of resistance (e.g., Horner, 1974), the contemporary acts and expressions of opposition as well as the organisations, such as the Aboriginal legal service, which appear to pose a challenge to the adequacy of the major institutions of our society. Is it that challenges to white hegemony are seen as a threat by power holders in the town? Labelling such responses as racist is one way in which the legitimacy of alternative ideas is disparaged.

Besides the expression of ironic humour towards whites described above, there are two forms that anti-white attitudes commonly take. One is within organisations which either have Aboriginal representatives or are Aboriginal organisations, and where whites may be unwelcome or face critical appraisal of their role. The other is the direct expression of hostility towards whites often by young people.

The latter consists mostly of general accusations made indiscriminately about white racism. They are expressions of resentment and anger made, often unjustly, to those people who are nearest, such as school teachers.

In both cases the authority relations that exist can be balanced, to some extent, by Aborigines grilling whites and making them account for their actions. In the larger centres most whites who work in the departments of Aboriginal Affairs, Education or any one of the bureaucracies charged with implementing the enlightenment policies, will be familiar with the claim made by some Aborigines that whites should no longer speak about Aboriginal matters. Aborigines are the experts and Aboriginal views must prevail. Many people recognise both the strength and weakness of such assertions. A person who is dedicated to their job, is married to an Aboriginal person, and whose children are Aboriginal may be in the painful situation of being told that he or she is a white and knows nothing. It is in circumstances where Aborigines are seen and see themselves as representing their race that such assertions are made. The experience of being black is considered more authoritative than that of someone who has married in. The fact that whites will not treat Aborigines as equals or listen to them or take their views seriously is stressed. Confronted with such assertions, whites tend to remain silent and deferential. The legitimacy of their views on any matter is suspect. But such attempts to control the exercise of authority by whites can hardly be deemed an expression of racism in anyone's language.

The danger of course is that the legitimacy of Aboriginal representatives might be established on the basis of the ability to control or bully whites. This advantages the most vociferous individuals rather than those with the soundest political knowledge. In fact other Aborigines are often angered, or 'shamed', if friendly and supportive whites are seen to be treated unfairly. The people most subject to such direct pressure are those who work in an official capacity most closely with Aborigines. Though perhaps least guilty of arrogance towards Aborigines they are in the firing line because of their proximity. But the circumstances are those of bureaucratic decision-making within a continuing structure of domination, even though it is solicitous rather than repressive. The white public servant is the bearer of the inadequacies of policy made by white policy-makers.

Not all Aboriginal communities have members who will challenge white authority. Sometimes there is no grassroots activity anyway, and the only criticism may be the curses of disillusioned youths. The aggressive assertion of the right of blacks to be heard would be valuable if it became prevalent in Brindleton, for it would achieve an avenue of expression of anger which otherwise continues to fuel indiscriminate destructiveness.

Of course not all whites are blind to what is occurring. One old resident with an old interest in social justice told me Aborigines are more family people than we are. He said:

> We have told them not to think and then told them to think for themselves. So we have earned any problem. We all say the shopkeepers are robbing us. The young ones think 'well, if he is robbing me why should I not rob him'. You can't on the one hand overcharge and then say theft is wrong. The feeling of being badly done by is the basis of the problem and poor whites are in the same boat.

THEORIES OF RACISM

Race

To understand the reasoning behind scientific racism as well as the more popular forms of racist belief it is necessary to give a brief account of the concept race. Race as a biological term refers to the same kind of category as sub-species. While species cannot, by definition, interbreed, sub-species or races are groups that happen not to have interbred for a period and as a consequence display some different genetic frequencies. That is, populations between which there has been some barrier to interbreeding, usually geographic, show some different frequencies of genetically given characteristics, some of which are observable, superficial and physical.

The human species is characterised by immense genetic variation and there is more variation within one population than there is between any two populations which are considered to be races. Furthermore any genetic differences between populations are differences of frequency. That is, only by taking a single genetically given characteristic can populations be divided into two discrete categories. Once two or more of the millions of such characteristics are considered, there will be problems of categorisation (Livingstone, 1962).

Skin colour is popularly considered to be the marker of racial categories, perhaps because of the visibility of the shading. In fact the genetic basis of skin colour is a minute part of the total genetic material which is inherited. Yet skin colour has immense meaning in our society at least. It is almost universally thought to denote a racial category, which popularly means fundamentally different kinds of human beings. Such categorisation has multi-faceted and changing consequences.

Perhaps the strongest challenge to the attribution of psychological and social characteristics to genetic causes, and to the logic of racial categorisation, comes from the process of miscegenation. In Australia the products of 'mixed-race' unions have almost always become part of the Aboriginal population. As the 'mixed-race' portion of the population increased, definitions of half, quarter and one-eighth Aboriginal were developed. No details of the proportion of English or Irish parentage was recorded; it was the Aboriginal heritage that defined a person's legal status. What did those who had some knowledge of the relatively precise science of genetics have to say about this biologically dubious classification system?

The categorisation process went unquestioned by scientists because those of mixed race joined the Aborigines and did not, or rather could not, by virtue of their European paternity, claim membership in the European population. Thus they did not constitute a public challenge to racial classification. Further this miscegenation was occurring in the rural areas of the colonies where it was ignored, not only by academic biologists, but by urban dwellers in general. The anthropologists continued to collect the bones of 'full-bloods'.

A pseudo-biological explanation developed for the consequences of miscegenation. The inferior class of Europeans were not only blamed at times for murdering Aborigines, but were also said to be the ones who were fathering infants of Aboriginal women. Thus, it was explained, the quality of the offspring could hardly show the superior European characteristics. In fact there is evidence that many of the self-styled superior Europeans, that is, the wealthy ones, fathered children of Aboriginal women in the outback. It would not be possible to discover if their trajectory in life was determined by any heritage from the father because the father usually disowned them. It would seem more useful to assume that the genetic heritage, which is as we have seen greatly variable in all populations, does not determine the position in society of any individual. Social groupings that are created over time may indeed be marked by certain inherited characteristics under certain circumstances, but the continuing existence and separateness of these groupings is determined not by their characteristics but by their relationship with other groups, and this is quite another matter. Such interrelationships have been the subject of this work.

There has been no consistent view of racism or of race in the Australian literature. Stevens' three volume collection *Racism; The Australian Experience* (1972, 1974, 1977) does not have one perspective. In his introduction Stevens depicts race conflict as a cancer, and discusses the difficulty of identifying 'What in fact was evidence of racism and what were the characteristics of other aspects of social disorder, namely mal-function or inequality.' There was also a 'semantic question of what was meant by race prejudice and precisely when it became racism' (Stevens, 1974:2). There is a reference to the notion of erroneous beliefs, and to the difference between racism and racialism, and generally a reliance on detecting a specific form of ideology which can be labelled as racism. Stevens' definition of racism relies on biological differences being present. He says that the problems (of analysis) were most difficult where biological differences were least (ibid., 3), and that the contributors deal with racism in its most patent form — 'discrimination between people based on biological grounds' (Stevens, 1972:2).

Despite some useful analyses in Stevens' three volumes, these references to the biological element of any racial situation are not taken up in any of the articles and there is virtually no reference to miscegenation. One comment from Encel points out that 'the emphasis on physical differences ignores the enormous amount of racial hostility directed against people who are socially rather than physically distinct, of which the prime example is anti-semitism' (Encel, 1974:30).

An implicit assumption about the importance of racial, meaning biological, differences as a part of the social problems associated with Aboriginal groups is embedded in many works. For instance the authors of a recent work on the history of race relations in Australia congratulate themselves on a new broad view of race relations as 'involving significant physical differences, marked typically by an awareness of skin colour' (Yarwood & Knowling, 1982:7). McConnochie's (1973) 'analysis of the concepts of race and racism' has an early section on population genetics and Aborigines are treated as a biologically distinct race throughout. Nowhere does the author discuss miscegenation. Broome (1982) uses the term 'half-castes' uncritically, and argues that ethno-centrism in the early days of European settlement gave way to hard-line racism. By racism he means negative prejudice based on a belief in genetic determination.

No one discusses how 'race' is to be redefined in a situation of genetic mixing. Skin colour is still in popular terms, and often in academic writings, a major though not essential part of defining who belongs to the category 'Aboriginal'. Much of the work demonstrating the quantitatively inferior position of Aborigines in health, education and before the law does not discuss this question either (e.g., Gale & Wundersitz, 1982). This implies not only that Aborigines are a self-evident category of the population, but also that the problems in these areas are specifically Aboriginal ones, different from other kinds of poor housing, ill health or unemployment.

The tendency to reify race is common. While denying that racial characteristics can explain behavioural variation or social inequality, most theories do accept by default that there are biological races. The consequences of the fact that racial categories are socially constructed have not been fully explored. If racial groupings are social constructs surely social analysis must begin with the question of how they are constructed.

Racism has been the subject of a good deal of academic writing. Much of this literature has considered the explicit expression of racial prejudice, discrimination or structural inequality without a close examination of how the processes operate at a community or an interpersonal level (e.g., Montagu, 1964; Rex, 1983). There have been a number of perspectives developed which relate to general theories of society or of personality and which are linked to popular usages of the concept of racism.

Socio-biology and the new racism

The socio-biologists have attempted to underpin the popular notion of prejudice by asserting in a pseudo-scientific jargon the innate basis of racism. This is a new version of an old and still popular idea that hostility towards those who are different from oneself is natural. Ideas of the naturalness of racist sentiments lead to dismissing enquiry into the social conditions which produce racism. Such views take any negative judgements expressed towards another group as a form of racism. Thus the fact that one Aboriginal group in Arnhem Land makes disparaging comments about other groups is taken to be evidence of the same kind of social process as that usually defined as racist. I would argue that such a phenomenon is more akin to the contemptuous attitudes of country people to the city dweller. In terms of individual psychology there may indeed be something common between all kinds of interpersonal or group hostility, but these are not necessarily encoded in a systematic ideology of domination.

Furthermore such a generalised notion of racism equates all kinds of denigration expressed by one group about another. It is premised on removing Aboriginal groups from their particular context to a general one, which involves a distortion. In fact sentiments towards other Aboriginal groups may vary with, for instance, the changing pattern of marriage alliance between close and distant kin, or changing relationships with mining companies. There may be common elements of ideologies which encode and evaluate group characteristics, but these are trivial features which do not account for the dynamic social processes I have discussed in this work.

The view that racism is a natural proclivity of humans has been scientised by the socio-biologists and has gained adherents even among those who earlier argued for political and economic explanations to do with exploitation. Pierre van den Berghe's book *The Ethnic Phenomenon*, which argues that 'ethnocentrism and racism are deeply rooted in our biology' (1981:xi), has convinced Rex that there is a 'primordial tendency to advance the interests of those thought of as one's own' (Rex, 1983:xx).

Socio-biologists are prone to posit tendencies and propensities as being biologically given and as explaining complex and heterogeneous areas of human behaviour, even the way societies are structured, in terms of biology. Frequently the tendency that is considered a determinant is a revamped popular notion which explains vast inequities in society (e.g., Ardrey, 1967; Tiger, 1969).

One aspect of van den Berghe's 'ethnic phenomenon', racism, is a way of recognising one's own kin, but only works when there has been long-distance migration making 'genetically inheritied phenotypes . . . the easiest, most visible and most reliable predictors of group membership' (1981:32). Racism is one way of distancing oneself from those to whom one should not, in the interests of one's genetic future, show nepotistic cooperation.[9] This lack of cooperation and hostility that are features of racism could be expected to keep the gene pools separated.

---

[9] It is difficult to treat the motivation proposed by socio-biologists seriously. If men are constantly motivated by the need or desire to maximise their fitness, why are they not more adulterous and randy than is the case? Explaining behaviour in terms of complex calculations of the probable outcomes seems equally ludicrous (Dickermann, 1984:432).

However there is another genetically given trait which the socio-biologists say interferes. 'Miscegenation almost invariably occurs because racism as such does little to inhibit it. Dominant group men, whether racist or not, are seldom reluctant to maximise their fitness with subordinate group women' (van den Berghe, 1981:33).

Australian history could presumably provide an example. It is quite clear that the populations which inhabited Australia in the 18th century, one indigenous and one European, had different gene frequencies, or, more accurately, different alleles at some loci, particularly those shown in skin colour and to a lesser extent in body shape and hair type. But it is equally clear that there has been massive intermingling of these gene pools so that the most striking phenotypical differences have virtually disappeared in many parts of the continent. Thus while racism is natural to the socio-biologists, miscegenation is even more natural.

This would seem to create problems for the theory. Nepotism, if genetically given, would surely have to be extended to one's off-spring across the racial boundary. Where there are two racial groups there is a contradiction between the tendency for men to increase their reproductive success (RS to the socio-biologists) by impregnating as many women as possible, and the tendency to nepotism, ethnism and other kinds of loyalty to those thought of as one's own. Van den Berghe comes to some kind of resolution by predicting that 'it is the long distance migration over genetic gradients that creates racism: conversely miscegenation attenuates it' (1981:32–3). But while this allows the theory to remain intact, the assertion that miscegenation reduces the level of racism does not accord with empirical observations in Brindleton and, I would venture to say, in a host of other places.

In fact it appears that those white men who continually and consistently impregnated Aboriginal women acted with biological insanity[10] as Aboriginal infant mortality was high and the population in decline. There is also doubt about the socio-biologist's prediction that subordinate group women maximised their fitness by mating with dominant group men, as they were quite likely to contract venereal disease. But more important for my purpose is the quite erroneous view that any kind of nepotism was practised by white

---

[10]The more popular explanation of the mingling of the gene pools is that Aboriginal women became a sexual commodity exploited to satisfy the sexual desires of the invading men. Socio-biological theory would argue that this fails to specify the real biological reason for these events.

men towards those kin who were defined as mixed-bloods. While in some cases the white fathers of these children did support them, in many they did not even know they existed. And as for any general cooperation extended to those thought of as one's own, nothing could be further from what in fact occurred.

The virulence of racism increased rather than decreased with the increase in genetic relatedness. Mixed-bloods were said to inherit the worst of both races. While there is no doubt that sexual exploitation occurred commonly, there have also been long-lasting and apparently felicitous relationships between black women and white men and less frequently between white women and black men. However this has not led to wider family unity. Rather the individual who crossed the racial divide has been rejected by the white community and has usually joined the black community. The children are not considered as warranting membership in the white community unless, as sometimes happens, they repudiate their black kin. Even then their status is tenuous.

Thus if biological relatedness leads to nepotistic sentiments or practices, how is it that the increase in relatedness between immigrant and indigenous populations in Australia led to enduring hostility? I would suggest there is no meaningful biological reason for this.

The notion that racism is natural is related to ideas of normal fear of strangers or of the unknown. However it seems that interest and curiosity about strangers is also natural, for instance to travellers and to anthropologists. There are many divisions into 'us' and 'them' based on place, profession, sex, age and interests as well as kin. The reason why some group boundaries are constantly broken and some loyalties are extended across major social barriers cannot be explained by any idea of natural cleaving to one's own kind. I would argue that it is no more natural to dislike those of a different skin colour, shape or hair type, than it is for women to dislike men! Inequalities of power though may tend to cause conflict.

Denying the accuracy of such scientistic nonsense may lend it a legitimacy that it does not deserve. Such constructions of racism should not be seen simply as part of a changing and incorrect field of representations, but as a sphere of social action which intersects and serves certain power relations. What enables them to circulate as 'truth' or 'science' if they are so fanciful? The logic of the arguments, or the innacuracy or accuracy with which they accord with empirical reality are not the only issues here, for there is also an attempt to construct such a reality. This attempt is evident in the 'new racism'.

Barker has called the new racism a theory of 'pseudo-biological culturalism' (1981:23), a consistent and complete theory of human nature concealed in innocent common sense language. He shows how ideas about race and place and identity in Britain are dedicated to showing why the 'aliens' should be kept out or sent home both in their own interests and in that of the British. This theory of human nature asserts that the instinct to preserve an identity and defend a territory is one of the 'deepest and strongest in mankind' (ibid., 22, quoting Powell), and that for the English that identity and territory is bound up with keeping England white. Britain is the natural home and birthright of its indigenous peoples, and 'foreigners too have their natural homes. Stopping immigration is being kind to them as well' (ibid., 21, quoting Powell). Here we can see how ideas stemming from the socio-biology enterprise are being used as part of powerful social messages.

Elements of the new racism are rather uncomfortable for Australians to contemplate. If Britain is the natural home of the British how did they manage to transplant so successfully to the antipodes? Some of the black immigrants to Britain have asserted 'We are here because you were there', a statement that nicely places their arrival in Britain in the context of colonialism. The title of a book studying racism in Britain is also apt; *The Empire Strikes Back* (C.C.C.S., 1982). But some of the British colonisers stayed 'there', for instance, in Australia. The Aborigines triumphant claim to 40,000 years of habitation sits ill with any notion of a natural home for the whites of this country. Thus the notions about race that hold sway in Australia do not share the emphasis on homeland which is evident in the new British racism. What they do share is the conviction that there is a tradition and an identity that is somehow connected with skin colour as well as place of origin. While conservative leaders in Britain appealed to feelings of belonging and to notions of legitimate home country to foster hostility, others can do the same in Australia only by ignoring the fact that Europeans are immigrants.

The historian Blainey has attempted to influence the immigration policy against the acceptance of immigrants from 'Asia' in ways that have something in common with the new ideas about race being promoted in Britain. There is the notion of a cultural tradition being swamped. He speaks of the threat to the Australian 'way of life' and of the 'limits of tolerance' which Australians in the past extended to immigrants. He sees himself voicing the 'genuine fears' that working-class Australians have of 'Asians flocking into their neighbourhood'.

'The poorer people in the cities are the real sufferers, and see themselves as such', not only because 'their' jobs are being competed for, but also because their way of life is being altered (Blainey, 1984). Thus Blainey makes a claim, on behalf of humbler citizens, for ownership of a cultural tradition and a continent. He assumes that 'Asians' will arouse a righteous anger in those who were here before, because they will change how they live. Aside from Blainey's right to speak for others, and the accuracy of his perception of poorer people's reactions,[11] this emphasis on the purity of tradition needs questioning. It is a part of the new racism which stresses the preciousness of a particular heritage to its bearers and makes that an excuse for excluding others. The dubious nature of white Australians claim to own the continent is matched by the dubious nature of the notion of a single and stable 'Australian way of life'.

Justifying ideology

An explanation of racism, widely espoused by sociologists, is as a justificatory ideology. Hartwig, for instance, argues that 'the efficient causes of Western racism appear to have been the need to rationalise dispossession and/or exploitation of non-European peoples' (Hartwig, 1972:12). Racism is a response to the psychology of the colonial situation, but he adds rather weakly that racism has become habitual (ibid., 21). While the socio-historical rather than psychopathological approach is one I fully concur with, the depiction of racism as a specific set of beliefs which function as a logical and consistent rationale for a particular situation is too limited.

In common with other explanations of racism it depends on specifying, as an antecedent condition, the existence of 'real' races. Further there is no clear distinction between sentiments and beliefs. This ideology is located in individual peoples' heads. Hartwig takes aspects of the theory directly from van den Berghe's earlier work (1967:13), which states that there must be *sufficient numbers* of people who *look different enough* so that at least some of their number can be readily classifiable; they also need to be *culturally different when they first meet*. Only then does he mention that there must be a situation of institutionalised inequality (quoted in Hartwig, 1972:11–12, my emphasis). It seems to me that only the latter is a necessary condition.

---

[11]Blainey gives no evidence of a lessening of tolerance towards 'Asians' among poorer people. He relies on the common sense notions to be gleaned from the occasional newpaper accounts of conflict which feed into the ideas that are already in place concerning the probability of tensions being generated by racial diversity.

Differences both in appearance and culture, far from simply being there, are attended to or are created, are reproduced or modified, according to processes that are independent of the degree to which the group members 'look different enough'.

There are many examples where imputed innate heritable characteristics of appearance were created and used as the basis of discrimination in exactly the way race is used. The innate inferiority held to be characteristic of the peasants and later the workers in Britain in earlier eras was conceived of in similar ways as racial inferiority. The anti-semites have never been quite sure about the visibility of the characteristics that are supposed to mark the Jew. Conversely there are many examples of group characteristics being extended to include those with quite different appearance and culture. Reay says that whites who mixed freely with Aborigines in Walgett were firmly categorised as being Aboriginal (1945:296). Stevens found examples of both kinds of confusion. The alleged inferior characteristics of Negro, Mexican and Caucasian Oklahoman workers (of which latter group he was temporarily a member) were, according to their employers, similar to each other and remarkably similar to the alleged characteristics of Australian Aborigines according to *their* employers (Stevens, 1974:xi). In all these cases 'looking different enough' is in the eyes of the observer, as are the other requirements of 'sufficient numbers' as well as 'cultural differences'. If we agree with Hartwig that racial, that is, gene pool characteristics cannot explain social inequality, then it makes little sense to allow them to explain racial sentiments.

Hartwig may be right in showing how certain ideas bridged the contradiction between Christian ideals and colonial reality. It is apparent that a particular form of racial ideology was promulgated in 19th-century Australia, and its multi-faceted nature is demonstrated in Reynold's work (1972). However those ideas did not consist of a static formula to be applied to any situation. Neither the murderous hostility nor the situations of cooperation and even passionate attachment between black and white people could be contained and comprehended by a rational theory of racial inequality. Rather scientific racial theories underwrote government policies and official attitudes and also formed the framework within which face-to-face situations were spelt out in common parlance. But these situations themselves influenced the theory and also the way in which government policy and public knowledge of race and racial conflict were formed. The formal theories about race and about Aborigines which were developed in the academy, as well as the more popular images and understandings, have undergone changes as a result of the Australian reality.

A curious terminological misrepresentation occurs in the literature with topics such as 'race relations', 'minority group relations', as well as 'ethnic groups' and 'ethnocentrism'. Such terms do not refer to races in any literal sense or to minorities in any numerical sense. Rather they purport to analyse the relationship between groups which are defined in terms of cultural characteristics. However what is being discussed is invariably a form of structural inequality. Why then are such studies not termed 'methods of domination' or 'oppression today'? There are, I think, two services performed by the terminology I am criticising. One is to give the appearance of even-handed objectivity. Using terms which focus on inequality, injustice or exploitation would upset a number of notions of the impersonal nature of research and science. Inequality can be presented as if it were a finding rather than the defined area of study. The other service this terminology performs relates to its explanatory implications. A minority could be expected to be swamped by the majority. It seems natural that ethnic or racial minorities lack power. Yet the wealthy and powerful are also a minority, and a culturally distinct one at that as I have tried to show in Brindleton. An explanation of the way such a minority retains its power and wealth would provide a more useful account of the disadvantaged groups than attention to their own characteristics.

Finally, Brown (1986) provides further evidence for the rejection of the individualistic prejudice model of racism. He shows that those who profess themselves to be anti-racists may, in action, continue to support racial inequality. By focussing on the everyday practices at the 'points of entry' into the social system (e.g., education and employment agencies), Brown showed that blacks are disadvantaged as much by the actions of avowed anti-racists as by formal discriminatory rules. The actions of anti-racists can accommodate and therefore facilitate and reinforce practices that disadvantage the blacks. The nature of their jobs (in an employment agency) in a racially structured society forces them to work in terms of the racial categories that are commonly used by those on whom they depend to get jobs for their clients. Unless these categories are resisted, the disadvantage is perpetuated. Brown asserts that while discrimination is written into the rules, it is the 'day to day practices of personnel working at the informal level' which explain how 'race, gender and class discrimination' are systematically reproduced (Brown, 1986:389). These findings, though occurring in the very different context of urban England, accord with my findings in Brindleton. That is, it is not racism expressed as overt prejudice that reproduces structural inequalities, for even those who profess to be anti-racists can contribute to the perpetuation of a racism which is embedded in common sense constructions of the social world.

Further a generalised level of ideas concerning worth and normality form a backdrop against which Aborigines are judged. Ideas concerning the importance of neat attire, hard work, tidy families, punctuality and diligence can all be brought to bear to judge the whole Aboriginal community as wanting. Such processes must be seen as essential elements of racism.

ABORIGINES AND THE ACADEMY

Aborigines in the literature

Australian Aborigines have long been famous among European intellectuals for their place as the central characters in a number of important origin myths developed within anthropology. The 'lowest level' of Morgan's (1870) kinship system was illustrated by Fison and Howitt's *Kamilaroi and Kurnai* (1880). Frazer (1915) used Baldwin Spencer's evidence of the most 'primitive' form of religion in Central Australia. Darwin referred to the Australian female as evidence that the difference between man and ape was one of degree, not of kind (Darwin, 1871:62). Freud's *Totem and Taboo* had the primal horde exemplified in Australia (Freud, 1950; first published 1912-13). Durkheim found the elementary forms of religion in the work of Spencer and Gillen and Strehlow (Durkheim, 1954; first published 1915). More recently Levi-Strauss found elementary structures of kinship there. Aborigines' existence in Australia has not been directly influenced by such writings and of course few Aborigines are aware of their renown in academic circles. However the work of intellectuals has been significant in determining how the category of Aboriginal Australians has been defined and reproduced for most of this century.

Historians have in recent years broken 'the great Australian silence' (Stanner, 1968:18) concerning Aborigines in accounts of Australia's past. That past silence reinforced the marginal place of Aborigines by ignoring them. Many texts made no mention of them at all, while others mentioned either the problems they posed for settlers or their immanent demise. Recently voices have been raised, often in outrage, both at the previous silence and at the events that had been hidden. Rowley's encyclopaedic work (1972a & b) has a mass of information and Robinson and York (1977) wrote a challenging reinterpretation of the colonial process. Reynolds (1981) has provided an account of Aborigines' responses to the colonisers in terms of a robust defence of their land. As well a whole host of oral histories, biographies and autobiographies from many different areas are being collected and published. These works will be of significance in the current reordering of the place of Aborigines in Australian society.

Psychologists have long been active in extending their scientific practices to the analysis of Aborigines. From the work of Porteus in 1917, which was criticised severely and effectively by Elkin (1932), psychologists have continued to measure and try to explain the different cognitive style and other mental and emotional characteristics of Aborigines. They have shown a good deal of ambivalence about the source of such differences, but the prevailing contemporary view seems to be that Aborigines are 'different but equal' (Kearney *et al.*, 1973:x). There is a touching faith in science shown both in the view that after the 1889 expedition, 'The earlier work of the phrenologists and other quasi-scientists . . . can be discarded as being pre-scientific and as not generating any useful data' (ibid., 1), and in the view that the evolutionary perspective which dominated early theories of Aboriginal intellect was replaced by scientific investigation (Chase & von Sturmer, 1973:13). They ignore the heritage from evolutionism in both psychology and anthropology. Porteus' article is reprinted without criticism in *The Psychology of Aboriginal Australians* (Kearney *et al.*, 1973).

Though psychologists have been influential in some circles, notably the field of education, and historians have recently been writing a lot, the history of the literature about Aborigines until the 1970s has been a history of anthropological hegemony. In the recent upsurge of interest and contributions from educationalists, historians, political scientists, psychologists, artists and musicologists, there is a tendency to rely on anthropologists' work for authoritative statements concerning Aboriginal traditions. It seems important therefore to define the limits of the anthropologist's area of expertise and admit that the discipline has no special authority in the area of what is called social or cultural change, or in the analysis of the kind of society into which Aborigines have been incorporated.

Parts of races and elements of cultures: the pitfalls of metaphor

Wolf (1982:4) shows how misleading is the attempt to separate cultural wholes and make distinct boundaries in situations where shifting relationships are the consequence of European expansion. Evidence from Australia is a case in point. The establishment of a British penal colony in 1788, and the subsequent colonisation of the continent of Australia, led to the virtual wiping out of the Aboriginal population in some areas, the confinement of others on reserves which shrank in size over the years, the employment of many on pastoral properties in serf-like conditions, and, in the more remote areas, the surveillance by missionaries and government welfare agencies (Rowley, 1972a,b). These different situations were of course marked by differing responses by Aborigines. Yet studies of Aboriginal culture continued to consider Aborigines as a self-evident category.

In the 20th century the study of the Australian race, through the examination of bones, artefacts and practices, became the study of the Aboriginal culture (Cowlishaw, 1987). The work of social anthropologists emphasised that it was the culture of Aborigines which made them distinct and unique. School textbooks described the nomadic hunter-gatherers, the cleverness of their artefacts and the exotic nature of their religious beliefs. Some of these descriptions were disparaging and some admiring. Intellectuals delivered papers on totemism and moieties to learned societies. But the people whose culture was being studied were the same people as those whose physical distinctiveness had been measured earlier as a part of the same enterprise.

Definitions of Aborigines were always dependent on notions of their cultural integrity and homogeneity. No concepts or theories have been developed which deal systematically and analytically with either relationships between the indigenous population and the invaders or with changes in either. When anthropologists did conduct research with non-traditional groups, the very vocabulary with which such groups were described relied on biological notions of race, and the search for the traditional also relies in the final analysis on the reification of race.

The interest in the authentic culture, that which was traditional and which defined Aborigines, led to the seekers of Aborigines, usually anthropology students, repairing to the remoter parts of the continent where miscegenation was less apparent. While in most parts of the continent the Aborigines had learned a great deal (though not of course scientifically) about the anthropologists' culture, the anthropologists' interest was only in those who had escaped, through geographical fortune, the direct invasion of their territory. In the closely settled areas, where often large Aboriginal minorities were to be found, there was little interest expressed by anthropologists. This equating of Aborigines with those deemed 'traditional' has meant an exclusion of NSW Aborigines and many others from the category.

The common view that after what was called 'culture contact' Aborigines began to 'lose' their culture can be directly related to the predominant view of what culture was. Culture was seen as unchanging and exotic. Those Aborigines commonly known as 'fringe dwellers' on the outskirts of country towns appear to have few cultural forms which are independent of the dominant society in which they are encapsulated. Those who write about Aborigines do not see them adapting or making strategic or rational judgements, much less striving to create a world of meaning under the judging gaze and physical intrusions of those with superior power. The changes that take place are nearly always seen in negative terms as a loss or breakdown and not as cultural adaptations to specifiable conditions.

The relationship between 'race' and 'culture' remained confusing in the literature from NSW. The use of the terms half-caste, mixed-bloods and part-Aborigine, without the relevance of 'caste' and 'blood' to what were supposedly studies of culture being spelt out, imply a casual connection between the dilution of the blood and the loss of Aboriginal, that is, traditional practices. In some cases there were references to these matters but no analysis or critique was attempted.

Elkin in 1938, R.M. & C.H. Berndt in 1964 and Maddock in 1972 (Elkin, 1974; Berndt & Berndt, 1977; Maddock, 1982), published the major textbooks on Aborigines. While markedly different in many respects, each shows the confusion of culture with racial categories, but also the static and mentalist notion of culture that drew the same kind of boundaries that race had previously done. Elkin, perhaps more than all other Australian academics, wanted to help the Aborigines but did not examine the institutions which were most directly oppressing them, particularly the Aborigines Protection Board. He did successfully influence the Board, but his efforts on behalf of Aborigines did not involve any analysis of the APBs political function and cultural context. The more recent widely used text by Maddock is called *The Australian Aborigines* (1982, first published 1972) but many Aborigines will not find themselves represented here. None of the Brindleton Aborigines would recognise themselves in any of these texts. They are in the category of those whose culture has been lost or destroyed, and so they merit no attention.

Given that Aborigines were defined as those with traditional culture, it is no wonder the NSW Aborigines were of little interest. Not only did they appear to have no rituals and few rules, they seemed to have no unique qualities. It is difficult to recognise a systematic and consistent ideology among subordinate groups. The very condition of powerlessness means that the material conditions are not present to independently create and control their social world. No one systematically studied Aboriginal responses and aims in new contexts, or how choices were systematically expressed or limited, organised or suppressed. There was little appreciation of the historical, political and economic forces that had created the community being studied. More surprisingly, there was no systematic attention to the way these Aboriginal communities were, in the contemporary situation, bounded by laws and practices that confined their activities to certain limited areas, both geographically and socially.[12] A notable exception was Beckett who was widely quoted in Chapter 2.

The few studies that were done in the 1940s and 1950s in NSW[13] would be rejected as theoretically inadequate today. The terms mixed-blood, part Aborigines or civilised Aborigines were used uncritically (e.g., Elkin, 1935; Reay 1945). While the process of change was dramatic and complex the analytic framework used was very simple. Elkin's work on 'southern' Aborigines was very much a response in terms of common sense welfare notions taken uncritically from his own cultural background (Elkin, 1935, 1937). These studies did not continue and little of the research was published (cf. Reay, 1964). One reason was that studies of such groups had low status in the academic world. Beckett has said that those who worked with half-castes were considered as apprentices, practising for the real anthropological work (pers. comm.). Recent discussions of the concept of Aboriginality (Thiele, 1984; Anderson *et al.*, 1985) show a growing awareness of the problem I have been discussing.

[12]The studies of 'traditional culture' suffered from this limitation also, as the changes which were occurring in even the remotest groups were not dealt with analytically. Given, for instance, that the hunter-gatherers were now fencing and mustering, were they still hunters and gatherers? Were people who had lived on government missions for many years behaving in ways simply determined by the fact that they were Aborigines? The use of the ethnographic present was an expedient convention which allowed the pretence that one could participate in an unchanging society. Questions about change could thus be avoided.
[13]Kelly, 1943, 1944; Reay, 1945,1949; Reay & Sitlington, 1948; Calley, 1956, 1957; Bell, 1956; Fink, 1957; Beckett, 1958a, 1964.

Theories that continue to define Aborigines in terms of one tradition and to ignore the particular ways that racial boundaries and definitions are created, will remain inadequate. If the study of race was the science that many of our academic forebears produced which explained and therefore justified the inequality between the colonisers and the colonised, it seems that social anthropology, by defining Aborigines as having a particular and unique culture, may be doing the same thing. Any connections between the specific characteristics of Aboriginal traditional culture and the political predicament of Aboriginal groups today is as invalid as earlier theories about race and disadvantage.

Current work

There are three distinguishable approaches taken by those writing about contemporary Aborigines in recent years. While some works incorporate a more complex set of determinants, the more popular works and some academic publications can be seen as typifying one of these approaches. In one Aborigines are seen as victims of racism, however that is understood (Lippman, 1973; McConnochie, 1973; Tatz, 1979). In another they are seen as victims of capitalism, exploited or dependent (Hartwig, 1972; Robinson & York, 1977). The third theme, which has appeared more recently, stresses Aboriginal resistance to invasion and hegemony (Reynolds, 1981; Morris, 1985).

This third theme is based on a more useful conception of culture than that described above, and also invites consideration of how and why changes have occurred in Aboriginal society or culture. Until a decade ago there was almost no recognition of the active part that Aborigines might have played in the retention or resurgence or even rejection of cultural forms as strategies, conscious or not, in a political struggle. Quite the opposite. As indicated, Aborigines were usually depicted either as having lost their culture, or as clinging rather pathetically to its remains. But there is quite a different interpretation of such clinging, or indeed of rejection of particular traditions.

Aborigines were not passive victims in a situation of cultural threat. We have seen the struggles and conflicting strategies and the active part Aborigines have taken in reforming their lives. There were dynamic cultural responses to external pressures and inevitable change in the meanings of cultural practices in the face of powerful forces.

The work of Gilroy develops a view of culture as essentially political. He says that terms such as coon and nigger (or boong) are cultural constructions in an ideological struggle, and that 'Cultures of resistance develop to contest them and the power they inform' (Gilroy, 1981:210). This is a quite different way of viewing culture from the old tradition-retained-or-lost one. If culture is a creation, an expression of a human group's responses to their social existence, then the changing conditions of that existence does not mean a loss of culture. One could as well lose one's biology. Rather it means a cultural response to a different situation which may involve rejecting previous practices and developing new ones. It is the relationship with the enveloping society, the conditions for cultural response, which must be examined if we are to understand Aboriginal culture today.

There may be psychological stress caused by pressure to change. There may be resistance to change. Some new practices may be destructive rather than generative. The difficulties of this kind in Australia were related not simply to a changed social environment but to the aggressive domination by whites described in previous chapters. While Aborigines have not chosen the weapons or the arena on which the struggle is played out, nonetheless they have, consciously or unconsciously, continually responded to and resisted the hegemony of white society.

Wolf provides an account of culture which is radically different from those which depend on some notion of authentic tradition. It is a view which could lead to a flowering of research into the humbler traditions which have flourished in Australia without being accorded the status of culture.

> In the rough and tumble of social interaction, groups are known to exploit the ambiguities of inherited forms, to impart new evaluations or valences to them, to borrow forms more express-ive of their interests, or to create wholly new forms to answer to changed circumstances. Furthermore if we think of such interac-tion not as causative in its own terms but as responsive to larger economic and political forces, the explanation of cultural forms must take account of that larger context, that wider field of force. 'A culture' is thus better seen as a series of processes that con-struct, reconstruct and dismantle cultural materials, in response to identifiable determinants (Wolf, 1982:387).

In NSW country towns there is an Aboriginal culture. One of its manifestations is the ironic humour which reinterprets events which threaten to engulf Aborigines' lives. Another part of it is the direct attacks on property. It is also manifested in the black power vocabu-lary which has been adopted by some of the young people, and in defiant public emphasis on values that are known to upset the dominant whites. These are indications of a wider ongoing re-creation of a distinct cultural heritage which also has its own vocabulary, its family form, pattern of interpersonal interaction and even its own economy (Cowlishaw, in press). Willis and Corrigan (1983) have discussed such 'oppositional culture' in Britain, and the work of Genovese (e.g., 1975) discusses equivalent cultural creations of the oppressed. I argue that Aborigines in all parts of Australia are Aborigines culturally through a dynamic tradition which is still being created in embattled situations. There has not been simply an attempt to cling to a past tradition but, wittingly or not, the creation of a set of new ones.

BIBLIOGRAPHY

Newspapers & Journals: Abbreviations

Australasian
Empire   The Empire
HB   The History of Bourke. Papers of the Bourke and District Historical Society. Volumes 1-10. Volume and page number given. Held in major NSW libraries.
Identity   Journal published July 1971 to October 1978, by Aboriginal Publishing Foundation. Vol 1 (1) to volume 3 (8).
MM   Maitland Mercury
PT   Pastoral Times and Southern Courier
SM   Sydney Mail
SMH   Sydney Morning Herald
T & C Journal   Town and Country Journal
WN   Walgett News and North-Western Grazier
Wellington Times
Western Herald

Books and Articles

Allen, H. n.d. Aborigines of the Western Plains of New South Wales. In *The Aborigines of New South Wales.* National Parks and Wildlife 2 (5):33-42.

Anderson, C. *et al.* 1985. On the notion of Aboriginality: a discussion. *Mankind,* 15(1):41-55.

Anti-Discrimination Board Report. 1982. *Study of Street Offenses by Aborigines.* NSW Anti-Discrimination Board.

Ardrey, R. 1967. *The Territorial Imperative.* London, Collins.

Baldwin, J. 1963 *The Fire Next time.* London, Joseph.

Barbalet, M. 1983. *Far from a low gutter girl.* Melbourne, Oxford University Press.

Barker, M. 1981. *The New Racism.* London, Junction Books.

Barwick, D. 1972. Coranderrk and Cumeroogunga: pioneers and policy. In S.Epstein and D.Penny (eds.), *Opportunity and Response.* London, Hurst & Company.

Bean, C.E.W. 1911. *The Dreadnought of the Darling.* London, Alston Rivers Ltd.

Bean, C.E.W. 1916. On The Wool Track. London, Hodder & Stoughton. (2nd edn. 1956, Angus & Robertson, Sydney.)

Beckett, J. 1958a. A Study of a Mixed-Blood Minority in the Pastoral West of New South Wales. MA thesis, Australian National University.

Beckett, J. 1958b. Aborigines Make Music. *Quadrant,* 2(4):32-42.

Beckett, J. 1958c. Marginal men: A study of two half-caste Aborigines. *Oceania,* 29(2):91-108.

Beckett, J. 1964. Aborigines, Alcohol and Assimilation. In M.Reay (ed.), *Aborigines Now.* Sydney, Angus & Robertson.

Beckett, J. 1965. The land where the crow flies backwards. *Quadrant,* 9(4):38-43.

Beckett, J. 1983. Internal colonialism in a welfare state: the case of the Australian Aborigines. Paper presented to American Anthropological Association, Chicago.

Bell, J.A. 1956. The economic life of mixed-blood Aborigines on the south coast of New South Wales. *Oceania,* 26(3):181-99.

Berndt, R.M. 1945. A Norther Territory problem: Aboriginal labour in a pastoral area. Typescript. Anthropology Dept., University of Sydney.

Berndt, R.M. & Berndt, C.H. 1977. *The World of the First Australians.* Sydney, Ure Smith.

Bird, N. 1961. *Born to Fly.* Sydney, Angus & Robertson.

Blainey, G. 1984. Report of speech in *The Age* (Melbourne). 20th March, 1984.

Bloch, J. M. 1958. *Miscegenation, Melalukation and Mr. Lincoln's Dog.* New York, Schaum Publishing Co.

Bottomley, G. 1979. *After the Odyssey*. St. Lucia, University of Queensland Press.

Broome, R. 1980. Professional Aboriginal boxers in eastern Australia 1930-1979. *Aboriginal History*, 4(1):49-71.

Broome, R. 1982. *Aboriginal Australians. Black responses to white dominance. 1788-1980*. Sydney, George Allen & Unwin.

Brown, K. 1986. Establishing difference: culture, 'race', ethnicity and the production of ideology. *A.N.Z.J.S*, 22(2):175-86.

Butlin, N. 1983. *Our Original Aggression. Aboriginal populations of southeastern Australia 1788-1850*. Sydney, George Allen & Unwin.

Calley, M. 1956. Economic life of mixed-blood communities in northern New South Wales. *Oceania*, 26(3):200-30.

Calley, M. 1957. Race relations on the north coast of New South Wales. *Oceania*, 27(3):190-209.

Cameron, W.J. 1978. *Bourke — A Centenary of Local Government*. Bourke Historical Society.

Cameron, W.J. 1982. *Bourke; A Pictorial History*. Bourke Wool Press.

C.C.C.S. Race and Politics Group. 1982. *The Empire Strikes Back*. London, Hutchinson.

Chase, A. & von Sturmer, J. 1973. 'Mental Man' and social evolutionary theory. In G.E. Kearney, P.R. de Lacey & G.R. Davidson (eds.), *The Psychology of Aboriginal Australians*. Australia, John Wiley & Sons.

Clune, F. 1952. *Roaming Round the Darling*. Sydney, Angus & Robinson.

Collmann, J. 1979. Fringe camps and the development of Aboriginal administration in Central Australia. *Social Analysis*, 2:38-57.

Cooper, J. 1976. The Politics of Consultation with Aboriginals, 1968-75. Unpublished MA thesis, University of Sydney.

Cowlishaw, G.K. 1978. Infanticide in Aboriginal Australia. *Oceania*, 48 (4):262-83.

Cowlishaw, G.K. 1983. Blackfella Boss: A study of a Northern Territory cattle station *Social Analysis*, 13:54-69.

Cowlishaw, G.K. 1987. Colour, Culture and the Aboriginalists. *Man*. 22(2):221-37.

Cowlishaw, G.K. in press. Material for identity construction. In J. Beckett (ed.), *Aboriginal identity and uses of the past*. Canberra, A.I.A.S.

Cuneen, C. 1986. The politics of law and order crises: the case of north-west NSW. Paper presented to ANZ society for criminology conference. Melbourne University, Melbourne.

Curr, E.M. 1886,1887. *The Australian Race*. (3 Vols.) London & Melbourne. John Ferres Government Printer.

Currawinya Diaries. 1870-1871. Transcriptions in *The History of Bourke*. 2:165-80.

Curthoys, A. 1973. Race and ethnicity: NSW 1856-81. PhD thesis, Melbourne University.

de Lepervanche, M. 1980. From race to ethnicity. *A.N.Z.J.S*, 16(1):24-37.

Dickermann, M. 1984. Concepts and classification in the study of human infanticide. In G. Hausfater & S. B. Hrdy (eds.), *Infanticide*. New York, Aldine.

Dowling, V.J. 1859 to 1863. Diaries of Vincent J. Dowling. Mitchell Library. Transcriptions in *The History of Bourke*. Vols. 3:5-30, 5:26-31, 6:131-202.

Eckermann, A-K., Watts, B.K. & Dixon, P.A. 1984. From here to there: a comparative case study of Aboriginal rural-urban resettlement in Queensland and New South Wales. Report to Department of Aboriginal Affairs, Canberra.

Edwards, C. 1982. Is the ward clean. In B. Gamage & A. Marcus (eds.), *All That Dirt. Aborigines 1938*. Canberra, History Project Incorporated.

Eggleston, E. 1976. *Fear, Favour or Affection*. Canberra, ANU Press.

Eipper, C. 1983. The Magician's Hat: a critique of the concept of ethnicity. *A.N.Z.J.S.*, 19(3):427-46.

Eipper, C. 1985. Double binds in the pursuit of prosperity. *Mankind*, 15(3):203-13.

Elkin, A.P. 1932. The social life and intelligence of the Australian Aborigine; A review of S.D. Porteus's 'Psychology of a Primitive People'. *Oceania*, 3(1):101-18.

Elkin, A.P. 1935. Civilized Aborigines and native culture. *Oceania*, 6(2):117-46.

Elkin, A.P. 1937. Native education with special reference to the Australian Aborigines. *Oceania*, 7(4):459-500.

Elkin, A.P. 1974. *The Australian Aborigines*. (5th edn.) Sydney, Angus & Robertson.

Encel, S. 1958. The concept of the state in Australian politics. In C. Hughes (ed.), *Readings in Australian government*. St. Lucia, University of Queensland Press.

Encel, S. 1974. The Nature of Race Prejudice in Australia. In F.S. Stevens (ed.), *Racism; the Australian Experience*. Vol.1. Sydney, ANZ Book Co. pp.30-42.

Fink, R. 1957. The caste barrier — an obstacle to the assimilation of part-Aborigines in north-west New South Wales. *Oceania*, 28(1):100-12.

Fitzpatrick, B. 1946. *The Australian People. 1788-1945*. Melbourne, Melbourne University Press.

Foott, B. 1958. Of Henrietta Marooned. *Bulletin*, 1st October 1958. pp.1,56-7.

Frazer, J.G. 1915. *The Golden Bough*. London, Macmillan.

Gale, F. & Brookman, A. 1975. *Race Relations in Australia — The Aborigines*. Sydney, McGraw-Hill Book Co.

Gale, F. & Wundersitz, J. 1982. *Adelaide Aborigines: A case study of urban life 1966-1981*. Canberra. ANU, Development Studies Centre.

Genovese, E. 1975. Class, culture and historical process. *Dialectical Anthropology*, 1:71-9.

Gibbs Diaries. Mitchell Library. Transcriptions in *The History of Bourke*. Vol.9:177-204.

Gilbert, K. 1978. *Living Black: blacks talk to Kevin Gilbert*. Ringwood, Vic., Allen Lane, Penguin Books.

Gilroy E. 1981. You can't fool the youths — race and class formation in the 1980s. *Race and Class*, XXIII (2/3):207-22.

Glazer, N. & Moynihan, D.P. (eds.), 1975. *Ethnicity: theory and experience*. Cambridge, Mass., Harvard University Press.

Glover, W.K. Some Early Settlers. In *The History of Bourke*, 1:31, 3:124.

Goodall H. 1982. A History of Aboriginal Communities in New South Wales, 1909-1939. PhD thesis, University of Sydney.

Gumbert, M. 1984. *Neither Justice nor Reason*. St. Lucia, University of Queensland Press.

Hall, S., Crichter, C., Jefferson, T., Clarke, J. & Roberts, B. 1978. *Policing the Crisis*. London, Macmillan.

Hanks, P. & Keon-Cohen, B. 1984. *Aborigines and the Law*. Sydney, George Allen & Unwin.

Hardy, B. 1977. *West of the Darling*. (2nd edn.) Adelaide, Rigby.

Hardy, B. 1981. *Lament for the Barkindji*. (2nd edn) Sydney, Alpha Books.

Harris, M. *et al.* 1986. Alcohol related admission in a country town. Unpublished typescript.

Harris, John W. 1976. Aboriginal Education in N.S.W. The past the present and the future. Unpublished paper presented at conference for teachers of Aboriginal children, Nowra, NSW. May, 1976.

Hartwig, M. 1972. Aborigines and Racism; an historical perspective. In F. Stevens (ed.), *Racism; the Australian experience*. Vol 2. Sydney, ANZ Book Co., pp.9-24.

Harvey, M.E. 1976. *The Impact of the Wool Crisis on the Bourke Economy Between 1968/69 and 1970/71*. University of New England, Armidale NSW. Miscellaneous publications 2.

Heathcote, R.L. 1965. *Back of Bourke*. Melbourne. Melbourne University Press.

Horner, J. 1974. *Vote Ferguson for Aboriginal Freedom*. Sydney, ANZ Book Co.

I.C.P.A. n.d. *History of Isolated Children's Parents' Association* booklet. Hamilton, Victoria, Magazine Art Pty Ltd.

Jervis, J. 1948. The West Darling: its exploration and development. In *Royal Australian Historical Society Journal*, 34(1):65-88; (2):146-83; (3):218-53.

Jervis, J. 1956. The Exploration and Settlement of the Western Plains. *Royal Australian Historical Society Journal*, 42(1):1-15.

Jervis, J. 1962. Exploration and Settlement of the North-Western Plains. *Royal Australian Historical Society Journal*, 48(4):377-94.

Kamien, M. 1978. *The Dark People of Bourke*. Canberra, A.I.A.S.

Kearney, G. E., de Lacey, P. R. & Davidson, G. R. 1973. *The Psychology of Aboriginal Australians*. Australia, John Wiley & Sons.

Keenan, J. 1981. The concept of mode of production in hunter-gatherer societies. In J.S. Kahn & J.R. Lobera (eds.), *The Anthropology of Pre-Capitalist Societies*. London, Macmillian.

Kelly, C. 1943. The reaction of white groups in country towns of New South Wales to Aborigines. *Social Horizons*. 1:34-40.

Kelly, C. 1944. Some aspects of culture contact in eastern Australia. *Oceania*, 15(2):142-53.

Kennedy, E. & Donaldson, T. 1982. Coming up out of the Nhaalya: reminiscences of the life of Eliza Kennedy. *Aboriginal History*, 6:5-27.

King, C.J. 1957. *An Outline of Closer Settlement in NSW. Part 1: The sequence of land laws 1788-1956*. Sydney, Department of Agriculture.

Lawrence, E. 1982. Just plain common sense: the 'roots' of racism. In *The Empire Strikes Back*. Centre for Contemporary Cultural Studies, Birmingham University, Hutchinson, pp.47-94.

Lewis, O. 1966. The Culture of Poverty. *Scientific American*, 215(4):19-25.

Lippmann, L. 1973. *Words or Blows. Racial attitudes in Australia*. Ringwood, Vic., Penguin Books.

Lippmann, L. 1981. *Generations of Resistance; the Aboriginal struggle for justice*. Melbourne, Longman Cheshire.

Livingstone, F.B. 1962. On the non-existence of human races. *Current Anthropology 3(3): 279–81*.

Lyons, G. 1984, Aboriginal legal services. In P. Hanks & B. Keon-Cohen (eds.), *Aborigines and the law*. Sydney, George Allen & Unwin.

McConnochie, K. 1973. *Realities of Race*. Sydney, ANZ Book Co.

McGrath, A. 1984. 'Black Velvet'; Aboriginal women and their relations with white men in the Northern Territory, 1910-40. In K. Daniels (ed.), *So Much Hard Work; Women and Prostitution in Australian History*. Sydney, Fontana/Collins.

Maddock, K. 1982. *The Australian Aborigines; a portrait of their society*.(2nd edn.) Ringwood, Vic., Penguin Books.

Mathews, J. 1977a. *The Two Worlds of Jimmie Barker*. Canberra, A.I.A.S.

Mathews, J. 1977b. Obituary to Eliza Kennedy. *A.I.A.S. Newsletter*. January, p.27.

Maxwell, Chas. F. n.d. *Australian Men of Mark 1788-1888*. Vol.1. Sydney, Chas. F. Maxwell.

Moffitt, P., Nurcombe, B., Passmore, M. & McNeilly, A. 1973. Intervention in cultural deprivation. In G.E. Kearney, P.R. de Lacey & G.R. Davidson (eds.), *The Psychology of Aboriginal Australians*. Australia, John Wiley & Sons.

Montagu, A. 1964. (4th edn.) *Man's most dangerous myth. The fallacy of race*. New York, World Publishing Co.

Morgan, L.H. 1870. *Systems of consanguinity and affinity of the human family*. Washington, Smithsonian Institute.

Morris, B. 1985. Cultural domination and domestic dependence: the Dhan-Gadi of New South Wales and the protection of the state. *Canberra Anthropology*, 8(1&2):87-115.

Newland, S. 1895. Some Aborigines I have known. *Proceedings of the Royal Geographical Society of S.A.*, 2:37-54.

Norton, A. 1907. Stray notes about our Aborigines. *Science of Man*, 9(5):68-9.

Nurse, G.T., Weiner, J.S. & Jenkins, P. 1985. The Peoples of Southern Africa and their Affinities. Oxford, Clarendon Press.

Perkins, C. 1975. *A Bastard Like Me*. Sydney, Ure Smith.

Porteus, S.D. 1973. (first pub.1917) Mental Tests with Delinquents and Australian Aboriginal Children. In G. E. Kearney, P. R. de Lacey & G. R. Davidson (eds.), *The Psychology of Aboriginal Australians*. Australia, John Wiley & Sons.

Read, P. 1982. *The Stolen Generations*. N.S.W. Ministry of Aboriginal Affairs, Government Printer.

Read, P. (ed.), 1984. *Down there with me on the Cowra mission*. Sydney, Pergamon Press.

Reay, M. 1945. A half-caste Aboriginal community in north-western New South Wales. *Oceania*, 15(3):296-323.

Reay, M. 1949. Native thought in rural New South Wales. *Oceania*, 20(1):89-118.

Reay, M.(ed.), 1964. *Aborigines Now*. Sydney, Angus & Robertson.

Reay, M. & Sitlington, G. 1948. Class and status in a mixed-blood community. *Oceania*, 18(3):179-207.

Rex, J. 1983 *Race Relations in Sociological Theory*. (2nd edn.) London, Routledge & Kegan Paul.

Reynolds, H. 1972. *Aborigines and Settlers*. Melbourne, Cassell.

Reynolds, H. 1981. *The Other Side of the Frontier*. Townsville, Qld., The James Cook University.

Robinson, F. & York, B. 1977. *The Black Resistance: an introduction to the history of the Aborigines' struggle against British colonialism*. Camberwell, Vic., Widescope.

Rowley, C.D. 1972a. *The Destruction of Aboriginal Society*. Ringwood Vic., Penguin Books.

Rowley, C.D. 1972b. *Outcasts in White Australia*. Ringwood Vic., Penguin Books.

Roy, A. 1984. The Bourke Water Polo Club. In M.T.Walker & J. Dixon (eds.), *Participation in Change*. Australian Case Studies. School of Social Science and Welfare Studies. M.C.A.E. Bathurst.

Ryan, W. 1972. *Blaming the Victim*. New York, Vintage books.

Sennett, R. & Cobb, J. 1973. *The Hidden Injuries of Class*. New York, Vintage Books.

Shepherd, T. 1976. *Children of Blindness*. Sydney, Ure Smith.

Smith, L. 1980. *The Aboriginal Population of Australia*. Canberra, ANU Press.

Stanner, W.E.H. 1968. *After the Dreaming*. Sydney, Australian Broadcasting Corporation.

Stevens, F.S. 1972. *Racism; the Australian Experience*. Vol.2. Sydney, ANZ Book Co.

Stevens, F.S. 1974 (2nd edn.). *Racism; The Australian Experience*. Vol.1. Sydney, ANZ Book Co.

Stevens, F.S. 1977 (2nd edn.). *Racism; the Australian Experience*. Vol.3. Sydney, ANZ Book Co.

Stevens, F.S. 1980. *The Politics of Prejudice*. Sydney, Alternative Publishing Cooperative Ltd.

Stevens, F.S. 1984. *Aborigines in the Northern Territory Cattle Industry*. Canberra, ANU Press.

Sykes, B. 1975. Black Women in Australia: a history. In J.Mercer (ed.), *The Other Half*. Ringwood, Vic., Penguin Books.

Tatz C. 1979. *Race Politics in Australia*. University of New England Publishing Unit, NSW.

Thiele, S.J. 1982. *Yugul, an Arnhem Land Cattle Station*. ANU North Australia Research Unit Monograph, Darwin.

Thiele, S.J. 1984. Anti-intellectualism and the 'Aboriginal problem': Colin Tatz and the 'self-determination' approach. *Mankind*, 14(3):165-78.

Tiger, L. 1969. *Men in Groups*. London, Nelson.

Valentine, C.A. 1969. Culture and Poverty: critique and counter proposals. *Current Anthropology*, 10:181-2.

van den Berghe P. 1967. *Race and Racism*. New York, John Wiley & Sons.

van den Berghe, P. 1981. *The Ethnic Phenomenon*. New York, Elsevier.

Ward, R. 1966. *The Australian Legend*. (2nd edn.) Melbourne, Oxford University Press.

Watson, P. 1983. *This Precious Foliage*. Oceania Monograph 26.

Watts, B.H. 1982. *Aboriginal Futures*. ERDC Report. Canberra, Australian Government Publishing Service.

Weaver, S. 1983. Australian Aboriginal policy: Aboriginal pressure groups or government advisory bodies. *Oceania*, 54(1):1-22; 54(2):85-108.

Wellman, D.T. 1977. *Portraits of White Racism*. Cambridge, Cambridge University Press.

Western Lands Commission. 1982. *An Economic Study of the Western Division of NSW*. Government Printer.

Wild, R.A. 1974. *Bradstow; a study of status, class and power in a small Australian town*. Sydney, Angus & Robertson.

Wilkie, M. 1985. *Aboriginal Land Rights in NSW*. Sydney, Alternative Publishing Cooperative Ltd.

Willis, P. & Corrigan, P. 1983. Orders of Experience: Working Class Cultural Forms. *Social Text*, 7:8-103.

Wilson, P.R. 1978. What is Deviant Language? In P. R. Wilson & J. Braithwaite (eds.), *Two Faces of Deviance: crimes of the powerless and the powerful*. St. Lucia, University of Queensland Press.

Wilson, P.R. 1982. *Black Death, White Hands*. Sydney, George Allen & Unwin.

Wolf, E. 1982. *Europe and the People without History*. Berkley, University of California Press.

Woods, J.E. 1879. *The Native Tribes of South Australia*. Adelaide, E.S. Wigg.

Yarwood, A.J. & Knowling, M.J. 1982. *Race Relations in Australia: a history*. North Ryde, NSW, Methuen.

Young, Dougie. Wilcannia Folk Songs. Recordings by J.Beckett held at Australian Institute of Aboriginal Studies, Canberra.

Index

Aboriginal Advancement Association, 132, 140, 143
Aboriginal community, *see* community
Aboriginal Development Commission, 148
Aboriginal Education Consultative Group, 116, 208, 214
Aboriginal Education Organisation (AEO), 184, 185
Aboriginal Housing Cooperative, 103, 109, 111, 115, 134, 138, 142, 144ff., 158, 159, 160, 162, 203, 218
Aboriginalisation policy, 127, 138, 190-1
Aboriginal Lands Trust, 109, 111, 140
Aboriginal Legal Service (ALS), 148, 174, 263
Aboriginal Liaison Officer(s), 150, 191, 242
Aboriginal Medical Service (AMS), 116, 148, 188
Aboriginal place names, 19
Aboriginal Protection Board (APB), 70, 72, 75ff., 85-6, 90, 91, 135, 171, 279
  charging of rent, 91
Aboriginal Reserve(s), 76, 79, 111, 130, 162, 202, 233, 278
  and Shire Council, 158, 216
  APB control of, 79-80
  as labour source, 78
  conditions on, 82, 210
  cultural significance, 149, 255
  DAA policy, 138, 146-7
  schooling on, 86
Aboriginal Secondary Grant (ASG), 180, 203ff., 207, 216-17
Aboriginal Studies courses, 181, 233
Aboriginal Teachers Aids (ATAs), 180-1, 214, 215, 225
Aboriginal Tent Embassy, 130, 133
Aborigines, *see also* community
  and alienation, 177
  and economic depression, 72, 78
  and law, 75ff., 170-1
  and resistance, 23-5, 31, 81, 89, 226, 281, 282
  as 'problems', 170, 179, 182, 207, 208, 211, 220, 258, 267
  classification of, 105-6, 107-9, 207, 250fn., 280
  definition of, 2, 107-9, 243, 278, *see also* culture
  exclusion of, 85-7, 90, 154, 252, 261, 263

experts on, 195, 237, 264
harassment of, 87, 93, 167
humour about, 62, 126, 184, 186-7, 262
humour of, 87, 235, 236, 243-4, 261-2, 263
identity,
  and colour, 105-6, 256, 258, 272
  as Aboriginal, 207, 242, 250-1
  rejection of, 114
  with community, 109-11, 231
images of, 16ff., 26, 30, 61ff., 70-1, 87, 111-12, 272, 276ff.
music, 92, 94
response to invasion, 72-4, 91ff., 280
ridicule of, 62ff.
theories about, 182, 276, 278-9
views of whites, 16fn., 146, 225-7, 234-6, 238, 242-4, 263-5
Aborigines Protection Act, 76, 77ff., 90-2
Aborigines Welfare Board (AWB), 77, 79, 81, 111, 140
activists, 225-7, *see also* 'stirrers'
Afghans, 64ff.,
alcohol,
  abuse, 188
  destructive, 87, 89
  illegality of, 93
  in Aboriginal communities, 92-5
  in public, 155, 234
  significance of, 81-2, 93ff., 240, 259
alcoholics, 221, 239, 263
Allen, H., 16
allocation of funds, 144-6, 201
ambulance, stealing of, 175
Anderson, C., 380
anthropologists, 14, 15, 77, 101ff., 248, 266, 277, 278, 280-1
Anti-Discrimination Board (ADB), 113, 258
  report, 171
anti-racists, 176, 220, 258, 275-6
architect, 141
Ardrey, R., 269
assimilation, 76, 82ff., 108, 127, 150, 157, 229, 242, 252
Assistance for Isolated Children (AIC), 204
Australasian, 69
Australian Broadcasting Commission (ABC), 222
Australian Labor Party, 154
Australian Workers Union (AWU), 69